CHAMBERS FIRST LEARNERS' DICTIONARY

Amy L Brown
John Downing
John Sceats

Pronunciation under the direction
of David Abercrombie and Alan Kemp
Department of Linguistics
University of Edinburgh

This dictionary gives the meanings and sounds of about 5000 simple English words. Near some words you will also find drawings which will help you to see what they mean.

Above each word you will find a guide to its pronunciation. In a very few cases, the dictionary gives two meanings of a word, which need separate pronunciations. The first meaning of the word is pronounced the first way; the second meaning is pronounced the second way.

As well as the letters which you already know, some special letters have to be used in the pronunciation. You will find examples showing the sounds of all the letters in the table below.

symbol	example	
a	[bag]	**bag**
a:	[ba:θ]	**bath**
e	[hed]	**head**
i	[milk]	**milk**
i:	[fi:l]	**feel**
o	[boks]	**box**
o:	[ho:l]	**hall**
u	[fut]	**foot**
u:	[blu:]	**blue**
ʌ	[sʌn]	**sun**
ə	['ribən]	**ribbon**
ə:	[fə:st]	**first**
ai	[fain]	**fine**
au	[laud]	**loud**
ei	['eibl]	**able**
eə	[heə]	**hair**
iə	[hiə]	**here**
oi	[dʒoin]	**join**
uə	[puə]	**poor**
ou	[gou]	**go**

symbol	example	
p	[peidʒ]	**page**
b	[bo:l]	**ball**
t	['teibl]	**table**
d	[dòg]	**dog**
k	[kik]	**kick**
g	[geˑt]	**get**
m	[mad]	**mad**
n	[neim]	**name**
ŋ	[baŋ]	**bang**
l	[leik]	**lake**
r	[reis]	**race**
f	[fi:t]	**feet**
v	[vois]	**voice**
θ	[θiŋ]	**thing**
ð	[ðou]	**though**
s	[seif]	**safe**
z	[zu:]	**zoo**
ʃ	[ʃip]	**ship**
ʒ	['meʒə]	**measure**
h	[ha:f]	**half**
w	[weit]	**wait**
j	['bju:ti]	**beauty**
tʃ	[tʃi:z]	**cheese**
dʒ	['dʒakit]	**jacket**

: means that the vowel which comes just before it is lengthened — [u:].

' comes just before the part of the word which is sounded with the greatest force (or *stress*) — ['meʒə].

Notes on the pronunciation

Pronunciation is indicated in that type of phonetic transcription often called "Extra Broad", using the alphabet of the International Phonetic Association.

Only one pronunciation is given for each word; where alternative forms exist, the most common has been selected. This has been done to make the system easier for the learner to understand; and a further aid is the clear phonetic key on the previous two pages.

['abəkəs]
abacus   a frame with beads on rods, used for counting

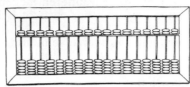

[ə'bandən]
abandon   to go away forever from something or somebody. The same word also means to stop what you are doing before you have finished it.

['abes]
abbess   a woman who is the head of the nuns in a convent or abbey

['abi]
abbey   a monastery or a convent; the big church of a monastery or convent

['abət]
abbot   a man who is the head of the monks in a monastery or abbey

[əbriːvi'eiʃən]
abbreviation   a short way of writing or printing a word, such as Dr. for Doctor, Jan. for January

['abdəmən]
abdomen   the lower part of the body which contains the stomach

[ə'biləti]
ability   strength, cleverness or skill

['eibl]
able   having the strength, cleverness or skill to do something

[ə'boliʃ]
abolish   to get rid of or to put an end to something

[ə'bʌv]
above   higher than; over

[ə'broːd]
abroad   away in another country

[ə'brʌpt]
abrupt   sudden; hurried

['absənt]
absent   missing; away; not present

[ə'bʌndənt]
abundant   more than enough; in great plenty

['aksənt]
accent   tone of voice; a way of pronouncing words.
  Londoners have a different accent from
  people living in other parts of Britain.

[ək'sept]
accept   to agree to receive something

['aksidənt]
accident   something that happens by chance, usually
  unpleasant

[ə'kaunt]
account   a statement of money owing or spent. The
  same word also means an explanation.

['akjurət]
accurate   correct; exactly right

[ə'kju:z]
accuse   to say someone has done something wrong

[eis]
ace   a card, domino or die with one spot or mark

[eik]
ache   a dull pain that goes on and on

['asid]
acid   a liquid which can burn your skin. The same
  word also means tasting sour or sharp.

['eiko:n]
acorn   the nut or seed that grows on an oak tree

['akrəbat]
acrobat   a person who does clever tricks, like
  balancing on a rope at a circus

[ə'kros]
across   from one side to the other side of something

[akt]
act   anything which is done is an act. The same
  word also means to pretend you are someone
  other than yourself, as in a play or film.

['akʃən]
action   something done; a series of acts performed

['aktiv]
active   doing something; being busy or lively

['aktə]
actor   a man or boy who acts in a play or film

['aktris]
actress   a woman or girl who acts in a play or film

['aktʃuəl]
actual   real; not imaginary

[ad]
add to put something together with something else.
You add two and two to make four $(2 + 2 = 4)$.

[ə'diʃən]
addition something added; the act of adding

[ə'diʃnl]
additional extra; added to something

[ə'dres]
address the name and number of your house and the
street and town where you are living. The same
word also means to write or speak to people.

['adinoidz]
adenoids two small fleshy lumps at the back of the
nose

['admərəl]
admiral a very important officer in the navy

[əd'maiə]
admire to think very well of someone or something

[əd'mit]
admit to agree that something is so. The same
word means to allow someone to come in.

['adʌlt]
adult a person who is fully grown-up

[əd'vaːns]
advance to move forward

[əd'ventʃə]
adventure an exciting or dangerous thing that you
do or that happens to you

['eəriəl]
aerial the metal rods or wires which receive or
send radio or television signals

['eərəplein]
aeroplane a flying machine

[ə'feə]
affair a happening or an event

[ə'fekt]
affect to do something that causes a change

[ə'fekʃən]
affection great liking; fondness

[ə'foːd]
afford to have enough money for something you
want to buy

[ə'flout]
afloat floating on the water
[ə'freid]
afraid frightened; full of fear
['a:ftə]
after later; behind; following on
[a:ftə'nu:n]
afternoon the time between midday and sunset
['a:ftəwədz]
afterwards at a later time
[ə'gen]
again once more
[ə'genst]
against in an opposite direction to; on the opposite
side to
[eidʒ]
age the number of years something or someone
has been alive, or has existed
['adʒail]
agile lively; nimble
[ə'gri:]
agree to consent to something, or to think the same
as someone else
[ə'griəbl]
agreeable friendly; easy to get on with
[ə'graund]
aground stuck on the sand or rocks. Ships
sometimes run aground and cannot move
without help.
[ə'hed]
ahead in front: before
[eim]
aim to point a gun or other weapon steadily at the
thing you want to hit
[eə]
air the mixture of gases which we breathe and
which surrounds the earth
['eəkra:ft]
aircraft any machine that can rise in the air and
move through it
['eəfi:ld]
airfield a place where aircraft can land and take off
['eəfo:s]
air force aircraft used for fighting and the people
who control them

['eəgʌn]
airgun   a gun in which the bullet is shot by the force
of compressed air

['eəmən]
airman   a man who flies or helps to fly aircraft

['eəpo:t]
airport   the place where aeroplanes come in to land
and take off

['eətait]
airtight   closed so tightly that air cannot get in or out

[ail]
aisle   a pathway between rows of seats in a church,
a cinema or theatre

[ə'la:m]
alarm   sudden surprise or fear. The same word also
means a warning of danger, often a bell.

['albəm]
album   a book of blank pages in which you keep a
collection of things like stamps or photographs

[eil]
ale   a kind of beer

[ə'lə:t]
alert   wide awake; active or watchful

['aldʒibrə]
algebra   a branch of mathematics in which you use
letters as well as figures

['alibai]
alibi   an excuse by someone that he could not have
done something, because he can prove that he
was somewhere else when it happened

[ə'lait]
alight   in flames; burning

[ə'laiv]
alive   living; not dead

[o:l]
all   the whole of; everything or everyone

['ali]
alley   a narrow passage between buildings in cities
and towns

['aligeitə]
alligator   a dangerous animal very like a crocodile,
but with a shorter nose

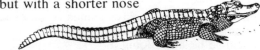

[ə'lau]
allow   to permit or let

['aloi]
alloy   a mixture of two or more metals

['o:l'rait]
all right   good; safe and sound; agreed

['o:lmənak]
almanac   a book that gives information about the
weather and other things that may happen in
the days. weeks and months of one year

['a:mənd]
almond   a kind of flat nut that grows inside the fruit
of an almond tree

['o:lmoust]
almost   nearly, but not quite

[ə'loun]
alone   all by yourself; with nobody else

[ə'laud]
aloud   out loud; the opposite of silent

['alfəbit]
alphabet   all the letters used in a language, arranged
in a special order

[o:l'redi]
already   sooner than expected

[al'seiʃən]
alsatian   a large wolf-like dog

['o:lsou]
also   as well as; too; in addition

['o:ltə]
altar   a kind of raised table inside a church

['o:ltə]
alter   to make a change in something. to make or
become different in some way

[o:ltə'reiʃən]
alteration   a change

[o:l'ðou]
although   even if; but; in spite of

[alju'miniəm]
aluminium   a lightweight, silver-coloured metal

['o:lweiz]
always   at all times; forever

['amətə]
amateur   someone who plays games or takes part
in something without being paid.
because he likes doing it

[ə'meiz]
amaze   to surprise greatly

[am'biʃən]
ambition   a wish to do very well, or to have power

['ambl]
amble   to walk along slowly

['ambjuləns]
ambulance   a special car for taking people who are
    ill or hurt to hospital

[ə'mʌŋ]
among   in the midst of

[ə'maunt]
amount   a quantity; the sum reached when several
    things are added together

['ampl]
ample   of a large size; in plenty

[ə'mju:z]
amuse   to make others smile or laugh by something
    you say or do

['aŋkə]
anchor   a heavy iron hook which is attached
    to a ship by a chain. When it is thrown
    over the side. it digs into the sea bed
    and stops the ship from moving.

['eindʒəl]
angel   a messenger from God

['aŋgl]
angle   the corner made when two lines meet at a
    point

[aŋ'go:rə]
angora   wool made from the long silky hair of the
    angora goat or rabbit

['aŋgri]
angry   very cross; in a bad temper

['animəl]
animal   any living creature which is not a plant

['aŋkl]
ankle   the thin bony part of your leg just above
    your foot

[ani'və:səri]
anniversary   a day which is remembered each year
    for something special which happened once.
    like a wedding anniversary

[ə'naʊns]
announce   to make something known by telling
   everyone

[ə'nɔɪ]
annoy   to make someone rather cross

['anərak]
anorak   a waterproof jacket, usually with a hood

[ə'nʌðə]
another   one more; a different one

['aːnsə]
answer   anything said or written in reply, usually to
   a question

[ant]
ant   a small insect

[ant'aːktɪk]
antarctic   at or around the South Pole

['anθəm]
anthem   a piece of music sung by a church choir.
   The same word also means the national song
   of a country.

[antɪ'klɒkwaɪz]
anti-clockwise   the opposite direction to the way
   clock hands move

['anvɪl]
anvil   an iron block on which pieces of metal can be
   hammered into shape

[aŋ'zaɪəti]
anxiety   worry; a feeling of fear about something
   you think might happen

['aŋkʃəs]
anxious   worried or afraid about something you
   think might happen

['eniθɪŋ]
anything   a thing of any kind

[ə'paːt]
apart   not together

[eɪp]
ape   a large monkey without a tail

['eɪpeks]
apex   the highest tip of something, such as the top
   point of a triangle

[apə'reɪtəs]
apparatus   a collection of things that help you to do
   something, such as ropes and bars in a
   gymnasium

[ə'pi:l]
appeal   to ask for help

[ə'piə]
appear   to come into sight

[ə'piərəns]
appearance   the way someone or something looks
   to you; the coming into sight of someone or
   something

['apitait]
appetite   the desire to eat

[ə'plo:d]
applaud   to show you like some entertainment or
   performance by clapping your hands together

['apl]
apple   a round red, green or yellow fruit which
   grows on a tree

[ə'prout∫]
approach   to go nearer to someone or something

[ə'proksimət]
approximate   nearly correct

['eiprikot]
apricot   a fruit which looks like a small yellow
   peach

['eiprən]
apron   a piece of cloth which you tie around you to
   keep your clothes clean

[ə'kweəriəm]
aquarium   a container, usually a glass tank, where
   fish and other water animals are kept for people
   to look at

[a:k]
arc   a part of a circle, a curved line

[a:t∫]
arch   a part of something, usually a building, that is
   curved, such as the top of a doorway or
   window

['a:t∫əri]
archery   shooting at a target with bow and arrow

['a:kitekt]
architect   someone who designs and plans buildings

['a:klait]
arc-light   a lamp lit by an arc of electricity

['a:ktik]
arctic   at or around the North Pole; very cold

['eəriə]
area   the extent of space on the ground or on a floor

[ə'ri:nə]
arena   a large open space with seats all around,
where you can watch games or sports

['a:gju:]
argue   to give reasons for or against something
which is being discussed

['a:gjumənt]
argument   reasons for or against your opinion about
something; a discussion

[ə'raiz]
arise   to get up

[ə'riθmətik]
arithmetic   working with numbers, like adding,
subtracting, multiplying and dividing

[a:k]
ark   the houseboat which saved Noah and his
family and the animals from drowning in the
Flood. The same word also means a chest in
which holy books are kept.

[a:m]
arm   the part of your body between your hand
and your shoulder

[a:'ma:də]
armada   a great fleet of warships

[a:mə'dilou]
armadillo   a small animal with an armour-like
covering

['a:mtʃeə]
armchair   a chair with sides on which to rest your
arms

['a:mə]
armour   a covering, usually made of metal, to
protect the body in battle

['a:mpit]
armpit   the hollow place under the top part of your
arm

[aːmz]
arms   war weapons, such as guns and cannons

['aːmi]
army   a large group of soldiers

[ə'raund]
around   on all sides

[ə'rauz]
arouse   to wake someone or stir him into action

[ə'reindʒ]
arrange   to put in a special order

[ə'raiv]
arrive   to reach the place you set out for

['arou]
arrow   a thin straight stick made of wood with a
sharp pointed tip. You shoot it with a bow.

[aːt]
art   drawing, painting and sculpture. The same
word is also used when something is done with
great skill.

['aːtful]
artful   cunning; clever in a rather sneaky way

['aːtikl]
article   a thing of a particular kind, such as an article
of clothing. The same word also means a piece
written in a newspaper or magazine.

['aːtist]
artist   a person who paints or draws pictures

[ə'send]
ascend   to go up; to move upward

[aʃ]
ash   the powdery stuff left when something has
completely burned up

[ə'ʃeimd]
ashamed   feeling shame

[ə'said]
aside   to one side; apart

[aːsk]
ask   to put a question to someone

[ə'sliːp]
asleep   sleeping; not awake

['aspərin]
aspirin   a pain-killing medicine, usually in
white tablets

[as]
ass   a donkey, an animal rather like a small horse

[ə'sembl]
assemble to meet together, as when the whole
  school is called together for assembly

[ə'sist]
assist to help

[ə'sistənt]
assistant a helper; someone who serves in a shop

[ə'sɔ:tid]
assorted of many different kinds

[əs'trolədʒə]
astrologer a fortune-teller who studies the stars

[əs'trolədʒi]
astrology the study of the stars as a way of telling
  your fortune

['astrənɔ:t]
astronaut someone who travels
  in space

[əs'tronəmə]
astronomer a scientist who studies the stars and
  other bodies in the sky

[əs'tronəmi]
astronomy the scientific study of stars and other
  bodies in the sky

['aθli:t]
athlete someone who is good at sports and games

['atləs]
atlas a book of maps

['atməsfiə]
atmosphere the air that is around the earth

['atəm]
atom an extremely small particle of anything

[ə'tatʃ]
attach to fasten, join or tie together

[ə'tak]
attack to make a move to hurt someone or
  something

[ə'tempt]
attempt to try; to make an effort

[ə'tend]
attend to be present. The same word also means
  to listen carefully to someone.

[ə'tendənt]
attendant   a helper or servant in a public place, such as a car-park, theatre or cinema

['atik]
attic   a room just under the roof of a building

[ə'trakt]
attract   to make something or someone come nearer

[ə'traktiv]
attractive   charming; lovely; having the power to make people want to be near you

['ɔ:kʃən]
auction   a public sale where things are sold to the people who offer the most money for them

['ɔ:diəns]
audience   a group of people listening to or watching something like a play or a concert

[a:nt]
aunt   the sister of your father or mother

[ɔ:'θɔrəti]
authority   the power to control what other people do. The headmaster of a school has authority over the teachers and pupils.

[ɔ:təbai'ogrəfi]
autobiography   the story of a person's life written by himself and not by someone else

['ɔ:təməbi:l]
automobile   any vehicle with an engine, meant to be driven on the road

['ɔ:təm]
autumn   the season between summer and winter, when the leaves fall

['avinju:]
avenue   a wide street or pathway, usually with trees on both sides

[eivi'eiʃən]
aviation   the art of flying aircraft

['eivieitə]
aviator   a pilot who flies an aircraft

[ə'void]
avoid   to escape; to keep out of the way of something

[ə'weit]
await   to wait for or look for

[ə'weik]
awake   not asleep. You can hear and see what is going on around you.

[ə'wo:d]
award   to give someone something he has won, like a prize or medal

[ə'weə]
aware   knowing about something, as when you are aware of the danger of crossing a road with heavy traffic

[ə'wei]
away   not here or with you; absent

[o:]
awe   great fear and wonder; great respect

['o:ful]
awful   very bad, ugly or nasty

['o:kwəd]
awkward   clumsy. The same word also means not convenient or not comfortable.

[aks]
axe   a sharp tool with a long handle, used for chopping wood

['aksis]
axis   a real or imaginary line through the middle of an object, around which the object turns

['aksl]
axle   the long bar on a vehicle to which the wheels are attached

[ə'zeiliə]
azalea   a shrub like a rhododendron, but smaller, with brightly coloured flowers

['eiʒə]
azure   a clear sky-blue colour

['babl]
babble   to talk or make sounds in a foolish way: to make a murmuring sound as water does in a stream or brook

[bə'bu:n]
baboon   a large monkey with a short tail and a long dog-like face

['beibi]
baby   a very young child who cannot walk yet

['beibiiʃ]
babyish   like a baby

['batʃələ]
bachelor   a man who has not married

['beikən]
bacon   pigmeat that has been dried and salted

[bad]
bad   not good; wrong; spoiled

[badʒ]
badge   a special sign or mark you wear to show you
   belong to a certain school or club

['badʒə]
badger   a grey, black and white striped animal
   which burrows in the earth with its long front
   claws

['badmintən]
badminton   a game rather like tennis, in which you
   use a smaller racket and a shuttlecock

['baflin]
baffling   too hard or puzzling to understand

[bag]
bag   a sack for holding things, often made of paper
   or plastic, but sometimes of leather or cloth

['bagidʒ]
baggage   another word for luggage

[beit]
bait   food used to attract fish or animals, so that
   they can be caught

[beik]
bake   to cook in an oven

['beikə]
baker   a person who bakes and sells bread and
   cakes

['baləns]
balance   to hold something steady so that it does
   not tip or fall over

['balkəni]
balcony   a platform, usually with railings or a low
   wall around it. It is built out from the side of a
   building.

[bɔ:ld]
bald   without any hair on the head

[beil]
bale a specially packed bundle of something, like straw or cotton

[bo:l]
ball an object which is completely round, often used for playing games. The same word also means a splendid dancing party.

[balə'ri:nə]
ballerina a girl ballet dancer

['balei]
ballet (*say balay*) a kind of dancing which tells a story in movement, with music, but without using words

[bə'lu:n]
balloon a bag filled with air or gas so that it can float above the ground

['bo:lpoint]
ballpoint a pen with a tiny ball instead of a point at the end

['bo:lrum]
ballroom a very big room used for dancing

[bam'bu:]
bamboo a kind of very tall grass with stiff hollow stems which are used for canes or for making furniture

[ban]
ban an order to put a stop to something

[bə'na:nə]
banana a long fruit with a thick yellow skin

[band]
band a group of people, sometimes playing musical instruments

['bandidʒ]
bandage a piece of cloth for covering up a wound

['bandit]
bandit a robber, usually one who robs people on the roads while they are travelling

[baŋ]
bang a loud and sudden noise. The same word also means to hit something hard.

['baŋgl]
bangle   a bracelet in the shape of a large ring

['banistə]
banister   a rail to hold on to at the side of a
staircase

['bandʒou]
banjo   a musical instrument which you play by
plucking the strings

[baŋk]
bank   a place where people put their money
so that it will be safe

['baŋknouts]
banknotes   paper money

['banə]
banner   a flag, sometimes with two poles

['baŋkwit]
banquet   a feast; a special dinner party

[ba:]
bar   a long shaped piece of hard material, usually
metal or wood. The same word also means
a counter where you can buy drinks.

['ba:bikju:]
barbecue   an outdoor party where meat is cooked
over an open fire

['ba:bd'waiə]
barbed wire   wire twisted so that sharp points stick
out. It is used as fencing.

['ba:bə]
barber   a man who cuts hair and shaves beards

[beə]
bare   without covering or decoration

['ba:gin]
bargain   something you buy that costs less than the
usual price. The same word also means to
argue with the seller about the price of
something you want to buy.

[ba:dʒ]
barge   a cargo boat which has a flat bottom

[ba:k]
bark   the tough covering on a tree trunk and
branches. The same word also means the loud
sharp noise dogs and some other animals make.

['ba:li]
barley   a plant from which we get a kind of grain;
     the name of that grain

[ba:n]
barn   a large farm building used mainly for storing
     grain, hay and other crops

['barən]
baron   a nobleman

['barəks]
barracks   the buildings where soldiers live

['barəl]
barrel   a container made of curved pieces of wood
     held together with hoops

['barən]
barren   not able to produce fruit, plants, babies or
     seeds. The land in deserts and on some
     mountains is barren because nothing will grow
     there.

['bariə]
barrier   something, like a fence or wall, that stops
     you from going further

['barou]
barrow   a two-wheeled cart that is pushed by a man

[beis]
base   the bottom of anything; the part on which
     something stands or is built

['beismənt]
basement   the lowest part of a building, usually
     below the ground

[baʃ]
bash   to hit something so hard that it is smashed or
     dented

['baʃful]
bashful   another word for shy

['beisn]
basin   a round bowl for holding water

[ba:sk]
bask   to warm yourself in the sun

['ba:skit]
basket   a container made of straw or thin pieces of
     wood. It has a handle so that you can carry
     things inside.

[bat]
bat a shaped piece of wood used to hit a ball in games. The same word also means a small mouse-like animal that flies at night.

[ba:θ]
bath a large container in which you can wash yourself all over

[beið]
bathe to take a bath or a swim

['ba:θrum]
bathroom a room with a bath in it

['batən]
baton a stick for beating time to music

['batə]
batter to beat or strike something over and over again. The same word also means a mixture of flour and liquid used in cooking.

['batəri]
battery a container for storing electricity

['batl]
battle a fight

['batlʃip]
battleship a warship with heavy armour and big guns

[bo:l]
bawl to cry out or shout very loudly

[bei]
bay a part of the sea or lake that makes a curve into the land

['beənit]
bayonet a long sharp blade attached to a rifle, so that it can be used like a spear

[bə'za:]
bazaar a market-place or fair where things are sold, usually to raise money for charity

[bi:tʃ]
beach the strip of land next to the sea, covered with sand or pebbles

['bi:kən]
beacon a signalling light, like a bonfire or lighthouse

[bi:d]
bead a small ball with a hole through it. You can
thread many beads together to make a necklace.

[bi:k]
beak the hard pointed part of a bird's mouth

['bi:kə]
beaker a tall cup, often without a handle

[bi:m]
beam a long thick piece of wood. The same word
also means a ray of light.

[bi:n]
bean a vegetable with large seeds that grow in pods

[beə]
bear a large heavy animal with thick shaggy fur and
a very short tail. The same word also means
to carry something or to put up with something.

[biəd]
beard the hair on a man's chin

['beəriŋ]
bearing the part of a machine on which another
part moves or slides. The same word also
means the way you carry yourself.

[bi:st]
beast an animal

[bi:t]
beat to hit over and over again; to keep regular
time in music. The same word also means
to do better than another person or team in a
game or a race.

['bju:təful]
beautiful lovely; very pretty

['bju:ti]
beauty great loveliness

[bi'kʌm]
become to grow to be something

[bed]
bed a soft place to sleep, with blankets and a pillow.
The same word is also used for a place where
flowers are grown, and for the bottom of the sea.

['bedkloυðz]
bedclothes   the covers on a bed

['bedrum]
bedroom   a room where there is a bed

['bedsaid]
bedside   the space next to a bed

['bedspred]
bedspread   the top cover on a bed

[bi:]
bee   an insect with four wings and a sting. It makes honey and wax.

[bi:tʃ]
beech   a kind of tree with smooth silver-grey bark

[bi:f]
beef   the meat from a cow or bull

['bi:haiv]
beehive   a house for bees

['bi:lain]
bee-line   a straight line between two places

[biə]
beer   a strong drink made from malt

['bi:tl]
beetle   an insect with four wings. The two front wings are hard, and protect the back wings when they are folded.

['bi:tru:t]
beetroot   a dark red vegetable

[bi'fo:]
before   ahead; in front

[beg]
beg   to ask earnestly or humbly for something

['begə]
beggar   someone who lives by asking for money and food from others

[bi'gin]
begin   to start

[bi'giniŋ]
beginning   the start of something

[bi'heiv]
behave   to act in a good or a bad way, showing good or bad behaviour

[bi'heivjə]
behaviour   how you act or behave; your manners

[bi'haind]
behind   at the back of; to the rear of

[bi'li:v]
believe   to accept what someone says as the truth;
     to have faith

[bel]
bell   a cup-shaped piece of metal
     which makes a ringing sound
     when struck

['belou]
bellow   to roar or yell loudly

['beli]
belly   another word for stomach

[bi'loŋ]
belong   to be the property of; to be part of

[bi'lou]
below   underneath; at a lower level

[belt]
belt   a long strip of material, usually leather, which
     fastens around the waist

[bentʃ]
bench   a long seat, usually made of wood

[bend]
bend   to make something crooked or curved

[bi'ni:θ]
beneath   under something

['berei]
beret   (*say berray*)   a round flat soft hat

['beri]
berry   any small round juicy fruit without a stone

[bə:θ]
berth   a bed or bunk in a ship or train

[bi'said]
beside   near; next to

[best]
best   most good

[bet]
bet   to risk your money against someone else's on
     the result of a game or race

[bi'trei]
betray   to give away secret information; to let
     someone down by breaking a promise

['betə]
better   more than good. The same word also means
     more clever or skilful than someone else.

[bi'twi:n]
between   in a space; among

[bi'weə]
beware to be very careful about something that may be dangerous, like a fierce dog or railway lines

[bi'wildə]
bewilder to puzzle someone or make him not sure what to do

[bi'jond]
beyond farther on, or farther away

[bib]
bib a cloth tied around a baby's neck, to stop food getting on his clothes

['baibl]
bible a holy book

['baisikl]
bicycle a two-wheeled vehicle with a saddle

[bid]
bid to command or invite: to make an offer

[big]
big large; important

[bil]
bill a written note of how much money is owing for work which has been done, or for something which has been bought. The same word also means a bird's beak.

['biljədz]
billiards a game played with hard balls and long sticks called cues, on a table covered with thick green cloth

['biligout]
billy-goat a male goat

[bin]
bin a container for corn, bread, coal, or rubbish

[baind]
bind to fasten or tie together

['biŋgou]
bingo a game of lucky numbers that can be played by lots of people at once, in a hall or theatre

[bi'nokjuləz]
binoculars a kind of double telescope with tubes for both eyes

[bəːtʃ]
birch   a tree with smooth silvery or white bark

[bəːd]
bird   a winged animal covered with feathers

['bəːdkeidʒ]
birdcage   a small cage for a pet bird

[bəːθ]
birth   coming into life, being born

['bəːθdei]
birthday   the day of the year when you were born

['biskit]
biscuit   a crisp flat cake

[bai'sekt]
bisect   to divide in two equal parts

[bit]
bit   a small piece of something

[bitʃ]
bitch   a female dog

[bait]
bite   to take a piece out of something with your teeth

['bitə]
bitter   tasting sharp and sour; not sweet or sugary

[blak]
black   the darkest colour of all. Coal is black.

['blakbəri]
blackberry   a small juicy black fruit which grows wild

['blakbəːd]
blackbird   a black songbird with a yellow beak

['blakbɔːd]
blackboard   a wooden board painted black. You write on it with chalk.

['blakkʌrənt]
blackcurrant   a small black berry

['blaksmiθ]
blacksmith   a man who makes and mends iron things. He also puts metal shoes on horses.

[bleid]
blade   one leaf of grass or wheat. The same word also means the cutting part of a knife.

[bleim]
blame   to find fault with

[blə'monʒ]
blanc-mange   (*say blah-monj*)   a milk jelly

[blaŋk]
blank   without any writing or marks, empty

['blaŋkit]
blanket   a woollen bed-cover

[bla:st]
blast   an explosion: a strong sudden gust of air

[bleiz]
blaze   a brightly burning fire

[bli:tʃ]
bleach   to take the colour out of something

[bli:k]
bleak   cold and windy: without cheer

[bli:t]
bleat   the crying sound made by a lamb, sheep or
      goat

[bli:d]
bleed   to lose blood

[blend]
blend   to mix together

[bles]
bless   to make holy; to ask God to show favour to
      someone or something

[blaind]
blind   not able to see

[bliŋk]
blink   to open and shut your eyes very quickly

['blistə]
blister   a swelling on the skin, like a small bubble,
      often filled with water or blood

['blizəd]
blizzard   a very windy snow storm

[blok]
block   a big piece of something, like wood, metal or
      stone. The same word also means to be in the
      way of something.

[blʌd]
blood   the red liquid which circulates round your
      body

[blu:m]
bloom   to come into flower

['blosəm]
blossom   another name for flower, especially the
      flowers on fruit trees and shrubs

[blot]
blot   a spot or mark, usually of ink

[blauz]
blouse   a loose garment covering the upper part of
the body. It is worn by girls and women.

[blou]
blow   to push air out of your mouth. The same word
also means a hard knock.

[blu:]
blue   a colour. When the sun shines the sky is blue.

['blu:bel]
bluebell   a wild flower with blue blossoms shaped
like bells

['blu:tit]
blue tit   a prettily coloured small wild bird

[blʌnt]
blunt   the opposite of sharp, having a dull edge or
point

[blə:]
blur   to make something look dim or not clear

[blʌʃ]
blush   to go pink in the face because you are shy,
ashamed or upset by something

[bo:]
boar   a male pig

[bo:d]
board   a long flat piece of wood

['bo:də]
boarder   someone who pays to sleep and eat in
someone else's house: someone who lives at
boarding school in term time

['bo:diŋsku:l]
boarding school   a school where children live during
term time

[boust]
boast   to talk a lot about how good you are at things,
to praise yourself or things which belong to you

[bout]
boat   a small ship

[bob]
bob   to move up and down

['bobin]
bobbin   a spool for holding thread or yarn

['bodis]
bodice   the part of a dress from the neck to the
waist. It is usually close-fitting.

['bodi]
body   the whole of a person or animal

['bodiga:d]
bodyguard   a person who guards and protects
someone

[bog]
bog   wet, marshy ground

[boil]
boil   to make water so hot that it bubbles and makes
steam. The same word also means a sore
swelling on your body.

['boilə]
boiler   a container for boiling water, often for
making steam

[bould]
bold   brave; without fear

[boult]
bolt   a metal fastening for doors and gates. The
same word also means to run away.

[bom]
bomb   a metal case that can be exploded

['bomə]
bomber   an aeroplane which carries bombs

[bond]
bond   anything which binds or fastens something
together

[boun]
bone   one of the hard white parts which are joined
together to make the skeletons of our bodies

['bonfaiə]
bonfire   a fire out of doors, usually in a garden

['bonit]
bonnet   a kind of hat that ties under the chin

['boni]
bonny   pretty; healthy-looking

[buk]
book   pages of print bound together in a cover

['bukkeis]
bookcase   a set of shelves for books

[bu:m]
boom a long deep noise, like the sound the word
    boom makes when you say it

['bu:mərəŋ]
boomerang a curved wooden weapon
    that turns in the air and comes back
    to the person who throws it

[bu:t]
boot a shoe that covers part of the leg as well as
    the foot

['bu:'ti:]
bootee a soft woollen boot for babies

['bo:də]
border the outside edge of something

[bo:]
bore to make a deep hole in something by twisting
    a tool round and round. The same word
    also means to make someone tired by dull talk.

[bo:n]
born starting to live

['borou]
borrow to take something which you intend to give
    back

['buzəm]
bosom another word for breast. The same word
    also means close, like a bosom friend.

[bos]
boss a chief or leader

['botəni]
botany the study of plants

['boðə]
bother to annoy or worry. The same word also
    means fuss or trouble.

['botl]
bottle a container, usually made of glass. It has a
    narrow neck and is used to hold liquids.

['botəm]
bottom the lowest part of anything

[bau]
bough (*rhymes with now*) the branch of a tree

['bouldə]
boulder a very large rock or stone

[bauns]
bounce to spring up again after hitting the ground

[baund]
bound   to leap forward. The same word also means
fastened or tied.

[bu'kei]
bouquet (*say bookay*)   a bunch of flowers

[bou]
bow (*rhymes with so*)   a kind of knot used to tie
ribbon or string. The same word also means a
curved strip of wood with a string, used for
shooting arrows.

[bau]
bow (*rhymes with now*)   a way of showing respect.
You bend forward and lower your head.

[boul]
bowl   a deep round dish for holding liquids or food.
The same word also means to throw a ball
overarm, as in cricket.

[boks]
box   a stiff-sided container

['boksə]
boxer   a man who fights with his fists, usually in
padded gloves

[boi]
boy   a male child who will grow up to be a man

['breislit]
bracelet   a pretty chain or ring
you wear on your arm

['breisiz]
braces   pieces of elastic which go over the shoulders
to hold trousers up

['brakit]
bracket   a piece of metal or wood that holds a shelf
up

[brag]
brag   another word for boast

[breid]
braid   to weave strips of hair or material in and out
to make a plait

[brein]
brain   the part inside your head that sends and
receives messages and thoughts and controls
what your body does

[breik]
brake   the part of a vehicle which stops the wheels
from going round

['brambl]
bramble   a blackberry bush

[bran]
bran   the skin of grains, which is separated from the
flour

[bra:ntʃ]
branch   the arm of a tree that grows out of its trunk

[brand]
brand   a mark on something to show whose it is
or who made it

[bra:s]
brass   a yellowish metal made by melting copper
and zinc together

[breiv]
brave   not running away from danger, even when
you are afraid

[bro:n]
brawn   strength; powerful muscle

[brei]
bray   the cry of a donkey

[bred]
bread   a food made mostly from flour, and baked
into a loaf

[bredθ]
breadth   how wide or broad something is

[breik]
break   to pull apart; to damage or spoil something

['brekfəst]
breakfast   the first meal of the day

[brest]
breast   the top front part of the body

[breθ]
breath   the air that is taken in and forced out by the
lungs

[bri:ð]
breathe   to take air into the body and force it out
again

[bri:d]
breed   to produce young ones

[bri:z]
breeze   a gentle wind

['bruəri]
brewery   a place where beer is made

[brik]
brick   a block of baked clay used in building

[braid]
bride a woman on her wedding day

['braidzmeid]
bridesmaid an unmarried woman who attends the
  bride on her wedding day

[bridʒ]
bridge something built over a road or river so that
  you can get across to the other side

[bri:f]
brief short; not long

[bri'geid]
brigade a group of men in uniform who work
  together, like a brigade of soldiers or a brigade
  of firemen

[brait]
bright shining; giving out light

['briljənt]
brilliant very bright; dazzling. The same word also
  means very clever.

[brim]
brim the upper edge of something, like the brim of
  a cup. The same word also means the part of a
  hat that sticks out all round.

[briŋ]
bring to carry something with you when you come

[brisk]
brisk quick; lively

['brisl]
bristle a short stiff hair

['britl]
brittle easily broken

[bro:d]
broad wide; the opposite of narrow

['bro:d'bi:n]
broadbean a bean with a wide pod

['bro:dka:st]
broadcast to send out radio or television
  programmes of news, music and entertainment

[broŋ'kaitis]
bronchitis an illness in the throat and chest that
  makes you cough a lot

[bronz]
bronze   a reddish-brown metal made by melting
    copper and tin together

[brout∫]
brooch (*say broach*)   an ornament which can be
    pinned to clothing

[bru:d]
brood   to sit quietly and think about something
    rather anxiously. The same word also means
    young birds all hatched in one nest at the
    same time.

[bruk]
brook   a small stream

[bru:m]
broom   a brush with a long handle, for cleaning
    floors

[broθ]
broth   a kind of thin soup

['brʌðə]
brother   a son of the same parents

[brau]
brow   the forehead

[braun]
brown   a colour. Chocolate is brown.

['brauni]
brownie   a junior member of the Girl Guides. The
    same word also means a kind of goblin who is
    supposed to help with housework.

[bru:z]
bruise   a dark-coloured mark where the skin has
    been hit but not broken

[brʌ∫]
brush   a bunch of hairs on a handle, used for
    cleaning or painting or doing your hair

['bʌbl]
bubble   a ball of liquid containing gas or air

['bʌkit]
bucket   a container with a handle for holding or
    carrying water

['bʌkl]
buckle   a fastening on a belt or strap

[bʌd]
bud   a flower or leaf not fully open

[bʌdʒ]
budge   to move a little

['bʌdʒərigaː]
budgerigar a bird like a very small parrot,
  often kept as a pet

['bʌfəlou]
buffalo a wild ox

['bʌfəz]
buffers flat metal plates at each end of a railway
  carriage or engine, or at the end of a railway
  track. They prevent damage from bumping.

[bʌg]
bug a tiny insect

[bild]
build to make or construct

['bildə]
builder a man who puts up buildings

['bildiŋ]
building anything with a roof and walls

[bʌlb]
bulb a small glass lamp which gives out electric
  light. The same word also means the rounded
  root from which some flowers grow.

[bʌldʒ]
bulge to swell out

[bʌlk]
bulk a large amount

[bul]
bull the male of cattle.
  Male elephants are
  also called bulls.

['buldog]
bulldog a heavily-built dog with a large head and
  powerful shoulders

['buldouzə]
bulldozer a powerful tractor used for shifting large
  loads of earth, sand or rubbish

['bulit]
bullet a small piece of metal which is shot from a
  gun

['bulfrog]
bullfrog a large frog with a deep voice

['bulək]
bullock a young bull

['buli]
bully someone who picks on others weaker or
  smaller than himself

['bulrʌʃ]
bulrush   a kind of tall reed that grows in or near water

['bʌmblbi:]
bumblebee   a large fluffy bee which makes a loud buzzing noise

[bʌmp]
bump   a swelling, or a raised part of anything. The same word also means to knock into something.

['bʌmpə]
bumper   a piece of curved metal on the front and back of cars to protect them if they bump into something

[bʌn]
bun   a small soft round cake

[bʌntʃ]
bunch   a group of things tied or growing together, like a bunch of flowers

['bʌndl]
bundle   a number of articles bound together, like a bundle of clothes

['bʌŋgəlou]
bungalow   a house without an upstairs

[bʌŋk]
bunk   a shelf-like bed attached to a wall

[boi]
buoy   (*say* boy)   something floating on the water but anchored to the sea bed. It marks the places where there is danger, or where small boats can be tied up.

['bə:dn]
burden   a load that is very heavy to carry

['bjuərou]
bureau   a chest of drawers with a writing desk on top. The same word also means an office.

['bə:glə]
burglar   someone who breaks into buildings at night and steals things

['beriəl]
burial   the burying of something, like a dead body, in the ground

[bə:n]
burn   to be on fire, or to set something on fire

['bʌrou]
burrow   a hole in the ground which has been dug by wild animals to live in. Rabbits and foxes live in burrows.

[bə:st]
burst   to give way suddenly; to rush forward

['beri]
bury   to put something somewhere deep, usually under the ground

[bʌs]
bus   a large vehicle which carries many people

['bʌzbi]
busby   a tall fur hat that some soldiers wear

[buʃ]
bush   a shrub, like a small tree with lots of branches growing close to the ground

['biznis]
business (*say bizness*)   occupation, work

[bʌst]
bust   a sculpture of someone's head, shoulders and chest. Sometimes the word means the breast.

['bʌsl]
bustle   to rush about busily

['bizi]
busy   having something to do all the time; working hard

['butʃə]
butcher   a man who cuts up meat and sells it

[bʌt]
butt   a large barrel for holding liquids

['bʌtə]
butter   a kind of soft yellow fat made from cream

['bʌtəkʌp]
buttercup   a bright yellow wildflower

['bʌtəflai]
butterfly   an insect with large coloured wings

['bʌtəskotʃ]
butterscotch   a sweet made from sugar and butter

['bʌtəks]
buttocks the two rounded parts which you sit on, at the back of your body below the waist

['bʌtn]
button a round fastening on clothes; any small knob

['bʌtnhoul]
buttonhole a narrow hole for a button to fit into

[bai]
buy to give money in exchange for something

[bʌz]
buzz the humming sound a bee makes

[kab]
cab the place in an engine or lorry where the driver sits. The same word also means a taxi.

['kabidʒ]
cabbage a vegetable with green or purple leaves growing tightly together in a round ball

['kabin]
cabin a small house or hut made of logs or other rough materials. The same word also means a room for passengers on a ship or aeroplane.

['kabənit]
cabinet a kind of cupboard with glass doors where you keep ornaments or collections of things

['keibl]
cable a very strong thick rope, sometimes made of pieces of wire twisted together

['kakl]
cackle the loud excited noise made by hens

['kaktəs]
cactus a plant with thick leaves and stems, often covered with prickles, which grows in hot dry countries. You can also grow small ones as house plants.

['kadi]
caddy a small airtight box to keep tea in

[kə'det]
cadet a boy or young man who is learning to be an officer in the army or navy or air force

['kafei]
café (*say caffay*) a place where you can buy a meal or a snack; a small restaurant

[kafə'tiəriə]
cafeteria an eating-place where you fetch your own food from a counter

[keidʒ]
cage   a box or room with bars, where birds or
   animals are kept

[keik]
cake   a sweet food made of flour, fat, eggs and sugar
   and baked in an oven. The same word also
   means a small flat lump of something, like a
   cake of soap.

[kə'laməti]
calamity   something awful that happens, like an
   earthquake or an aeroplane crash in which
   many people are killed or hurt

['kaləndə]
calendar   a list of all the days and dates in each
   week and each month of a year

[ka:f]
calf   a young cow or bull. The same word also
   means the thick part of the back of your leg
   below the knee.

[kɔ:l]
call   to shout or cry out. The same word also means
   to stop at someone's house for a short time.

[ka:m]
calm   quiet; still. The same word also means not
   getting upset or excited when something
   unusual happens.

['kaməl]
camel   a big animal with a long neck and one or two
   humps on its back. It carries people or things
   from place to place in some hot countries.

['kamərə]
camera   a kind of box for taking photographs

['kaməfla:ʒ]
camouflage   to disguise something so that it is
   hidden from the enemy

[kamp]
camp   to live outdoors in a tent. The same word
   also means the place where the tents are set up.

[kan]
can a small airtight metal container for food or liquids. The same word also means to be able to do something.

[kə'nal]
canal a very big ditch, dug across land and filled with water so that ships and boats can move along it

[kə'neəri]
canary a small yellow bird kept as a pet because of its sweet song

['kandl]
candle a rounded stick of wax with a wick through the middle. It burns and gives light.

['kandlstik]
candlestick a holder for a candle

[kein]
cane the hard stem of a plant or small palm tree. The same word also means a light walking stick.

['kanən]
cannon a big heavy gun, sometimes on wheels

[kə'nu:]
canoe a narrow light boat. You use a paddle to make it move through the water.

['kanəpi]
canopy a covering hung over a throne or a bed

[kan'ti:n]
canteen a place in a factory or office building where food and drinks are sold to the people who work there

['kanvəs]
canvas tough strong cloth used for tents and sails and for painting pictures on

[kap]
cap a small soft hat, usually with a peak

[kə'pasəti]
capacity the greatest amount a container will hold

[keip]
cape a piece of clothing without sleeves that goes over the back and shoulders and fastens round

the neck. The same word also means a point of
land sticking out into the sea.

['keipə]
caper   to leap or jump about happily

['kapitl]
capital   a large letter of the alphabet, like A, B, C.
The same word also means the chief city in a
country.

['kapsju:l]
capsule   a tiny container for medicine, which melts
after you have swallowed it. The same word
also means the closed cabin of a spacecraft.

['kaptən]
captain   a person who is in charge of a group of
people, like soldiers, sailors or a football team

['kaptiv]
captive   someone who has been captured and held
prisoner

['kaptʃə]
capture   to catch someone and hold him by force

[ka:]
car   a motor for driving from place to place

['karəmel]
caramel   a kind of sweet, like toffee, made with
sugar and butter cooked together until the
mixture is sticky and brown

['karəvan]
caravan   a small house on wheels, pulled by a car or
a horse. The same word also means a group of
people travelling together for safety, especially
in the desert.

['ka:bjuretə]
carburettor   part of a car engine that mixes air and
petrol

[ka:d]
card   stiff paper. Sometimes it is cut into pieces
with pictures and greetings for special days like
birthdays and Christmas. Cards are also used
in playing games.

['ka:dbo:d]
cardboard   very thick stiff paper

['ka:digən]
cardigan   a knitted woollen jacket

[keə]
care   a worry or trouble. The same word also means
    to look after someone who needs help.

['keəful]
careful   giving special attention to what you are
    doing

['keəlis]
careless   not taking trouble or thinking about what
    you are doing

['keəteikə]
caretaker   a person who looks after a building or
    part of a building

['ka:gou]
cargo   a ship's load

[ka:'neiʃən]
carnation   a pink, red, yellow or white flower with a
    spicy smell

['karəl]
carol   a song of joy or praise, most often heard at
    Christmas time

['ka:pintə]
carpenter   a man who makes things out of wood

['ka:pit]
carpet   a thick soft woven covering for the floor

['karidʒ]
carriage   a vehicle for carrying passengers from
    place to place. The same word also means
    part of a railway train.

['karət]
carrot   a long pointed orange vegetable that grows
    under the ground

['kari]
carry   to take something from one place to another

['karikot]
carry-cot   a bed with handles, used to carry a small
    baby about

[ka:t]
cart   an open wagon with only two wheels

[ka:'tu:n]
cartoon   a short funny film or drawing in a
    newspaper

['ka:tridʒ]
cartridge   a case for holding the gunpowder and
    bullet to be shot from a gun

[ka:v]
carve   to shape a piece of wood or to cut patterns
   on it with a knife. The same word also means
   to cut meat into slices.

[keis]
case   a kind of box to keep or carry things in

[kaʃ]
cash   coins and banknotes

[ka'ʃiə]
cashier   someone who looks after the money in a
   bank, a shop or an office

[ka:st]
cast   to throw something with force. The same word
   also means to shape something by pouring hot
   metal or liquid plaster into a mould.

['ka:stəwei]
castaway   a person who has been shipwrecked

['ka:sl]
castle   an old building with thick stone walls to
   resist enemy attacks

[kat]
cat   a furry animal, usually kept as a pet

['katəlog]
catalogue   a list of things in a special order, like a
   list of books in a library

['katəpʌlt]
catapult   a Y-shaped stick with elastic attached,
   used for shooting stones

[katʃ]
catch   to get hold of something

['katəpilə]
caterpillar   a grub that turns into a moth or butterfly

[kə'θi:drəl]
cathedral   a very large and important church

['katkinz]
catkins   small fluffy flowers without petals. They
   grow on willow and hazel trees.

['katl]
cattle   cows, bulls and oxen

['kɒliflauə]
cauliflower a cabbage-like vegetable with a large
    white part in the middle that is good to eat

[kɔːz]
cause to make something happen

['kɔːʃən]
caution carefulness; watchfulness

['kavəlri]
cavalry soldiers on horseback

[keiv]
cave a big hole in rocks or in the side of a hill

['kavən]
cavern a large cave

[kɔː]
caw the loud hoarse cry of a crow

[siːs]
cease to stop

['siːliŋ]
ceiling the top of a room

['seləndain]
celandine a yellow wildflower

[selə'breiʃən]
celebration a party on a special day like a
    birthday or a national holiday

['seləri]
celery a vegetable with long white stalks and pale
    green leaves

[sel]
cell a room where prisoners are kept. The same
    word also means the small bare room a monk
    lives in.

['selə]
cellar an underground room where coal and wine
    and other things are kept

[si'ment]
cement a greyish powdered clay mixture that
    hardens when it is mixed with sand and water.
    It is used to stick bricks and other building
    materials together.

['semətri]
cemetery a place where people who have died are
    buried

['sentigreid]
centigrade divided into a hundred degrees. On a
    centigrade thermometer freezing point is shown
    as zero and boiling point at 100.

['sentimi:tə]
centimetre a hundredth part of a metre

['sentə]
centre the middle part of anything

['sentʃuri]
century a hundred years

['siəriəl]
cereal any kind of grain used as food

['serimə ni]
ceremony an important and special happening, like
    a wedding or a coronation

['sə:tn]
certain sure; without any doubt

[sə'tifikət]
certificate something written or printed which
    proves that something is true; written proof
    that you have passed an examination

['tʃafintʃ]
chaffinch a small wild bird with a cheerful song

[tʃein]
chain metal rings joined together

[tʃeə]
chair a single seat with a back to lean against

['ʃalei]
chalet (*say shalay*) a small wooden house, usually
    with overhanging eaves

[tʃo:k]
chalk a soft white stone which can be made into
    sticks for writing on the blackboard

['tʃalindʒ]
challenge to invite someone to try to beat you at
    something, such as running, swimming or
    wrestling

['tʃampiən]
champion someone who is better at a sport than
    anyone else. The same word also means to
    stick up for someone or defend him.

[tʃaːns]
chance something that happens without being planned. The same word also means an opportunity.

[tʃeindʒ]
change to make something different from what it was before

['tʃanl]
channel a deep narrow strip of sea-water between two pieces of land. The same word also means a kind of path through the air used for television programmes.

[tʃap]
chap a boy or a man

['tʃapəl]
chapel a small church or a separate part of a large church

['tʃaptə]
chapter a section of a book divided off by numbers — chapter 1, chapter 2

['kariktə]
character what a person is like. Someone's character may be good or bad, honest or dishonest, nice or nasty.

[ʃəˈraːd]
charade (*say sharahd*) a game in which you act out parts of a word and then the whole word

['tʃaːkoul]
charcoal a hard blackened piece of burnt wood. You can draw pictures with it.

[tʃaːdʒ]
charge the cost of something. The same word also means to rush at something. To be in charge is to be in control.

['tʃariət]
chariot an open two-wheeled carriage drawn by horses. In olden days chariots were used in wars and in races.

['tʃarəti]
charity   a feeling of kindness and affection towards
    other people: a gift of money, food or shelter
    to people in need

[tʃa:m]
charm   to make others think you are nice and
    pleasant to know. The same word also means
    something that has magic powers or can
    bring good luck.

[tʃa:t]
chart   a map, usually of the sea

[tʃeis]
chase   to run after

['ʃasi]
chassis (*say shassee*)   the framework which forms
    the base of a car

[tʃat]
chat   to talk with someone in a friendly way

['tʃatə]
chatter   to talk a lot about things that are not
    important

['tʃatəboks]
chatterbox   someone who is always talking

['ʃoufə]
chauffeur (*say shofer*)   a man who is paid to drive
    someone else's car

[tʃi:p]
cheap   not costing much money

[tʃi:t]
cheat   to do something that is not honest or right,
    like copying someone else's answers during a
    test

[tʃek]
check   to go back over something to make sure it is
    correct. The same word also means a pattern
    with squares in it.

[tʃi:k]
cheek   the soft side of your face below your eyes
    and either side of your nose

['tʃi:ki]
cheeky   saucy; a bit rude

[tʃiə]
cheer   to shout at someone to do his best or to
    show you are pleased. The same word also
    means joy, happiness.

['tʃiəful]
cheerful   happy; joyful

[tʃi:z]
cheese   a food made from milk

['kemist]
chemist   a man who makes up medicines and sells
them, as well as things like toothpaste and
soap

['kemistri]
chemistry   the study of what things are made of

[tʃek]
cheque (*say check*)   a special piece of paper you
write on to ask your bank to pay some of your
money to someone

['tʃeri]
cherry   a sweet round red or yellow fruit with a
stone in it

['tʃerəb]
cherub   a winged creature
with a child's face

[tʃes]
chess   a game for two people, using pieces called
chessmen on a board marked with black and
white squares

[tʃest]
chest   a large strong box with a lid. The same word
also means the front part of your body
between your neck and your waist.

['tʃesnʌt]
chestnut   a nut. One kind is good to eat when it is
roasted, and the other kind is a conker.

[tʃu:]
chew   to crush or grind with your teeth

['tʃuiŋʌm]
chewing gum   a sweet that you keep chewing but do
not swallow

[tʃik]
chick   a baby bird

['tʃikin]
chicken   a young hen or cock

['tʃikinpoks]
chicken-pox   an illness. You have a high temperature
and lots of spots all over you.

[tʃiːf]
chief   a leader or ruler. We also use the word to mean that something is the most important, like the chief city in a country.

[ˈtʃilblein]
chilblain   a painful itchy swelling on your hands or feet in cold weather

[tʃaild]
child   a boy or girl who is older than a baby, but who is not yet grown up

[ˈtʃildrən]
children   boys and girls

[ˈtʃili]
chilly   feeling cold

[tʃaim]
chime   a musical sound made by a set of bells, usually in a clock

[ˈtʃimni]
chimney   an opening from the fireplace to the roof to let the smoke out

[tʃimpənˈziː]
chimpanzee   a very clever ape, smaller than a gorilla

[tʃin]
chin   the part of your face under your mouth

[ˈtʃainə]
china   cups and plates made from a kind of clay

[tʃiŋk]
chink   a narrow crack or slit. The same word also means a clinking sound, as when you rattle coins together.

[tʃip]
chip   to knock a small piece off something like a cup or vase. The same word also means a small piece of fried potato.

[ˈtʃipmʌŋk]
chipmunk   a small wild animal, like a squirrel with stripes

[tʃəːp]
chirp   a short shrill sound made by some birds and insects

['tʃizl]
chisel a tool with a cutting edge at the end, used for cutting stone or wood

['tʃokələt]
chocolate a sweet brown food or drink made from cocoa

['kwaiə]
choir (*say kwire*) a group of people trained to sing together

[tʃouk]
choke to find it hard to breathe because there is something in your throat or because there is smoke in your lungs

[tʃuːz]
choose to take one thing rather than another

[tʃop]
chop to cut something with hard blows. The same word also means a small piece of meat on a bone.

['tʃopə]
chopper something you use to chop with, like an axe

['tʃopstiks]
chopsticks two thin pieces of wood or ivory used for eating food by people living in some far-eastern countries

['koːrəs]
chorus the part of a song that comes after each verse, when everyone joins in the singing. The same word means the people on a stage who dance and sing together.

['krisn]
christen to give a baby its first or Christian name, usually in a church

['kristjən]
Christian a follower of Jesus Christ

['krisməs]
Christmas the birthday of Jesus Christ

[kroum]
chrome a silvery-looking metal

[kri'zanθəməm]
chrysanthemum   an autumn flower with lots of
     brightly coloured curving petals

[tʃʌk]
chuck   to throw

['tʃʌkl]
chuckle   to laugh quietly

[tʃʌm]
chum   a close friend

[tʃəːtʃ]
church   a building where people go to worship God

[tʃəːn]
churn   a machine for making butter: a milk can

[si'gaː]
cigar   tobacco leaves rolled tightly together, for
     smoking

[sigə'ret]
cigarette   finely cut pieces of tobacco rolled in thin
     paper, for smoking

['sindəz]
cinders   coal or wood that has been burned but not
     burned away to ashes

['sinəmə]
cinema   a building where films are shown

['səːkl]
circle   a completely round ring

['səːkjuleit]
circulate   to move around and come back to the
     beginning. The blood in our veins circulates
     through every part of our bodies.

['səːkəs]
circus   a travelling show with acrobats and animals
     and clowns who do all sorts of tricks

['siti]
city   a very large town

['sivl]
civil   to do with people or the government, like the
     civil service, but not the armed forces. The
     same word means polite.

[kleim]
claim   to demand something because you believe
     you should have it

[klaŋ]
clang   a loud deep echoing noise, usually made by
     big bells

[klaŋk]
clank   a deep ringing sound such as the noise made by rattling heavy chains

[klap]
clap   to slap the palms of your hands together

[klaʃ]
clash   a loud noise when things are banged together

[klaːsp]
clasp   to hold tightly. The same word also means a fastening for a brooch or other jewellery.

[klaːs]
class   a number of children or older people learning something together

['klaːsrum]
classroom   a room in school where children learn things

['klatə]
clatter   a rattling noise, as when you are washing up crockery and cutlery

[kloː]
claw   one of the sharp curved nails on the foot of an animal or bird

[klei]
clay   soft sticky earth that can be baked to make bricks or crockery

[kliːn]
clean   without dirt or dust

['kliːnə]
cleaner   someone or something that cleans things

[klenz]
cleanse   to make clean

[kliə]
clear   bright, or with nothing in the way, so that you can see things easily

[klentʃ]
clench   to close your teeth or fists tightly together

[klaːk]
clerk   someone who does office work, such as answering letters and keeping accounts

['klevə]
clever   quick to learn; able to do things very well

[klik]
click a short snapping sound

[klif]
cliff a high steep rock

['klaimət]
climate the kind of weather a country usually has. Africa and India have hot climates.

[klaim]
climb to move upwards using your feet and sometimes your hands to hold on

[kliŋ]
cling to hold on to something tightly

['klinik]
clinic a place where people go to see doctors or nurses

[kliŋk]
clink a small ringing sound, as when you gently touch coins or glasses together

[klip]
clip to cut or trim something with scissors. The same word also means a small metal fastening for holding letters or papers together.

['klipə]
clipper a large fast ship with many sails

[klouk]
cloak a loose garment without sleeves, usually longer than a cape

['kloukrum]
cloakroom a place where you can leave hats and coats: a lavatory

[klok]
clock a machine that tells you what the time is

['klokwaiz]
clockwise the direction in which clock hands move

['klokwə:k]
clockwork machinery like that which is inside a clock

[klog]
clog to block up something like a drainpipe. The same word also means a wooden shoe.

[klouz], [klous]
close   to shut. The same word also means very near.

[kloθ]
cloth   a woven material that clothes and coverings
are made of

[klouðz]
clothes   all the things you wear, except jewellery

['klouðiŋ]
clothing   another word for clothes

[klaud]
cloud   millions of tiny drops of water floating close
together in the sky. Clouds may look white or
grey.

[klaut]
clout   a blow. The same word also means a piece
of cloth.

['klouvə]
clover   a wild plant with leaves in three rounded
parts and small tight pink or white heads

[klaun]
clown   a man in a circus. He has a funny painted
face and makes us laugh.

[klʌb]
club   a group of people who meet to do things
together, like playing tennis or golf. The same
word also means a heavy stick.

[klʌk]
cluck   the soft short sound a hen makes to her
chicks

[kluː]
clue   something that helps you to find the answer
to a puzzle or mystery

[klʌmp]
clump   a number of plants or trees growing close
together

['klʌmzi]
clumsy   not graceful; not good at handling things

['klʌstə]
cluster   a bunch; a group

[klʌtʃ]
clutch   to grab something and hold on to it tightly.
The same word also means a part of machinery
used for starting and stopping an engine.

[koutʃ]
coach   a large carriage pulled by horses, with an

outside seat in front for the driver. The same
word also means a large motor vehicle for long
journeys.

[koul]
coal a hard black mineral used for fuel

['koulmən]
coalman a man who delivers coal

[ko:s]
coarse rough

[koust]
coast the border of land next to the sea. The same
word also means to go downhill in a car
without using the engine, or on a bicycle
without pedalling.

[kout]
coat an outer garment with sleeves

['koblə]
cobbler someone who makes or mends boots and
shoes

['kobweb]
cobweb a very thin net made by a spider to trap
insects

[kok]
cock a male bird: a rooster

['kokərəl]
cockerel a young cock

['koukou]
cocoa a brown powder made from cocoa beans. It
is used to make hot drinks and chocolate.

['koukənʌt]
coconut a very large nut with milky liquid inside

[kod]
cod a large sea fish caught for food

[koud]
code secret words or signals used to send
messages

['kofi]
coffee a hot drink made from ground-up roasted
coffee beans

['kofin]
coffin a large wooden or metal box that a dead
body is put into

[koil]
coil to wind in rings

[koin]
coin a piece of money made of metal

[kouk]
coke fuel made from coal when the gas has been
baked out of it

[kould]
cold the opposite of hot. A fire is hot and ice is
cold. The same word also means an illness
which affects the nose and throat.

[kə'laps]
collapse to fall to pieces or to fall down

['kolə]
collar the part of a garment round the neck

[kə'lekt]
collect to bring together or gather together

[kə'lekʃən]
collection the things you collect, such as a collection
of stamps, seashells or old coins

['kolidʒ]
college a place where you can go on studying after
you have left secondary school

[kə'laid]
collide to bump or run into something

['koli]
collie a large longhaired sheepdog

['koljəri]
colliery a coal mine

['kʌlə]
colour Red, yellow, blue and green are colours.

[koult]
colt a young horse

['koləm]
column a pillar. The same word also means a line
of soldiers and a list of numbers.

[koum]
comb a short piece of plastic or metal with teeth in
it, used to tidy your hair

[kəm'bain]
combine to mix or join together

['kombain'ha:vistə]
combine-harvester a farm machine that does two
jobs. It harvests the grain and then threshes it.

[kʌm]
come to move near

[kə'mi:diən]
comedian an actor who makes people laugh

['komədi]
comedy a funny play or film

['kʌmfətəbl]
comfortable to be feeling at ease, without pain or
worry

['komik]
comic a picture paper for children

[kə'ma:nd]
command to tell someone he must do something

[kə'mens]
commence to begin

[kə'mit]
commit to do something, usually something wrong
like a crime

[kə'miti]
committee a small number of people who meet
together to arrange things

['komən]
common ordinary; usual. The same word also
means an open piece of ground that doesn't
belong to one person.

[kə'mouʃən]
commotion noise and fuss

[kəm'panjən]
companion someone who goes somewhere with
you; a friend

['kʌmpəni]
company a group of people working together in a
business. The same word also means a group of
people who are guests at a party.

[kəm'peə]
compare to say how things are alike or different; to
show whether one thing is better or worse than
another

['kʌmpəs]
compass an instrument for
showing north. south.
east and west

['kʌmpəsiz]
compasses   a tool for drawing a circle

[kəm'pel]
compel   to force someone to do something

[kəm'pi:t]
compete   to be in a test or race to see who is best

[kompi'tiʃən]
competition   a test of how much people know or
   how good they are at something. The winner
   usually gets a prize.

[kəm'plein]
complain   to tell about something that is upsetting
   you, or that you think is wrong

[kəm'pli:t]
complete   whole, with nothing missing

['komplikeitid]
complicated   not easy or simple; difficult to
   understand

['kompləmənt]
compliment   something nice said about someone to
   please him

[kompə'ziʃən]
composition   things put together to make a whole
   thing. A number of notes make a musical
   composition, and words written down make a
   written composition.

[kompri'henʃən]
comprehension   the ability to understand

[kəm'pres]
compress   to press together

[kən'si:l]
conceal   to hide; to keep secret

[kən'si:tid]
conceited   thinking too highly of yourself

['konsəntreit]
concentrate   to bring together in one place: to think
   hard about one thing

[kən'sə:n]
concern   to do with; to interest or trouble yourself
   with

['konsət]
concert   a musical entertainment

[kən'klu:d]
conclude   to end or finish something

['kɔŋkri:t]
concrete a mixture of cement, gravel and water that dries as hard as stone

[kən'dens]
condense to make something smaller or shorter by taking part of it away. Condensed milk has some of the liquid taken out of it to make it thicker and smaller in quantity.

[kən'diʃən]
condition how something or someone is

[kən'dʌkt], ['kɔndʌkt]
conduct to guide; to lead; to be in charge. The same word also means behaviour.

[kən'dʌktə]
conductor someone who collects bus or train tickets. The same word also means a man who stands in front of an orchestra and beats time.

[koun]
cone something round at the bottom and pointed at the top, like an ice-cream cone or a clown's hat. The same word also means the fruits of pine or fir trees, which are cone-shaped.

[kən'fes]
confess to say that you have done wrong; to own up to something

[kən'feti]
confetti tiny bits of coloured paper thrown at a wedding for good luck

[kən'fju:z]
confuse to mix up; to mistake one thing for another

[kən'gratjuleit]
congratulate to tell a person you are glad about something good that has happened to him

[kɔŋgri'geiʃən]
congregation people gathered together in a church

['kʌndʒərə]
conjuror someone who can do magic tricks

['kɔŋkə]
conker a round hard shiny brown nut in a prickly outer covering. It grows on a horse chestnut tree.

[kə'nekt]
connect to join or fasten together

['koŋkə]
conquer   to win; to overcome

['konʃəs]
conscious   knowing what is going on; able to hear and understand what is happening around you

[kən'sent]
consent   to agree

[kən'sə:vətri]
conservatory   a heated greenhouse where plants can be grown

[kən'sidə]
consider   to think carefully about something

[kən'sidərəbl]
considerable   rather large; much

[kən'sidərət]
considerate   kind to others; thoughtful about how other people feel

['konsənənts]
consonants   the sounds of a language other than vowels. They are written by all the letters of the alphabet except *a e i o u.*

['kʌnstəbl]
constable   a policeman

[kən'strʌkt]
construct   to build or make

[kən'tein]
contain   to hold something inside. A bottle contains milk.

[kən'teinə]
container   something that holds things inside, such as a box or bottle

[kən'tentid]
contented   happy; pleased with what you have

['kontents]
contents   what is contained in something

[kən'tinjuəl]
continual   keeping on; frequent

[kən'tinju:]
continue   to go on doing something, or to begin doing something again

[kən'tinjuəs]
continuous   keeping on without stopping

[kən'trakt], ['kontrakt]
contract   to become smaller. The same word also means an agreement.

[kontrə'dikt]
contradict   to disagree entirely; to say that
    something someone has said is not true
[kən'troul]
control   to guide or check something, such as a
    vehicle or a machine. The same word also
    means to be in command of other people.
[kən'vi:njənt]
convenient   easy to use or reach
['konvənt]
convent   a building for nuns to live in
[konvə'seiʃən]
conversation   talk between two or more people
['konvikt]
convict   someone who has been sent to prison
[kən'vins]
convince   to persuade someone that you are right
[kuk]
cook   to heat food and make it ready for eating
['kukə]
cooker   a stove on which food is cooked
['kukəri]
cookery   the art or practice of cooking
[ku:l]
cool   not quite cold
['kopə]
copper   a reddish-brown metal. The same word
    also means a copper-coloured coin.
['kopi]
copy   to make or do something exactly the same as
    something else
['korəl]
coral   a hard, stony pink or white material made
    from millions of piled-up skeletons of tiny sea
    animals, sometimes used to make jewellery
['ko:dəroi]
corduroy   cotton cloth with ridges in it
[ko:]
core   the middle part of something, like the part
    where the seeds are in an apple or pear
['ko:gi]
corgi   a small dog with short legs
[ko:k]
cork   a stopper put in the top of a bottle to keep
    the liquid from spilling out

[ko:n]
corn   the seeds of grain plants, like wheat, barley
and oats. The same word also means a hard
lump of skin on your toe, that hurts when your
shoe is too tight.

['ko:nə]
corner   where two walls or roads meet

['ko:nit]
cornet   a musical instrument like a trumpet. The
same word also means an ice cream in a kind
of biscuit shaped like a cone.

['ko:nfleiks]
cornflakes   a breakfast cereal eaten cold with milk
and sugar

['ko:nflauə]
cornflower   a bright blue summer flower

[korə'neiʃən]
coronation   the crowning of a king or queen

[ko:pə'reiʃən]
corporation   a group of people who run the business
of a town

[kə'rekt]
correct   right; true; with no mistakes

['korido:]
corridor   a long narrow passage with rooms
leading off it

['kozməno:t]
cosmonaut   someone who travels in space

[kost]
cost   what you have to pay for something

['kostli]
costly   expensive; not cheap

['kostju:m]
costume   style of clothing worn at different times in
history. The same word also means clothes
worn by actors on the stage.

['kouzi]
cosy   comfortable; snug and warm

[kot]
cot   a bed for a small child

['kotidʒ]
cottage   a small house in the country

['kotn]
cotton   thread or cloth made from the cotton plant

['kɔtn'wul]
cottonwool   the fluffy part of the cotton plant

[kautʃ]
couch   a long soft seat where more than one person can sit

[kɔf]
cough   the loud noise you make when you choke
or when you have a sore throat
or bronchitis

['kaunsəl]
council   a group of people who meet to talk and
decide about problems to do with controlling a
town or city

[kaunt]
count   to name numbers in their proper order. The
same word also means a nobleman.

['kauntdaun]
countdown   the counting backwards of seconds of
time before a rocket is fired

['kauntə]
counter   a kind of long table in a shop or café

['kʌntri]
country   the land outside a town. Another country
means another part of the world.

['kaunti]
county   a part or section of a country

['kʌpl]
couple   two of anything; a pair

[ku:pɔn]
coupon   a printed piece of paper which can be
exchanged for something else

['kʌridʒ]
courage   without fear even when there is danger;
bravery

[kɔ:s]
course   the direction in which anything goes. The
same word also means a number of lessons on
one special subject.

[kɔ:t]
court   the place where a king or a judge does his
work

['kɔ:tja:d]
courtyard   an enclosed space near or within a
building

['kʌzn]
cousin   the child of your aunt or uncle

['kʌvə]
cover   to put one thing over another so as to hide it

[kau]
cow   the female of cattle

['kauəd]
coward   someone who is not brave

['kauboi]
cowboy   a man on a ranch
who looks after cattle

['kauʃed]
cowshed   a farm building where cattle are kept

['kauslip]
cowslip   a small yellow spring wildflower

[krab]
crab   a water animal with a hard shell and
big claws

[krak]
crack   a split or long thin opening in something. The
same word also means a sharp, sudden noise.

['krakə]
cracker   a small firework. The same word also
means a thin crisp biscuit.

['krakl]
crackle   a crisp sound, like the sound made by the
word when you say it. Dry twigs crackle on a
fire.

['kreidl]
cradle   a baby's bed with rockers instead of legs

['kra:ftsmən]
craftsman   someone who is good at making things
with his hands

['kra:fti]
crafty   artful; cunning

[krein]
crane   a machine for lifting heavy things. The same
word also means a long-legged bird.

[kraʃ]
crash   a loud smashing noise

[kreit]
crate   a container for packing vegetables, eggs, fruit
and bottles. It is made of thin pieces of wood
fastened together.

[kro:l]
crawl to move forward on your hands and knees.
The same word means a stroke used in
swimming.

['kreiən]
crayon a soft kind of pencil that you use to colour
a picture

['kreizi]
crazy silly; mad

[kri:m]
cream the rich fatty part of milk

['kri:məri]
creamery a place where butter and cheese are made
or sold

[kri:s]
crease a mark made by folding or doubling
something like paper or cloth

[kri'eit]
create to make or bring into being

[kri'eitə]
creator maker or producer

['kri:tʃə]
creature a living thing, such as a bird, insect or
other animal

[kri:k]
creek a small stream or part of a river

[kri:p]
creep to move slowly and quietly, sometimes on
your hands and knees

[kreip]
crêpe (*say crayp*) thin wrinkly cloth

['kresnt]
crescent anything shaped like the new moon

[kres]
cress a plant used in salads

[kru:]
crew people who work on a ship or aeroplane

[krib]
crib a small bed with bars to keep a young child
from falling out

['krikit]
cricket a game played with a bat and ball and
several players. The same word means an
insect something like a grasshopper, which
makes a chirping sound.

[kraim]
crime   something wrong that can be punished
by law

['krimzn]
crimson   a deep red colour with some blue in it

['kriŋkl]
crinkle   to wrinkle something by squeezing it tightly

['kripl]
cripple   a person who is lame or whose arms or legs
have been damaged in some way

[krisp]
crisp   hard and dry; easily broken, like a potato
crisp or a piece of toast

['kriskros]
crisscross   straight lines crossing over each other

[krouk]
croak   a deep, hoarse noise, like the sound a frog
makes

[krok]
crock   a pot or a jar

['krokədail]
crocodile   a dangerous scaly reptile which lives in
or near water in hot countries

['kroukəs]
crocus   a small garden plant, with bright purple,
yellow or white flowers

[kruk]
crook   a long hooked stick or staff carried by
shepherds. The same word also means someone
who is not honest.

['krukid]
crooked   not straight

[krop]
crop   grain, fruit or vegetables grown on the land
for food. The same word also means a short
whip used in hunting.

[kros]
cross   anything shaped like × or +. The same
word also means rather angry.

['krospatʃ]
crosspatch   someone who is bad-tempered

[krou]
crow   a large black bird, with a harsh croaking
voice. The same word also means the sound a
cock makes.

[kraud]
crowd a lot of people all together in one place

[kraun]
crown the gold head dress worn by a king or queen

[kruəl]
cruel very unkind

[kruːz]
cruise a sea voyage for pleasure

[krʌm]
crumb a very small piece of bread, cake or biscuit

['krʌmbl]
crumble to break into little pieces

['krʌmpl]
crumple to crush something into wrinkles

[krʌntʃ]
crunch to make a loud noise when you are chewing
    something hard and crisp like an apple or toast

[krʌʃ]
crush to press together or squash something

[krʌst]
crust the hard outer covering of something like a
    loaf of bread or a pie

[krʌtʃ]
crutch a special stick with a padded top piece that
    fits under the armpit. Lame people use crutches
    to help them to walk.

[krai]
cry to weep tears. The same word also means to
    make a loud sound of joy or sorrow.

['kristl]
crystal a hard mineral that is transparent

[kʌb]
cub the name given to some young animals such as
    bears and foxes

[kjuːb]
cube a shape having six sides of equal
    measurement, like a cube of sugar

['kukuː]
cuckoo a bird that lays its eggs in other birds'
    nests. It makes a noise that sounds like its
    name, cuckoo.

['kjuːkʌmbə]
cucumber a long green watery vegetable used in
    salads

['kʌdl]
cuddle   to hug with affection

[kju:]
cue   a stick used in the game of billiards

[kʌf]
cuff   the end of a sleeve at the wrist. The same
   word also means a blow with the palm of your
   hand.

['kʌniŋ]
cunning   clever in a rather unpleasant way; crafty

[kʌp]
cup   a small bowl-shaped container with a handle,
   used for drinking

['kʌbəd]
cupboard   a set of shelves with doors

[kə:b]
curb   to stop or hold something back

[kə:dz]
curds   the thick part of milk, when it is separated to
   make cheese. The thin watery part is called
   whey.

[kjuə]
cure   to help someone who is ill to get well again;
   to heal

['kjuəriəs]
curious   wanting to know or find out. The same
   word also means odd or strange.

[kə:l]
curl   to twist hair into curves or rings

['kə:ləz]
curlers   rollers or pins which girls and women put
   into their hair to make it curly

['kə:li]
curly   not straight; going around in curves

['kʌrənt]
currant   a small dried grape: a red, black or white
   sour-tasting berry that grows on bushes

['kʌrənt]
current   a flow or stream of air, water or electricity.
   The same word also means at present,
   happening now.

['kə:tn]
curtain   a piece of cloth hanging down to cover
   a window or a stage in a theatre

['kə:tsi]
curtsey   a bow girls and women make by bending
their knees

[kə:v]
curve   a line shaped like part of a circle

['kuʃən]
cushion   a soft pillow covered with pretty material.
It is used to rest against on a chair or settee.

['kʌstəd]
custard   milk, eggs and sugar cooked together to
make a pudding or sauce

['kʌstəm]
custom   what is usually done; habit

['kʌstəmə]
customer   someone who wants to buy something,
usually in a shop

[kʌt]
cut   to make pieces of something smaller by using
scissors or a knife

['kʌtləri]
cutlery   what you eat food with – knives, forks and
spoons

['saikl]
cycle   another word for bicycle

['saikloun]
cyclone   a very bad storm in which a strong wind
goes round and round in a circle

['silində]
cylinder   a hollow rounded piece of metal often used
in machinery

['simbəlz]
cymbals   two metal musical instruments,
shaped like plates

[dab]
dab   to touch something lightly

['dafədil]
daffodil   a yellow spring flower shaped rather like a
trumpet

[da:ft]
daft   foolish or silly

['dagə]
dagger   a short sword

['deiljə]
dahlia   a garden plant with brightly coloured flowers

['deili]
daily every day

['deinti]
dainty pretty; delicate

['deəri]
dairy a place where milk, butter and cheese are
    kept

['deizi]
daisy a small field flower with white or pink petals
    around a yellow centre

[deil]
dale low ground between hills; a small valley

[dam]
dam a special kind of wall which checks a flow of
    water

['damidʒ]
damage harm or injury

[damp]
damp slightly wet

[da:ns]
dance to move in time to music

['dandilaiən]
dandelion a wild plant with bright yellow flowers

['dandi]
dandy a man who spends a lot of time on his
    clothes and the way he looks

['deindʒə]
danger risk; the opposite of safety

['deindʒrəs]
dangerous not safe

[deə]
dare to have the courage to do something

['deəriŋ]
daring full of courage; plucky

[da:k]
dark without light. When the sun goes down, the
    sky grows dark.

['da:liŋ]
darling someone dearly loved. We may call a
    person or animal we love, darling.

[da:n]
darn   to mend a hole by sewing it over with wool or
      cotton
[da:t]
dart   a kind of small arrow thrown by hand
['da:tbo:d]
dartboard   the target at which you aim in the game
      of darts
[daʃ]
dash   to rush suddenly. The same word also means
      a short straight line in writing, like this –.
[deit]
date   a time when something happens; a certain
      hour, day, month or year. The same word also
      means a sweet sticky fruit with a stone.
['do:tə]
daughter   a female child of a father and a mother
['do:dl]
dawdle   to waste time
[do:n]
dawn   the first light of day
[dei]
day   the time between sunrise and sunset
[deizd]
dazed   being confused or bewildered
['dazl]
dazzle   to blind someone for a short time by
      suddenly shining a strong bright light into
      his eyes
[ded]
dead   without life
[def]
deaf   not able to hear
[di:l]
deal   an amount. The same word also means to do
      business with.
[diə]
dear   much loved, precious. The same word also
      means highly priced.
[deθ]
death   the end of life
[det]
debt   what someone owes to someone else
[di'kei]
decay   to become rotten or to fall into ruins

[di'si:v]
deceive   to make someone believe something that is
    not true; to cheat

['di:snt]
decent   proper; acceptable to most people

[di'said]
decide   to make up your mind; to settle something

['desiməl]
decimal   numbered by tens

[dek]
deck   the flooring on a boat or ship

['dektʃeə]
deck chair   a folding chair used for resting out of
    doors

[di'kleə]
declare   to say something clearly; to make
    something known

['dekəreit]
decorate   to make something look pretty. We
    decorate a Christmas tree.

[di:d]
deed   an act; something done

[di:p]
deep   a long way down

[diə]
deer   a wild animal with four long legs. The male
    has large branched horns.

[di'fi:t]
defeat   to beat someone at a game; to conquer

[di'fend]
defend   to try to keep yourself from being beaten;
    to guard someone or something against attack

['definit]
definite   certain; without doubt

[di'fai]
defy   to refuse to obey

[di'gri:]
degree   a unit of measurement. Temperature is
    measured in degrees centigrade or fahrenheit.

[di'lei]
delay   to put off to a later time

[di'libərət]
deliberate   not by accident; done on purpose

['delikət]
delicate   easily broken or damaged; fragile

[delikə'tesn]
delicatessen   a shop that sells food ready to eat,
      such as cooked meats or special cheeses and
      salads

[di'liʃəs]
delicious   very good to taste and eat

[di'lait]
delight   great pleasure or joy

[di'livə]
deliver   to hand something over to someone else.
      The same word also means to rescue or set
      free.

[del]
dell   a little valley in a wood or forest

[di'ma:nd]
demand   to ask for something in a commanding way,
      without saying please

['di:mən]
demon   an evil spirit or devil

[den]
den   a cave or shelter where some kinds of wild
      animals live

[dens]
dense   closely-packed; thick; difficult to make your
      way through, like a dense forest

[dent]
dent   a bent place in something, usually caused by
      a blow

['dentist]
dentist   someone who takes care of your teeth

[di'nai]
deny   to say that something someone says is not
      true

[di'pa:t]
depart   to go away or leave a place

[di'pa:tmənt]
department   a part or section of a shop, office or
      factory

[di'pend]
depend   to count on someone; to rely

[di'pozit]
deposit   to put something down and leave it. The same word also means a small amount of money left in part payment for something.

['depou]
depot (*say depo*)   a storehouse

[depθ]
depth   how deep something is

[di'send]
descend   to go down

[dis'kraib]
describe   to say what something or someone is like

['dezət]
desert   land on which very little can grow because there is no water. Deserts are often made of sand.

[di'zə:v]
deserve   to earn something, like deserving a reward for working hard

[di'zain]
design   to draw a pattern; to make a plan or drawing

[di'zaiə]
desire   to want something very much. The same word also means a wish or request.

[desk]
desk   a table used for reading or writing

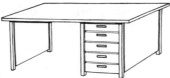

[dis'peə]
despair   to give up hope

[dis'paiz]
despise   to dislike something or someone very much because you think they are no good and worthless

[di'zə:t]
dessert   the fruit or pudding served after the main part of a meal

[dis'troi]
destroy   to kill or ruin completely

[dis'trɔiə]
destroyer   a warship that guards a fleet of ships
against attack

['diːteil]
detail   a small part

[di'təːmin]
determine   to settle or decide; to make up your
mind to do something

[di'test]
detest   to hate very much

[di'veləp]
develop   to grow gradually, as a puppy develops into
a dog, or a bud develops into a flower

['devl]
devil   an evil spirit. The word is often used to
describe a wicked or cruel person.

[djuː]
dew   drops of moisture which cover the ground in
the very early morning

[dai'agənl]
diagonal   a line drawn from one corner of something
to the opposite corner

['daiəgram]
diagram   a plan or drawing to show what a thing is,
or how it works

['daiəl]
dial   the flat round part of something with numbers
on it, like a clock, a watch or a telephone

['daiəlekt]
dialect   a special way of speaking a language in
one part of a country

[dai'amitə]
diameter   a straight line drawn from one side of a
circle to the other, passing through the centre

['daiəmənd]
diamond   a very hard colourless precious stone
which sparkles

['daiəri]
diary   a book in which you write down what you
do from day to day

[dais]
dice   a pair of small cubes with different numbers of
spots on each side. They are
used in games like ludo
and snakes and ladders.

['dikʃənəri]

dictionary a book which tells you the meanings of
words and how to spell them

[dai]

die to stop living or to come to an end. The same
word also means one of a pair of dice.

['diːzəl'endʒin]

diesel engine an engine that burns a special kind of
oil

['difə]

differ to be unlike; to disagree

['difrəns]

difference what makes something not like
something else

['difrənt]

different not the same

['difəkəlt]

difficult hard to do or to understand

[dig]

dig to make a hole in the ground

['dignifaid]

dignified acting in a serious manner

[dim]

dim not bright

['dimpl]

dimple à little hollow, usually in your cheek or chin

[din]

din loud noise, usually going on for a long time

[dain]

dine to eat dinner

['dindʒi]

dingy dull and dirty looking

['dinə]

dinner the main meal of the day

['dainəsoː]

dinosaur a very large reptile that lived millions and
millions of years ago

[dip]

dip to go in and out of something quickly. You dip
your spoon into a bowl of soup.

['daiə]
dire dreadful; terrible

[di'rekt]
direct straight; the quickest or shortest way. The same word also means to show someone the way.

[di'rekʃən]
direction the way something goes, such as a road going north, south, east or west

[dəːt]
dirt mud, soil, or earth

['dəːti]
dirty not clean; in need of washing

[disə'griː]
disagree to have a different opinion about something

[disə'piə]
disappear to go away very quickly; to vanish

[disə'point]
disappoint to find that things are not as you had hoped they would be. When you do not win a game you may be disappointed.

[di'zaːstə]
disaster a calamity; a great misfortune

[disk]
disc anything which is round and flat, such as a gramophone record

[di'saipl]
disciple a follower or pupil

[dis'kʌridʒ]
discourage to make someone feel that what he is doing is not worth while so that he will stop trying

[dis'kʌvə]
discover to find out; to see something for the first time

[dis'kʌvəri]
discovery something which has been found out

[dis'kʌs]
discuss to talk about

[dis'kʌʃən]
discussion an argument or talk with other people

[di'ziːz]
disease illness; sickness

[dis'greis]
disgrace   shame

[dis'gaiz]
disguise   to change your appearance by wearing
different clothes, a wig or a false moustache, so
that people do not recognize you

[dis'gʌst]
disgust   a feeling of dislike so strong that it makes
you feel sick

[diʃ]
dish   a plate for food

[dis'onist]
dishonest   the opposite of honest

[dis'laik]
dislike   the opposite of like

[dis'mei]
dismay   fear; a feeling of being upset and sad

[dis'mis]
dismiss   to send someone away or tell him they
can leave

['distəns]
distance   the length of space between two places

['distənt]
distant   far away. A far-off place is distant.

[dis'tempə]
distemper   an illness which young dogs get. The
same word also means a kind of paint used on
walls in rooms.

[dis'tiŋkt]
distinct   separate; clearly seen or heard

[dis'tres]
distress   a feeling of great pain, sorrow or worry

['distrikt]
district   a part of a town or county

[dis'tə:b]
disturb   to interrupt or cause trouble

[dis'tə:bəns]
disturbance   a noisy interruption, as when people
upset a meeting by shouting out

[ditʃ]
ditch   a very long narrow trench which is dug in the
ground to drain water away

[di'van]
divan   a couch

[daiv]
dive to plunge headfirst into water or down through the air

['daivə]
diver someone who goes down into very deep water

[di'vaid]
divide to separate into parts

['dizi]
dizzy feeling that your head is spinning round and round; giddy

[du:]
do to perform or make

[dok]
dock a place where ships are unloaded or repaired

['doktə]
doctor someone who helps you to get better when you are ill

[dodʒ]
dodge to jump quickly to one side so as not to bump into something

[dog]
dog a four-legged animal which is often kept as a pet

[dol]
doll a toy made to look like a person

[doum]
dome a curved roof like half a ball

['dominou]
domino a small oblong piece of wood either painted black with white dots or white with black dots. You play a game with dominoes.

['doŋki]
donkey an animal like a small horse with long ears

['du:dl]
doodle to draw or scribble while thinking about or doing something else

[do:]
door a kind of barrier which has to be opened to go in or out of a building or room. It is usually made of wood and fitted with a handle.

['do:step]
doorstep the step just outside a doorway

['do:wei]
doorway the frame into which a door is fitted

['do:mitri]
dormitory   a big room with lots of beds

['do:maus]
dormouse   a kind of mouse with a furry tail, rather like a squirrel

[dous]
dose   the exact amount of medicine you should take at one time

[dot]
dot   a small round mark

['dʌbl]
double   twice as much

['dʌbl'dekə]
double-decker   a bus with an upstairs

['dautful]
doubtful   not being sure, not quite believing

[dou]
dough   a thick floury mixture which is baked into bread or cakes

[dʌv]
dove   a pretty bird, rather like a pigeon

[douz]
doze   to close your eyes because you are sleepy, but not quite asleep

['dʌzn]
dozen   twelve of anything

[drag]
drag   to pull something heavily along the ground

['dragən]
dragon   an imaginary animal which breathes fire. You read about dragons in fairy stories.

['dragənflai]
dragonfly   a large flying insect with transparent wings

[drein]
drain   to take away water or some other liquid

[dreik]
drake   a male duck

[dra:ft]
draught a gust of cold air. The same word also
means a small wooden disc used in the game of
draughts.

[dro:]
draw to make a picture with pencils or crayons.
The same word also means to pull.

['dro:bridʒ]
drawbridge a bridge that can be let down or drawn
up

[dro:]
drawer a kind of box that fits into a piece of
furniture. It slides in and out.

['dro:iŋpin]
drawing pin a pin with a large flat head

[dred]
dread great fear

['dredful]
dreadful causing great fear; terrible; awful

[dri:m]
dream the thoughts that go on in your mind after
you are asleep

[drentʃ]
drench to soak right through

[dres]
dress to put on clothes. The same word also means
a garment worn by girls and women.

['dresiŋgaun]
dressing-gown a garment which you wear over your
nightdress or pyjamas

['dresiŋteibl]
dressing table a table with a mirror where you can
sit to do your hair

['dresmeikə]
dressmaker a person who makes clothes for women,
girls and small children

['dribl]
dribble to let food or liquid trickle out of the mouth
on to the chin. The same word also means to
run with a football at your feet.

[drift]
drift to be floated or blown along

[dril]
drill to bore a hole in something with a special tool.
The same word also means regular practice.

[driŋk]
drink   to swallow water, milk, or some other liquid
[drip]
drip   to drop in little drops. A tap drips when
    only a little water comes out very slowly.
[draiv]
drive   to make something move along
['draivə]
driver   someone who drives
['drizl]
drizzle   light rain
[dru:p]
droop   to bend or flop over
[drop]
drop   to let something fall. The same word also
    means a tiny bead of water.
[draun]
drown   to die under water because there is no air to
    breathe
['drauzi]
drowsy   feeling very sleepy
[drʌm]
drum   a hollow instrument that you beat to make
    music
['drʌmstik]
drumstick   the stick you use to beat a drum. The
    same word also means the leg of a chicken or
    turkey.
[drai]
dry   not wet; without water
[dʌk]
duck   a rather large web-footed bird which swims.
    The same word also means to dip underwater
    for a moment; to lower your head; to dodge
    something.

[dju:]
due   owing; not paid
[dju:k]
duke   a nobleman of high rank

[dʌl]
dull uninteresting, not lively or sharp, with no
 sparkle

[dʌm]
dumb not able to speak

['dʌmi]
dummy a model made to look like a person:
 something in place of the real thing

[dʌmp]
dump to throw down or get rid of something

['dʌmpliŋ]
dumpling a lump of flour and fat cooked in a stew

[dʌns]
dunce a fool; someone who is slow to learn things

['dʌndʒən]
dungeon a dark prison cell, usually under the
 ground

['djuəriŋ]
during throughout: while something is happening

[dʌsk]
dusk the part of the evening just before the sky
 gets really dark

[dʌst]
dust tiny bits of powdery dirt

['dʌsbin]
dustbin a container for dirt and rubbish

['dʌstə]
duster a cloth used for wiping away dust

['dʌsmən]
dustman a man who empties dustbins

['dʌspan]
dustpan a container into which you sweep dust

['dju:ti]
duty what you ought to do or have to do

[dwɔ:f]
dwarf an animal, plant, or person who is much
 smaller than most others of the same kind

[dai]
dye colouring powder or liquid used to change the
 colour of cloth or other material

['dainəmait]
dynamite a powerful exploding substance

['i:gə]
eager wanting very much to do something; keen

['i:gl]
eagle   a large bird of prey, with a sharp curved beak and claws

[iə]
ear   the part of the body you hear with. The same word means a spike of grain such as an ear of corn or barley.

[ə:l]
earl   a nobleman of high rank

['ə:li]
early   in good time; near the beginning

[ə:n]
earn   to get something, usually money, in return for working: to deserve

['ə:nist]
earnest   serious; sincere

['iəriŋ]
earring   jewellery which is worn on the ear

[ə:θ]
earth   the planet we live on; the world. The same word also means the ground in a garden or field.

['ə:θkweik]
earthquake   a violent shaking of the earth's surface

[i:z]
ease   freedom from pain or worry: rest from work

['i:zl]
easel   a special stand on which a painter can put his picture while he is working on it

['i:zəli]
easily   with no difficulty

[i:st]
east   the direction in which the sun rises; the opposite direction to west

['i:stə]
Easter   the time when Christians believe Jesus came back from the dead

['i:zi]
easy   not difficult; not hard to do or understand

[i:t]
eat   to chew and swallow food

[i:vz]
eaves   the edges of the roof sticking out over the top
of the walls

[eb]
ebb   the going back of the sea from the shore when
the tide goes out

['ekou]
echo   a sound that comes back to you, as when you
shout in a tunnel or cave

[i'klips]
eclipse   a cutting off of light from the sun when the
moon comes between the sun and the earth

[edʒ]
edge   the cutting side of a knife. The same word
also means the end of something like a table or
a shelf.

['edʒukeit]
educate   to help someone to learn

[edʒu'keiʃən]
education   helping people to learn, usually in schools
or colleges

[i:l]
eel   a very long fish that looks like a snake

[i'fekt]
effect   the result caused by something, as when the
effect of cold weather is to make you shiver

['efət]
effort   a hard try. When you use all your strength
you are making an effort.

[eg]
egg   an oval object with a thin shell. A chicken, like
other baby birds, lives inside an egg before it
is born.

['aidədaun]
eiderdown   a quilt, usually filled with feathers from
an eider duck

[i'lastik]
elastic   material made with rubber which stretches
easily

['elbou]
elbow   the joint in the middle of your arm

['eldə]
elder   older. The same word also means a large
shrub with clusters of white blossoms which
turn into purple berries later.

['eldəberi]
elderberry   a purple berry from which wine can be made

[elek'trisəti]
electricity   an invisible force which is used to make light and heat. It also makes power for engines and machinery.

['eləfənt]
elephant   a very large animal with a long nose called a trunk

[elf]
elf   a tiny mischievous fairy

['els'weə]
elsewhere   not here; somewhere else; in another place

[im'barəs]
embarrass   to make someone feel shy by teasing or by making difficulties for them

[im'broidə]
embroider   to make pretty designs on material using a needle and thread

['emərəld]
emerald   a bright green precious stone

['empərə]
emperor   the male ruler of an empire

['empaiə]
empire   a group of countries or states which is ruled by one king or queen, called an emperor or empress

[im'ploi]
employ   to give work to someone, usually for payment

['empris]
empress   an emperor's wife, or the female ruler of an empire

['empti]
empty   with nothing or no one inside

[i'naməl]
enamel   a hard shiny paint used on such things as bathtubs, cookers and saucepans

[in'klouz]
enclose   to put something in an envelope or package:
   to surround or shut in by a fence or wall

[in'kʌridʒ]
encourage   to help someone to keep on trying; to try
   to give courage to someone

[ensaiklə'pi:diə]
encyclopaedia   a book or set of books which tells
   you something about every subject

[end]
end   the last part; the finish

[in'djuə]
endure   to bear trouble or pain with courage and
   patience

['enəmi]
enemy   someone who fights against you or your
   country

[in'geidʒ]
engage   to hire someone to work for you

[in'geidʒd]
engaged   bound by a promise. as when a man and a
   woman are engaged to be married to each other

['endʒin]
engine   a machine which makes things work.
   Aeroplanes, cars and trains are all moved by
   engines.

[endʒi'niə]
engineer   someone who makes or looks after
   machines. The same word also means someone
   who plans and builds dams, roads, railways and
   bridges.

[in'dʒoi]
enjoy   to take pleasure in something

[i'no:məs]
enormous   very large; huge

[i'nʌf]
enough   as much as is needed and no more

[in'kwaiə]
enquire   to ask. The word is also spelled inquire.

['entə]
enter   to go or come into a place

[əntə'tein]
entertain   to amuse. The same word also means to
   have someone as your guest.

[entə'teinmənt]
entertainment   a show or concert that entertains or
     amuses you

[in'θu:ziazəm]
enthusiasm   keenness; eagerness; great interest in
     something

[in'taiə]
entire   complete; whole

['entrəns]
entrance   a doorway or way into a place

['entri]
entry   the act of entering

['envəloup]
envelope   a folded piece of paper in which you put
     letters for posting

['envi]
envy   a wish to have something that belongs to
     someone else

['episoud]
episode   an event in a story; a complete short story
     which is part of a longer story

['i:kwəl]
equal   of the same size, quantity or value as
     something else

[i'kweitə]
equator   an imaginary line around the middle of the
     earth's surface

[i'kwipmənt]
equipment   all the things needed to do a job, play a
     game, or go on an expedition

[i'rekt]
erect   upright; standing up straight

['erənd]
errand   a short journey to take a message or to
     deliver or collect something

['erə]
error   a mistake; something that has been done
     incorrectly

['eskəleitə]
escalator   a moving staircase

[is'keip]
escape   to get free, usually from something
     unpleasant

[is'peʃəli]
especially   most of all; of greatest importance

['estimeit]
estimate to guess the size, quantity or value of something

[i:v]
eve evening. The same word also means the day before a special event, like Christmas Eve.

['i:vn]
even level; smooth. The same word also means any number that can be divided exactly by two.

['i:vniŋ]
evening the time between afternoon and night

[i'vent]
event something that happens

['evə]
ever always; for all time

['evəgri:n]
evergreen a shrub or tree that keeps its leaves and stays green all the year round

['evri]
every each one

['evribodi]
everybody each person

['evri'dei]
everyday daily. The same word also means usual or common.

['evriwʌn]
everyone another word for everybody

['evriθiŋ]
everything all things

['evriweə]
everywhere in all places

['i:vl]
evil very bad; wicked; the opposite of good

[ju:]
ewe a female sheep

[ig'zaktli]
exactly just right; correctly; with no mistakes

[ig'zadʒəreit]
exaggerate to say that something is bigger or more important than it really is

[igzami'neiʃən]
examination a number of questions that you have to answer, usually in writing, to show how much you know about something; another word for test

[ig'zamin]
examine   to look at closely and carefully

[ig'za:mpl]
example   a sample; a single one of many. The same
word also means a pattern to be copied, as
when you follow somebody's good example.

['eksələnt]
excellent   very, very good

[ik'sept]
except   leaving out; apart from

[iks'tʃeindʒ]
exchange   to give one thing in return for another

[ik'saitiŋ]
exciting   Something which makes you feel strongly
is exciting. You can feel excited if something
nice is going to happen.

[iks'kleim]
exclaim   to speak or call out suddenly

[iks'kju:s]
excuse   a reason for not doing something. It may be
a good excuse or a poor excuse.

['eksəsaiz]
exercise   the training of your mind or body

[ig'zo:st]
exhaust   to use up or tire out completely. The same
word also means the pipe which lets out the
gases from a motor engine.

[eksi'biʃən]
exhibition   a public show of things such as works of
art, flowers, or furniture

[ig'zist]
exist   to be; to continue to live

['eksit]
exit   the way out of a place

[iks'pand]
expand   to grow bigger; to swell

[iks'pekt]
expect   to look forward to; to think something will
happen

[ekspi'diʃən]
expedition   a journey to explore a place or to search
for something, such as rare plants and animals

[iks'pens]
expense   cost; payment of money

[iks'pensiv]
expensive   costing a lot of money; dear

[iks'piəriəns]
experience   knowledge of something because you
      have seen or done it

[iks'perimənt]
experiment   something tried out to see what will
      happen: a test to find out something

['ekspə:t]
expert   someone who knows a lot about a particular
      subject

[iks'plein]
explain   to give the meaning of something; to make
      something clear

[eksplə'neiʃən]
explanation   anything said or written that helps you
      to understand clearly the reason for something

[iks'ploud]
explode   to burst or blow up with a loud bang

[iks'plo:]
explore   to travel to places to try to find out all
      about them

[iks'plouʒən]
explosion   the act of blowing up or exploding: a
      sudden burst with a loud noise

[iks'pres]
express   to put thoughts into words, music or
      pictures. The same word also means a fast train.

[iks'preʃən]
expression   the look on faces when people are happy,
      sad, or worried. The same word also means a
      way of saying things.

[iks'tend]
extend   to stretch out: to make longer

[iks'tent]
extent   the length, size or area of anything

['ekstrə]
extra   more than necessary or expected

[iks'tro:dənəri]
extraordinary   very unusual: not ordinary: surprising

[ai]
eye   one of the two parts of your face that you see
      with

['aibrau]
eyebrow   a little line of hairs over each eye

['ailaʃ]
eyelash   one of the little hairs that grow along the
edge of the eyelid

['aipiːs]
eyepiece   the glass part of a telescope or microscope
which you look through

['feibl]
fable   a short story, usually about animals, which is
meant to teach us a lesson

[feis]
face   the front of your head

[fakt]
fact   a thing that everyone knows is true and not
imaginary

['faktəri]
factory   a building where things are made in large
quantities, usually by machine

[feid]
fade   to lose colour or freshness

['fagət]
faggot   a bundle of sticks

['farənhait]
fahrenheit   a measurement of heat having the
freezing point of water marked at 32 degrees
and the boiling point at 212 degrees

[feil]
fail   not to be able to do something you try to do;
to be unsuccessful

['feiliŋ]
failing   a fault or a bad habit

[feint]
faint   pale or weak. The same word also means
feeling weak and dizzy.

[feə]
fair   a place with roundabouts where you have fun.
The same word also means light in colour (as
in fair hair) and right or good (as in fair play).

['feəli]
fairly   not bad; reasonably good

['feəri]
fairy   a very small person who can do magic. You
read about fairies in stories for young children.

[feiθ]
faith   what you believe in: trust that what is said is
true

['feiθful]
faithful   keeping your promises; believing

[feik]
fake   something that looks valuable but is not; a cheap copy of something

[fɔ:l]
fall   to drop through the air

[fɔ:ls]
false   wrong; not keeping your promises; not faithful; not real or true

['fɔ:ltə]
falter   to stumble; to hesitate when speaking

[fə'miljə]
familiar   well known or close to you

['faməli]
family   a mother and father and their children

['famin]
famine   great scarcity of food; starvation

['famiʃt]
famished   starving

['feiməs]
famous   well known

[fan]
fan   something which makes a cool breeze. The same word also means someone who is very fond of a certain sport, hobby or famous person.

['fansi]
fancy   decorated. The same word also means imagination.

[faŋ]
fang   a long pointed tooth

[fa:]
far   a long way away

[feə]
fare   the price you pay for travelling on a public vehicle such as a bus

[feə'wel]
farewell   an old-fashioned word for goodbye

[fa:m]
farm   a place where a farmer keeps animals and grows food

['fa:mə]
farmer a man who looks after a farm
['fa:mja:d]
farmyard ground surrounded by barns, cowsheds
and other farm buildings
['fa:ðə]
farther at a greater distance away; more distant
['fasineitiŋ]
fascinating very attractive; very charming
[fa:st]
fast very quick
['fa:sn]
fasten to join together
['fa:sniŋ]
fastening something that fastens or closes things
tightly
[fat]
fat big and round. The same word also means the
whitish greasy part of meat and bacon. Other
kinds of fat are found in fish and in nuts.
['feitl]
fatal causing death; disastrous
['fa:ðə]
father a man who has children in his family
[fɔ:lt]
fault a mistake; anything which spoils something
which is otherwise good
['feivə]
favour an act of kindness which is done for
someone
['feivərit]
favourite a person or thing which is liked better
than any other
[fɔ:n]
fawn a young deer

[fiə]
fear a feeling of alarm when you think you are in
danger
['fiəful]
fearful afraid. The same word also means terrible
or awful.

['fiəlis]
fearless   without fear; brave

[fi:st]
feast   a large special meal with lots of good things
      to eat and drink

[fi:t]
feat   an act of great skill or strength

['feðə]
feather   part of the wing or the soft coat of a bird

['fi:bl]
feeble   very weak; not strong

[fi:d]
feed   to give food to someone or some animal

[fi:l]
feel   to find out what something is like by
      touching it

[fi:t]
feet   more than one foot

['felou]
fellow   a man: a companion

[felt]
felt   a thick woollen material used for hats

['fi:meil]
female   people and animals who can become
      mothers. Girls and women are of the female
      sex but boys and men are of the male sex.

['feminin]
feminine   like. or to do with. women or girls

[fens]
fence   something put round a field or garden to keep
      animals and people in or out

['fendə]
fender   a metal guard in front of a fire

[fə:n]
fern   a plant which has lacy, feathery leaves but no
      flowers

['ferit]
ferret   a small animal used for hunting out rabbits
      and rats

['feri]
ferry a boat used to take people or cars across
  water where there is no bridge

['fə:tail]
fertile able to produce seeds or plants abundantly

['festə]
fester to rot; to become infected

['festəvəl]
festival a joyful celebration with dancing, music and
  often feasting

[fetʃ]
fetch to go and get

[feit]
fête (*rhymes with gate*) an outdoor entertainment or
  party, usually to raise money

['fi:və]
fever an illness which makes your body very hot
  and makes you feel weak and thirsty

[fju:]
few not many

[fib]
fib a small lie; something which is not quite true

['fikʃən]
fiction a made-up story or book about people and
  happenings that are not really true

['fidl]
fiddle a violin. The same word also means to play
  about with something in a careless sort of way.

['fidlə]
fiddler a man who plays a fiddle

['fidʒit]
fidget to move about in a restless way

[fi:ld]
field an open piece of land, often surrounded by
  hedges

[fiəs]
fierce angry; wild

['faiəri]
fiery like fire; flaming or burning

[fig]
fig a soft sweet fruit which grows on a fig tree

[fait]
fight to struggle against someone or
  something

['figə]
figure the shape of something, such as a person's body. The same word also means a number.

[fail]
file a metal tool with a rough surface, used to make things smooth. The same word also means a line of people following one behind the other.

[fil]
fill to put so much in a container that you cannot get any more in

[film]
film a moving picture. The same word also means a strip of material used in a camera.

['filtə]
filter a special strainer used to separate dirt and other solids from liquid

['filθi]
filthy very dirty

[fin]
fin one of the wing-like parts of a fish which help it to balance and swim

['fainl]
final the very last; coming at the end

['fainəli]
finally at last; at the end

[faind]
find to see something you are looking for; to discover

[fain]
fine excellent; very good. The same word also means sunny and dry.

['fiŋgə]
finger a part of your hand. You have five fingers on each hand.

['fiŋgəprint]
fingerprint the pattern made when you press your finger or thumb on the surface of something

['finiʃ]
finish to get to the end; to complete

[fə:]
fir a kind of evergreen tree with leaves like needles

['faiə]
fire the flames, light and heat made by something burning

['faiərendʒin]
fire engine   a big motor vehicle that carries the
firemen and their equipment to put out a fire.

['faiəmən]
fireman   a man who helps to put out fires

['faiəpleis]
fireplace   the open place under the chimney where
a fire burns

['faiəsaid]
fireside   the space next to a fireplace where you can
sit and warm yourself

['faiəwə:ks]
fireworks   Fireworks are usually made of gunpowder
in a cardboard tube. They are set alight after
dark on special days.

[fə:m]
firm   solid; strong and not easily moved

[fə:st]
first   at the very beginning

[fiʃ]
fish   a swimming animal which cannot live out of
water. It has fins and breathes through its gills.

['fiʃəmən]
fisherman   a man who catches fish

['fiʃiŋ]
fishing   the sport or business of catching fish

['fiʃiŋnet]
fishing-net   a net used for catching fish

['fiʃiŋrod]
fishing-rod   a long thin stick with a string and hook
attached for catching fish

[fist]
fist   a tightly closed hand

[fit]
fit   to be the right size and shape for something.
The same word also means in good health.

[fiks]
fix   to mend something. The same word also means
to tie or fasten something firmly.

[fiz]
fizz   to bubble and make a hissing sound

[flag]
flag   a piece of cloth with a coloured pattern. Each
country in the world has its own flag with its
own pattern.

[fleik]
flake a very small thin piece of something, such as a snowflake

[fleim]
flame the bright fire that leaps from something burning

[flan]
flan an open piece of cooked pastry which is filled with custard, fruit, or some other filling

['flanl]
flannel a soft warm woolly material

[flap]
flap to move up and down, as a bird flaps its wings. The same word also means anything which hangs loose or is hinged, such as a table flap.

[fleə]
flare to burst into bright light, as when a piece of wood suddenly bursts into flame

[flaʃ]
flash a sudden bright light that appears only for a moment, like a flash of lightning

[fla:sk]
flask a kind of bottle, usually made of metal or glass, for holding liquids

[flat]
flat smooth; without bumps and being the same height all over. The same word also means a home on one floor which is part of a larger building.

['flatn]
flatten to make something flat

['fleivə]
flavour what makes foods taste differently from each other. Ice cream comes in lots of flavours, like strawberry, vanilla and chocolate.

[flaks]
flax a plant from which strong threads can be obtained. The cloth woven from these threads is called linen.

[fli:]
flea a tiny jumping insect

[fli:]
flee to run away, usually because of danger

[fli:s]
fleece the coat of wool on a sheep

[fli:t]

fleet   a number of ships or vehicles that belong
together

[fleʃ]

flesh   the soft parts of your body

[fleks]

flex   a wire for electricity, covered with plastic or
some other material

[flik]

flick   to hit something very lightly

['flikə]

flicker   to burn brightly and then dimly so that the
light is not steady

[flait]

flight   the act of flying through the air

['flimzi]

flimsy   not strong or thick, easily broken

[fliŋ]

fling   to throw something away from you

[flint]

flint   a very hard kind of stone which gives off
sparks when you strike it with steel

[flit]

flit   to move about very lightly and quickly

[flout]

float   to rest on top of a liquid or on air. A boat
floats on water, and a bubble floats on air.

[flok]

flock   a large group of birds or of some animals

[flʌd]

flood   a great overflowing of water, usually over dry
land

[flo:]

floor   the part of a room you walk on

[flop]

flop   to let yourself fall down heavily

['flauə]

flour   a white powder made from grain. It is used to
make bread and cakes.

[flou]

flow   to move along smoothly, like water

['flauə]

flower   the pretty coloured part of a plant

['flauəpot]

flower-pot   a pot in which you plant flowers

[flu:]
'flu a shortening of the word influenza, which is an illness causing a fever and a sore throat

[flʌf]
fluff a light soft stuff that comes off woollen cloth and similar materials, such as blankets and carpets

['fluid]
fluid something that can flow, such as liquid or gas

[flu:k]
fluke something lucky that happens by chance

[flu:t]
flute a long thin musical instrument which you blow into

['flʌtə]
flutter to flap about; to move the wings quickly

[flai]
fly to move through the air. The same word also means a flying insect.

['flaiiŋ'fiʃ]
flying fish a fish with large fins that help it to move through the air when it leaps out of the water

[foul]
foal a young horse

[foum]
foam a lot of tiny white bubbles, usually on the top of liquid or soapy water; froth

['foukəs]
focus to get a clear picture

[fou]
foe an enemy

[fog]
fog thick cloudy air

[fould]
fold to double something over

['fouliidʒ]
foliage the leaves on trees and plants

[fouk]
folk people

['folou]
follow to come after someone or something

['foli]
folly   silliness; a foolish action

[fond]
fond   loving; liking very much

[font]
font   a stone basin in a church, which contains the water for christening a baby

[fu:d]
food   the things we eat to keep us alive

[fu:l]
fool   a silly person

['fu:liʃ]
foolish   silly; stupid; not wise

[fut]
foot   the part of the body you stand on. The same word also means a measure of 12 inches.

['futbo:l]
football   a team game in which you kick a ball and try to score goals

['futpa:θ]
footpath   a path or part of the road where people can walk but vehicles are not allowed

['futprint]
footprint   the mark someone's foot leaves in wet sand or soft earth

['futstep]
footstep   the sound a foot makes when walking

[fə'bid]
forbid   to command or order someone not to do something

[fo:s]
force   power; strength

[fo:d]
ford   a place in a river where the water is shallow enough for you to walk or drive through it safely

['fo:ra:m]
forearm   the part of your arm between your wrist and elbow

['fo:ka:st]
forecast   to say that something will happen before it does

['forid]
forehead   the part of your face above your eyes

['forən]
foreign   of another country: strange

['forist]
forest   a large area of land where lots of trees are growing close together

['fo:θo:t]
forethought   a thought or plan for the future

['fo:fit]
forfeit   something you have to give up because of something you have done

[fo:dʒ]
forge   a blacksmith's workshop, with a furnace for heating the metal. The same word also means to copy someone else's handwriting for a dishonest purpose.

['fo:dʒəri]
forgery   something written or painted which is not genuine: someone else's handwriting copied for a dishonest purpose

[fə'get]
forget   not to remember

[fə'getminot]
forget-me-not   a little blue flower

[fə'giv]
forgive   to pardon, to stop being cross with someone who has done something wrong

[fo:k]
fork   a tool used to pick up food

[fo:m]
form   shape. The same word also means a class in school, or a paper asking questions which are to be answered.

[fo:t]
fort   a strong building made to keep enemies out

[fo:θ]
forth   onwards; out

['fo:tnait]
fortnight   fourteen days; two weeks

['fo:tris]
fortress   another word for fort

['fo:tʃənət]
fortunate   lucky

['fo:tʃən]
fortune   what comes by luck or chance: great riches or wealth

['fɔːwəd]
forward   towards the front

['fɔsl]
fossil   the remains of an animal or plant that has turned to stone after being buried for many millions of years

[faul]
foul   dirty; horrible

[faun'deiʃənz]
foundations   the solid part of a building below ground level

['fauntən]
fountain   water pushed up into the air continuously in one or more jets

[faul]
fowl   a bird, usually a hen

[foks]
fox   a wild animal which has a long bushy tail

['frakʃən]
fraction   a part of a whole, such as one-half ($\frac{1}{2}$) or one-third ($\frac{1}{3}$)

['fradʒail]
fragile   delicate; easily broken or damaged

['fragmənt]
fragment   a bit or piece broken off something

[freim]
frame   the wood or metal around something, like a window or a picture

['freimwɔːk]
framework   the outline or main parts of something that the rest is built on to

[frɔːd]
fraud   dishonesty; a cheating trick

[frei]
fray   a fight or quarrel

[friːk]
freak   a person, plant or animal whose appearance is not ordinary or normal, such as a white blackbird

['frekl]
freckle   a small brown spot on the skin

[fri:]
free   not a prisoner; able to do or say what you like.
The same word also means without payment.

[fri:z]
freeze   to become hard because of the cold, as when
water turns into ice

['fri:kwənt]
frequent   happening often

[freʃ]
fresh   new: healthy: not tired

[fret]
fret   to be discontented; to worry

[frend]
friend   someone you know well and like a lot

['frendli]
friendly   kind; showing friendship

[fri:z]
frieze   a picture or pattern around the top of a wall

[frait]
fright   sudden fear; alarm

['fraitnd]
frightened   afraid of something

['fraitful]
frightful   terrible; awful

[fril]
frill   an edging of lace or light material on clothing
or curtains

[frindʒ]
fringe   hair cut straight across the forehead. The
same word also means an edging of loose
threads, usually on clothing, lampshades and
rugs.

['friski]
frisky   lively; playful

['fritə]
fritter   to waste something a little at a time. The
same word also means a piece of meat or fruit
fried in batter.

['frizi]
frizzy   very tightly curled

[frok]
frock   a dress

[frog]
frog   a small animal which lives
in or near water and can jump a long way

['frolik]
frolic   to have fun; to dance and play games

[frʌnt]
front   the opposite to back; the most forward part of anything

[frost]
frost   a thin icy covering on the ground when it is cold

[froθ]
froth   a lot of tiny white bubbles. usually on top of liquid; foam

[fraun]
frown   to wrinkle your forehead when you are angry or not pleased

['frouzn]
frozen   solid with ice

[fru:t]
fruit   a part of a bush or tree which can be eaten

['fru:tful]
fruitful   producing much fruit

[frai]
fry   to cook something in fat or oil

['fraiiŋpan]
frying pan   a round shallow pan for frying

[fjuəl]
fuel   anything used to make heat, such as coal, gas or wood

[ful]
full   no room for any more

['fuli]
fully   completely; entirely

[fʌn]
fun   to have fun is to have a good time and enjoy yourself

['fju:nərəl]
funeral   the ceremony of burying a dead person

['fʌnl]
funnel   a kind of chimney on a ship. The same word also means a tube that is wide at the top so that you can pour liquid into something without spilling it.

['fʌni]
funny   amusing; laughable. Anything that makes you laugh is funny.

[fə:]
fur the soft hair on animals

['fə:nis]
furnace a place where great heat is produced by fire. Steel is made in a furnace.

['fə:nitʃə]
furniture the things you use in a house, such as chairs, tables and beds

['fʌrou]
furrow a long narrow cut made in the ground by a plough

['fə:ðə]
further more distant

['fjuəri]
fury very great anger

[fju:z]
fuse a piece of string or material attached to something that will explode. It burns slowly to give you time to get to safety before the explosion. The same word also means a piece of wire used for safety in an electric system.

[fʌs]
fuss a bother or worry, usually about something unimportant: unnecessary noise and bustle

['fju:tʃə]
future the time to come: the days, months and years ahead of us

['fʌzi]
fuzzy covered with tiny hairs or fluff. The same word also means not clear or easily seen.

['gabl]
gabble to speak so quickly that people find it hard to understand what you are saying

['gadʒit]
gadget a small cleverly designed tool or piece of apparatus

[gein]
gain to earn or win: to add to what you already have

[geil]
gale a strong wind

['galiən]
galleon a large sailing ship which was used by the Spaniards hundreds of years ago

['galəri]
gallery the upper floor of seats in a theatre or church. The same word also means a room or building where works of art are on show.

['galən]
gallon a measure of liquid, equal to 4 quarts or 8 pints

['galəp]
gallop the fastest speed at which a horse can move

[gə'loʃiz]
galoshes a special kind of waterproof overshoes. Sometimes the word is spelled goloshes.

['gambl]
gamble to play a game for money

['gambl]
gambol to skip and jump happily

[geim]
game a way of playing which has rules

['geimiŋ]
gaming another word for gambling

['gandə]
gander a male goose

[gaŋ]
gang a group of people working together. The same word also means a band of robbers or thieves.

['gaŋstə]
gangster a member of a gang of robbers and thieves

['gaŋwei]
gangway a narrow passage between rows of seats: a movable bridge between ship and shore

['gantri]
gantry a bridge built over railway lines to carry signals: a support for a crane

[dʒeil]
gaol (*say jail*) another word for prison. The word is also spelled jail.

[gap]
gap an opening or break in something

['gara:ʒ]
garage a place where motor cars are kept or repaired

['ga:dn]
garden a piece of land where flowers, fruit or vegetables are grown

['ga:lənd]
garland a circle of leaves or flowers worn on the head or around the neck or hung on something as a decoration

['ga:mənt]
garment any article of clothing

['ga:tə]
garter a ring made of elastic which keeps a stocking from falling down

[gas]
gas something like air, neither solid nor liquid, which can fill space. It is usually invisible. Gas that burns comes through pipes and is used for cooking and heating.

[gaʃ]
gash a long deep cut or wound

[ga:sp]
gasp to take a quick deep breath: to struggle for breath

[geit]
gate a door in a fence, wall or hedge

['gaðə]
gather to collect; pick up one by one

[gei]
gay happy and lively

[geiz]
gaze to look at something steadily; to stare

[giə]
gear things that belong to you, such as clothes or tools. The same word also means the working part of a car or bicycle which changes the speed.

[gi:s]
geese more than one goose

[dʒem]
gem any precious stone; a jewel

['dʒenərəl]
general a commander in the army. The same word also means usual; happening everywhere.

['dʒenərəs]
generous   kind in sharing or giving things to others

['dʒentl]
gentle   quiet; soft or soothing

['dʒentlmən]
gentleman   a kind and honourable man

['dʒenjuin]
genuine   real; true; not a fake or copy

[dʒi'ogrəfi]
geography   the study of the surface of the earth and
the people and animals living there

[dʒi'omətri]
geometry   the part of mathematics to do with lines,
angles and figures such as triangles and circles

[dʒə'reiniəm]
geranium   a plant, usually with scarlet, white or
bright pink flowers

[dʒə:m]
germ   a very tiny bit of animal or plant life that you
can only see under a microscope. Some germs
cause diseases.

[get]
get   to receive; to fetch. The same word also means
to become, as when we say someone will get
well, or get rich.

[goust]
ghost   the spirit of a dead person

['dʒaiənt]
giant   a very big strong person, usually in fairy
stories

['gidi]
giddy   having a feeling that things are going round
and round

[gift]
gift   something which is given as a present

[dʒai'gantik]
gigantic   enormous; giant-like

['gigl]
giggle   to laugh in a silly way

[gil]
gill   an opening for breathing in a fish's skin

['dʒindʒə]
ginger   the root of a plant. It tastes spicy and makes
your mouth feel hot.

['dʒindʒəbred]
gingerbread   a cake or biscuit which is made with
ginger

['dʒipsi]
gipsy   someone who belongs to a race of dark
people who originally came from India. Gipsies
wander from place to place and usually have no
permanent home. The word is sometimes
spelled gypsy.

[dʒi'ra:f]
giraffe   a tall animal
with a very long neck

['gə:də]
girder   a long heavy piece of metal or wood used to
strengthen buildings, bridges and parts of
railways

[gə:l]
girl   a female child; a child who will grow up to be
a woman

[giv]
give   to hand something over freely to someone else

['glasiə]
glacier   a mass of ice that moves very slowly down
a mountainside

[glad]
glad   pleased; happy

[gla:ns]
glance   a quick look

[gleə]
glare   a dazzling bright light. The same word also
means to stare angrily at someone.

[gla:s]
glass   a hard material you can see through. Windows
are made of glass.

['gla:siz]
glasses   two framed pieces of a special kind of glass.
If you cannot see well, glasses help you to see
better.

[gli:m]
gleam   to shine, but not brightly. Old metal gleams
when it is polished.

[glen]
glen   a narrow valley

[glaid]
glide   to move smoothly and easily; to flow gently

['glaidə]
glider   a light aeroplane which can fly for some time
without an engine after being launched

['glimə]
glimmer   to shine faintly and unsteadily

[glimps]
glimpse   a very brief sight of someone or something

[glint]
glint   to gleam or glimmer

['glisn]
glisten   to shine or gleam

['glitə]
glitter   to sparkle; to reflect light brightly

[gloub]
globe   a round object, like a ball or the world

['glu:mi]
gloomy   dark; dim: miserable; the opposite of
cheerful

[glʌv]
glove   a covering for the hand. It fits around each
finger.

[glou]
glow   to burn without flames; to give out a steady
light

[glu:]
glue   a strong paste which sticks things together

[glʌm]
glum   silent and sad; gloomy

['glʌtn]
glutton   a person who is greedy and eats too much

[na:ld]
gnarled   twisted and lumpy, like the trunk of a very
old tree

[naʃ]
gnash   to grind your teeth together when you are
very angry

[nat]
gnat   a small flying insect which stings

[nɔ:]
gnaw   to wear something away by scraping at it
with teeth, as when a dog gnaws at a bone

[noum]
gnome   a dwarf you read about in stories

[gou]
go   to start off or move

[goul]
goal   a kind of target. In football you have to kick
the ball into the goal which is the space
between two posts.

[gout]
goat   an animal rather like a sheep. It usually has
horns and a little beard.

['gobl]
gobble   to swallow food quickly without chewing it

['goblit]
goblet   a kind of drinking cup with no handle

['goblin]
goblin   a mischievous elf or fairy

[god]
God   the Creator of everything

[gould]
gold   a yellow shiny metal which is worth a lot of
money

['gouldən]
golden   the colour of gold; made of gold

['gouldfiʃ]
goldfish   a small fish often kept as a pet. It is
usually a pretty reddish-gold colour.

[golf]
golf   a game which is played with a small white ball
and a set of long-handled clubs

[gə'loʃiz]
goloshes   another way of spelling galoshes

[goŋ]
gong   a round metal disc which makes a deep
ringing sound when you hit it

[gud]
good   right or satisfactory; kind; nice

[gud'bai]
goodbye   a word said to someone who is just
going away

['gudnis]
goodness   the act of being good or kind

[gudz]
goods   things bought and sold

[gu:s]
goose   a big bird, like a duck with a long neck

['guzbəri]
gooseberry   the fruit of the gooseberry bush. It is
     usually green with a rather hairy skin.

['go:dʒəs]
gorgeous   splendid; magnificent; richly coloured and
     beautiful

[gə'rilə]
gorilla   the largest kind of ape. It lives in Africa.

[go:s]
gorse   a prickly shrub with bright yellow flowers

['gozliŋ]
gosling   a young goose

['gosip]
gossip   chatter about other people, sometimes
     spiteful and unkind

['gʌvən]
govern   to rule or control

['gʌvənmənt]
government   a group of people who have the power
     to make laws and decide what is best for the
     country

[gaun]
gown   a woman's dress. The same word also means
     a long loose-fitting robe or cloak.

[grab]
grab   to seize hold of something suddenly

['greisful]
graceful   easy and smooth in movement; the
     opposite of clumsy

['greiʃəs]
gracious   kind; charming

[greid]
grade a way of deciding how good something is. If one kind of apple is better than another, it will be graded higher.

['gradʒuəl]
gradual happening slowly, a bit at a time

[grein]
grain the seeds of some plants that are used as food. The same word also means a very small piece of something hard, like a grain of sand.

['gramə]
grammar the study of the way people put words together when they speak or write

[gram]
gramme a very small weight, the thousandth part of a kilogramme

['graməfoun]
gramophone an instrument on which you can play records of music or words; another word for record-player

[grand]
grand important; large; splendid

['granfa:ðə]
grandfather the father of your mother or father

['granmʌðə]
grandmother the mother of your mother or father

['granit]
granite a very hard rock used for buildings and for kerbstones

[gra:nt]
grant to give, to allow as a favour

[greip]
grape green, purple or red fruit that grows in bunches on a vine

['greipfru:t]
grapefruit a round fruit like a large orange with a yellow skin and a sharp taste

[gra:f]
graph a diagram, usually on squared paper, that shows how a series of measurements changes

[gra:sp]
grasp to seize and hold tightly

[gra:s]
grass a low green plant which has many thin leaves and covers fields and lawns

['gra:shopə]
grasshopper   a hopping, leaping insect. It makes a
      chirping noise by rubbing its wings or legs
      together.

['gra:ssneik]
grass-snake   a small and harmless snake
[greit]
grate   a framework of iron for holding a fire in a
      fireplace. The same word also means to rub
      something, such as a piece of cheese, against
      a rough surface to reduce it to small particles.
['greitful]
grateful   giving thanks, thankful
[greiv]
grave   very serious. The same word also means a
      hole in the ground where a dead person is
      buried.
['gravəl]
gravel   lots of little pebbles which can be used to
      make paths
['greivi]
gravy   the juices of cooked meat, sometimes mixed
      with flour to make it thicker
[greiz]
graze   to eat grass. The same word also means to
      scrape the skin.
[gri:s]
grease   a thick oily substance; softened animal fat
[greit]
great   large; big. The same word also means
      important or famous.
[gri:d]
greed   a great longing to have more of something,
      even though you already have enough
[gri:n]
green   the colour of grass in springtime
['gri:ngrousə]
greengrocer   a man who sells vegetables and fruit
['gri:nhaus]
greenhouse   a glass house where plants are grown
[gri:t]
greet   to welcome; to speak to someone when
      you meet

['gri:tiŋ]
greeting   a welcome: a kind wish often written on a
birthday or Christmas card

[grei]
grey   the colour of the sky when there is no sun

['greihaund]
greyhound   a very thin dog with long legs, used for
racing

[gri:f]
grief   great sadness

[gri:v]
grieve   to be very sad about something; to be very
unhappy

[grim]
grim   stern, unsmiling, and often cruel

[graim]
grime   dirt that sticks on and is hard to get off

[grin]
grin   to smile broadly

[graind]
grind   to crush something into a powder. The same
word also means to rub together, like grinding
your teeth.

[grip]
grip   to hold on to something tightly

[grit]
grit   a small piece of dirt or sand. The same word
also means to grind.

[groun]
groan   a deep unhappy sound of pain or sorrow

['grousə]
grocer   a man who sells many kinds of food and
household supplies

[gru:v]
groove   a long narrow cut hollowed out, usually in
wood or metal

[group]
grope   to feel for something with your hands
because you cannot see well

[grous]
gross   very fat or big. The same word also means
12 dozen (144).

[graund]
ground   the earth we walk on

['graundʃiːt]
groundsheet a waterproof sheet which you lie on
    when you camp

[gruːp]
group a number of people or things together in
    one place

[graus]
grouse a bird that lives on the moors. The same
    word also means to grumble.

[grouv]
grove a small wood, a few trees

[grou]
grow to get bigger

[graul]
growl to make a low rumbling noise deep down in
    the throat. Dogs and lions growl when they are
    angry or afraid.

['grounʌp]
grown-up fully grown, adult

[grʌb]
grub a soft fat new-born insect

[grʌdʒ]
grudge a feeling of unfriendliness or dislike for
    someone

[grʌf]
gruff rough in manner; stern

['grʌmbl]
grumble to find fault and say you are not satisfied

['grʌmpi]
grumpy bad-tempered

[grʌnt]
grunt to make a noise like a pig

[gaːd]
guard to look after someone or something and see
    that nothing harms it, or is harmed by it

['gaːdiən]
guardian someone who guards or looks after
    someone or something

[ges]
guess to answer a question without knowing for
    sure that it is the right answer

[gest]
guest a visitor; someone you invite to your house,
    or to a restaurant

['gaidəns]
guidance   explaining or showing the way to
    someone

[gaid]
guide   someone who shows people the way. He
    leads and helps them.

[gilt]
guilt   a feeling of having done something wrong

['gini]
guinea   one pound and one shilling or one pound
    and five new pence

['ginipig]
guinea-pig   a small furry animal with short ears and
    tail, often kept as a pet

[gi'ta:]
guitar   a musical instrument. It has strings which
    you pluck to make music.

[gʌlf]
gulf   a very large bay that cuts into the land: a very
    deep hollow in the earth

[gʌl]
gull   a web-footed sea bird, usually coloured grey
    and white

['gʌlit]
gullet   a part inside your body which is like a tube.
    It leads from your mouth to your stomach.

[gʌlp]
gulp   to take a quick deep swallow of food or air

[gʌm]
gum   sticky stuff which you use to fasten things
    together. The same word also means a soft
    sweet which you chew but don't swallow.

[gʌn]
gun   a machine which shoots bullets

['gʌnpaudə]
gunpowder   a special powder which explodes when
    you set light to it

['gə:gl]
gurgle   to make a bubbly sound, as when water is
    let out of a bath

[gʌʃ]

gush   to rush out suddenly, as when water rushes out of a burst pipe

[gʌst]

gust   a sudden burst or rushing out of wind or laughter

['gʌtə]

gutter   a narrow hollow for draining off rain water, usually on a roof or at the roadside

[dʒim'neiziəm]

gymnasium   a large room fitted with ropes, bars and all kinds of equipment for exercise

['dʒipsi]

gypsy   another way of spelling gipsy

['habit]

habit   something you do regularly and often, almost without thinking about it, such as brushing your teeth

['hadək]

haddock   a sea fish, rather like a cod

[heil]

hail   frozen rain which falls as little lumps of ice

[heə]

hair   the soft covering which grows on your head

['heəbrʌʃ]

hairbrush   a special brush you use for tidying and arranging your hair

['heədresə]

hairdresser   someone who cuts and arranges people's hair

[ha:f]

half   one of two equal parts. When you cut something in half, you divide it into two parts which are exactly the same size.

[ho:l]

hall   the space inside the entrance of a building. The same word also means a large room used for special occasions, like a town hall.

['heilou]

halo   a ring of light around the sun or moon, or around the heads of holy people in paintings

[ho:lt]

halt   to stop

[ha:v]

halve   to divide into two equal parts

['hamə]
hammer   a heavy tool for hitting or breaking things

['hamək]
hammock   a swinging bed of netting or canvas hung up by ropes at each end

['hampə]
hamper   a large basket with a lid, often used for carrying food. The same word also means to hinder.

['hamstə]
hamster   a little furry animal, usually golden-brown in colour. It is often kept as a pet.

[hand]
hand   the end of your arm which you use to hold things

['hanbag]
handbag   a small light bag that you can carry in your hand

['handful]
handful   as much as your hand will hold; a small number or quantity

['handikap]
handicap   to make something more difficult for someone

['handikraːft]
handicraft   work in which things are made by hand and not by machine

['haŋkətʃif]
handkerchief   a small piece of cloth for wiping your nose or eyes

['handl]
handle   the part of something by which you can hold it, like the handle of a cup. The same word also means to touch or hold things with your hands.

['handlbaː]
handlebar   the part of a bicycle you hold on to and steer with

['hansəm]
handsome   good-looking

['handwə:k]
handwork work, like sewing or clay modelling,
     which you do with your hands

['handi]
handy useful and clever with your hands. The
     same word also means near; close at hand.

[haŋ]
hang to fasten something to a firm support so that
     it swings freely, but cannot fall

['haŋə]
hangar a large shed for aircraft

['haŋə]
hanger a shaped piece of metal or wood to hang
     clothes on so that they don't get wrinkled

[hap'hazəd]
haphazard not planned; happening by chance

['hapən]
happen to take place

['hapinis]
happiness joy; gladness

['hapi]
happy full of joy

['ha:bə]
harbour a sheltered place where ships stay before
     going out to sea

[ha:d]
hard not soft. Stones are hard. The same word also
     means difficult.

['ha:dn]
harden to make or become hard

['ha:dli]
hardly scarcely; only just

['ha:di]
hardy tough; brave

[heə]
hare an animal like a large rabbit

[ha:m]
harm to damage or hurt

['ha:mful]
harmful doing harm or damage

['ha:mlis]
harmless the opposite of harmful; doing no harm

['ha:nis]
harness the straps and other equipment worn by a
     horse

[ha:p]
harp a big musical instrument shaped like
a triangle. It has strings which you
pluck to make music.

[ha:'pu:n]
harpoon a sharp spear attached to a rope,
used for hunting whales

[ha:ʃ]
harsh rough or unkind

['ha:vist]
harvest the gathering of grain and fruit

[heist]
haste hurry

['heisn]
hasten to hurry up

[hat]
hat a covering for the head

[hatʃ]
hatch to break out of the eggshell, as when baby
birds and chicks are hatched

['hatʃit]
hatchet a small axe

[heit]
hate to dislike someone or something very much

['ho:ti]
haughty full of pride

[ho:l]
haul to drag along; to pull

[ho:nt]
haunt to visit a place very often

['ho:ntid]
haunted lived in or visited by ghosts

[hav]
have to own or to hold

['havək]
havoc very great damage, as when trees are blown
down in a strong wind

[ho:k]
hawk a bird of prey that hunts small birds and
animals

['hɔ:θɔ:n]
hawthorn   a kind of large bush which grows wild. It
   has pink or white flowers in spring and red
   berries in the autumn.

[hei]
hay   dried grass used for feeding animals

[heiz]
haze   mist or thin cloud

['heizl]
hazel   a small nut tree

[hed]
head   the part of your body above your neck. The
   same word also means a person who is in
   charge; a chief or leader.

['heddres]
head dress   something very decorative worn on the
   head on special occasions or as part of a
   costume

[hed'ma:stə]
headmaster   a man who is responsible for all the
   teachers and pupils in a school

[hed'mistris]
headmistress   a woman who is responsible for all the
   teachers and pupils in a school

[hi:l]
heal   to make someone well again

[helθ]
health   how your body feels. You have good health
   when you are not ill.

['helθi]
healthy   well in body and mind; free from illness

[hi:p]
heap   a pile, like a heap of dead leaves

[hiə]
hear   to use your ears to listen to sounds

[ha:t]
heart   the part of your body which pumps the blood
   around inside you

[ha:θ]
hearth   the floor of a fireplace

[hi:t]
heat   to make something hot

['hi:tə]
heater   something that produces heat, such as an
   electric fire

[hi:θ]
heath   an open area where nothing much grows
    except small shrubs; a moor

['hi:ðən]
heathen   a person who does not believe in God.
    Sometimes heathens worship idols.

['heðə]
heather   a small wild plant which has white or
    purple flowers. It often grows on moors and
    heaths.

[hi:v]
heave   to haul or lift something up with a great
    effort

['hevn]
heaven   the home of God. The same word also
    sometimes means the sky.

['hevi]
heavy   difficult to pick up and carry away; weighing
    a lot

[hedʒ]
hedge   lots of bushes growing close together in a
    line, like a fence

['hedʒhog]
hedgehog   a little animal with a coat like sharp
    needles mixed with hair

[hi:l]
heel   the back of your foot. The same word also
    means the back part of your shoe.

[hait]
height   how tall or high something is

[eə]
heir   a man or boy who will receive money,
    property, or a title when the present owner dies

['eəris]
heiress   a woman or girl who will receive money,
    property, or a title when the present owner dies

['helikoptə]
helicopter   a kind of aircraft without wings which
    can go straight up or down in the air as well as
    along

[hel]
hell   a place of misery

['helmit]
helmet   a covering, usually made of metal, which protects the head. Soldiers, racing-drivers, and motorbike riders wear them.

[help]
help   to make something easier for a person to do. You help your mother to wash the dishes.

['helpful]
helpful   being of help

['helplis]
helpless   not able to help yourself or others, often because of weakness

['heltə'skeltə]
helter-skelter   a slide where you go round and round as you go down

[hem]
hem   an edge of cloth which is folded over and sewn to make it neat

[hen]
hen   a mother bird

[hə:b]
herb   a plant which is used for flavouring food or for medicine

[hə:d]
herd   a group of animals kept together, such as a herd of cows

[hiə]
here   in this place

['hiərou]
hero   a man or boy who does something brave. The same word also means the most important man in a book or play.

['herouin]
heroine   a girl or woman who does something brave. The same word also means the most important woman in a book or play.

['herouizəm]
heroism   great bravery

['heriŋ]
herring   a small seafish

[hə:'self]
herself   she and no one else

['heziteit]
hesitate   to pause because you are not sure what
     to do or to say next

['haibəneit]
hibernate   to sleep all through the winter, as some
     animals do

['hikʌp]
hiccup   to make a sharp noise in your throat,
     usually when you have eaten or drunk too
     quickly. Sometimes the word is spelled
     hiccough.

[haid]
hide   to go where no one can see you or to put
     something where no one can see it. The same
     word also means the skin of an animal.

['haidən'si:k]
hide-and-seek   a game where one person hides and
     another tries to find him

['hidiəs]
hideous   very ugly; horrible

['haidiŋ]
hiding   a beating or whipping

[hai]
high   a long way up. Mountains are high.

['haiwei]
highway   a public road

['haiweimən]
highwayman   a robber on horseback who held up
     travellers on the road in olden days

[hil]
hill   part of the ground that is higher than the rest,
     but lower than a mountain

[him'self]
himself   he and no one else

['hində]
hinder   to delay or prevent someone from doing
     something

[hindʒ]
hinge   a joint, usually of metal. Doors are fitted with
     hinges so that they can be opened and shut.

[hint]
hint   to suggest something without actually saying it
     in so many words. You might say to someone
     that it is getting late as a hint that you wish
     he would go home.

[hip]
hip   one of the sides of your body just below your waist

[hipə'potəməs]
hippopotamus   a very big animal which lives in hot countries

['haiə]
hire   to pay for the use of something for a certain length of time. You can hire a taxi. The same word also means to employ.

[his]
hiss   to make a noise that sounds like s-s-s-s-s. Snakes and geese make hissing sounds.

['histəri]
history   the study of what has happened in the world in the past

[hit]
hit   to knock something. The same word also sometimes means a show or a tune which is a big success.

[haiv]
hive   a house for bees

[ho:d]
hoard   a store or stock of something hidden away. Squirrels have a hoard of nuts hidden away for the winter.

[ho:s]
hoarse   having a rough-sounding voice, as when you have a sore throat

[hob]
hob   a place near the hearth where things can be kept hot

['hobl]
hobble   to walk with difficulty because you are lame

['hobi]
hobby   something you very much like to do in your spare time, such as collecting stamps or making models

['hoki]
hockey   a team game where you try to hit a ball into the goal with a long stick curved at one end.

Sometimes the game is played on ice, with a rubber disc instead of a ball.

[hou]
hoe   a long-handled garden tool for clearing weeds and loosening the earth

[hould]
hold   to have in your hand or your arms; to contain. The same word also means the part of a ship where cargo is kept.

[houl]
hole   an opening in or through something

['holədi]
holiday   a time when you do not have to work or go to school

['holou]
hollow   having a space or a hole inside: a valley

['holi]
holly   a tree with evergreen prickly leaves and bright red berries. It is often used for decoration at Christmas.

['holihok]
hollyhock   a tall plant with many large flowers on each stalk

['houlstə]
holster   a leather case on a belt for holding a gun

['houli]
holy   anything specially belonging to, or to do with God

[houm]
home   the place where you live

['houmwə:k]
homework   work done at home, usually school work

['onist]
honest   truthful; not likely to steal from others

['hʌni]
honey   a sweet food which is made by bees

[hoŋk]
honk   the loud cry of a wild goose: the noise of a motor horn

['onə]
honour   to show respect for someone or something

[hud]
hood   a loose cloth covering for the head. It is
         sometimes fastened to a coat or jacket.

[hu:f]
hoof   the hard part of a horse's foot. Cattle, deer
         and some other animals also have hooves.

[huk]
hook   a curved pointed piece of metal for catching,
         holding, or pulling things

['hu:ligən]
hooligan   a rough noisy person who goes about
            the streets bullying people and damaging
            property

[hu:p]
hoop   a large ring made of metal or wood

[hu:t]
hoot   to shout scornfully at someone. The same
         word also means the cry of an owl at night; the
         sound of a motor horn.

['hu:tə]
hooter   a whistle blown by steam; a siren

[hop]
hop   to jump on one leg or move in short jumps

[houp]
hope   to wish that something may happen, although
        you know it may not

['houpful]
hopeful   hoping; full of hope

['houplis]
hopeless   without hope; impossible

[ho:d]
horde   a crowd or mass of people

[hə'raizn]
horizon   the place where the sky and earth appear
           to meet

[ho:n]
horn   one of the hard sharp bony parts that grow
        out of the heads of some animals such as cows
        and goats. The same word also means a
        musical instrument that you blow.

['horəbl]
horrible   dreadful; ugly and awful

['horid]
horrid   nasty; very unpleasant

['horə]
horror   a very great fear or loathing
[ho:s]
horse   an animal used for riding
and for pulling carts,
coaches and carriages

['ho:sbak]
horseback   on the back of a horse
['ho:s'tʃesnʌt]
horse chestnut   a kind of chestnut tree that conkers
grow on. It has cone-shaped bunches of white
or pink flowers in spring.
['ho:ʃʃu:]
horseshoe   a curved iron shoe which is nailed to the
bottom of a horse's hoof
[houz]
hose   a long thin tube used for carrying water from
a tap. The same word also means socks or
stockings.
['hospitl]
hospital   a place where people who are ill or hurt
are looked after by doctors and nurses
[houst]
host   a boy or man who has other people as his
guests: an old fashioned word for innkeeper.
The same word sometimes means a crowd or a
large number.
['houstis]
hostess   a girl or woman who has other people as
her guests
[hot]
hot   very warm
[hə'tel]
hotel   a building with many rooms, where you pay
for a bedroom and food when you are travelling
[haund]
hound   a hunting dog
['auə]
hour   60 minutes
[haus]
house   a building to live in
['hausbout]
houseboat   a large flat-bottomed boat used as a
floating house

['haushould]
household   all the people who live in the same house

['hovə]
hover   to float or stay in one place in the air

['hovəkra:ft]
hovercraft   a vehicle without wheels that can glide
   very quickly over the earth's surface, both
   land and water

[hau]
how   in what way

[haul]
howl   to make a long loud whining noise

[hʌb]
hub   the middle of a wheel

['hʌdl]
huddle   crowded closely together, sometimes to
   keep warm

[hʌg]
hug   to hold someone or something close to you in
   your arms

[hju:dʒ]
huge   enormous; very big

[hʌl]
hull   the main part of a ship

[hʌm]
hum   to make a musical sound in your nose as
   though you are saying m-m-m-m without
   opening your mouth

['hju:mən]
human   a man, woman or child. The same word also
   means having to do with people, not with
   other animals or plants.

['hʌmbl]
humble   the opposite of proud or boasting, meek

['hju:mərist]
humorist   someone who makes you laugh at his
   jokes and sayings

['hju:mərəs]
humorous   funny; amusing

['hju:mə]
humour   fun; jokes

[hʌmp]
hump a lump or large bump, often on the back of an animal, like a camel's hump

[ˈhʌŋgə]
hunger a need for food

[ˈhʌŋgri]
hungry feeling you want something to eat

[hʌnt]
hunt to chase after something which you want to catch

[ˈhʌntə]
hunter someone who hunts wild animals or birds for food or sport

[ˈhəːdl]
hurdle a kind of wooden fence which animals or people have to jump over in some races

[həːl]
hurl to throw something away from you with all your strength

[ˈhʌrikən]
hurricane a very great windstorm

[ˈhʌri]
hurry to move fast in order to get somewhere more quickly, or to finish what you are doing sooner

[həːt]
hurt to give pain

[ˈhəːtl]
hurtle to rush or dash with great force and speed

[ˈhʌzbənd]
husband a married man

[ˈhʌzbəndmən]
husbandman a farmer

[hʌʃ]
hush to become quiet or silent

[ˈhʌsl]
hustle to hurry; to make someone hurry along by pushing and shoving

[hʌt]
hut a small wooden house

[hʌtʃ]
hutch a little wooden house for a pet rabbit

[ˈhaiəsinθ]
hyacinth a spring flower which has spikes of bright, sweet-smelling blossoms

[hai'i:nə]
hyena   a wild animal rather like a dog. It makes a
high laughing sound and lives in some
hot countries.

[him]
hymn   a song which praises God

[ais]
ice   water which has been frozen hard by the cold

['ais'kri:m]
ice cream   a frozen food made with milk and sugar

['aisikl]
icicle   a long thin spike of ice, usually hanging from
a roof

['aisiŋ]
icing   a sugar coating for cakes

[ai'diə]
idea   a plan which you think of, or a picture in your
mind

[ai'diəl]
ideal   perfect; exactly right

['idiət]
idiot   a person whose mind does not work properly;
a crazy person

['aidl]
idle   lazy; not working; doing nothing

['aidl]
idol   an image or statue of a person or animal that is
worshipped as a god

['iglu:]
igloo   a hut made of blocks of hard snow. It has a
domed roof.

['ignərənt]
ignorant   without knowledge; not knowing

[ig'no:]
ignore   to take no notice; to pretend someone or
something is not there

[il]
ill   not well; not healthy

[i'lu:mineit]
illuminate   to light or throw light upon

[iləs'treiʃən]
illustration   a picture, usually in a book. The same

word also means an example that helps to explain something.

['imidʒ]
image   an exact likeness or copy of something; a statue

[i'madʒinəri]
imaginary   something you think of that is not real

[i'madʒin]
imagine   to picture in your mind what something or someone is like

['imiteit]
imitate   to copy, to do something the same as someone else

[i'miːdiətli]
immediately   at once

[i'mens]
immense   enormous; very big

[imp]
imp   a little devil: a naughty child

[im'poːtənt]
important   of great interest or value. The same word also means powerful.

[im'posəbl]
impossible   not able to be done

[im'pres]
impress   to make something stick in someone's mind

[im'preʃən]
impression   an idea or thought that is fixed firmly in your mind. The same word also means a mark that is made by pressing or printing.

[im'presiv]
impressive   making a deep impression on the mind

[im'pruːv]
improve   to make better; to become better

['impjudənt]
impudent   cheeky; not respectful

[intʃ]
inch   a measure of length. There are 12 inches in one foot.

['insidənt]
incident   something that happens; an event

[in'kluːd]
include   to count something in; to contain

[in'kri:s]
increase   to get bigger or more in number

['indeks]
index   a list in alphabetical order, usually at the end
     of a book. It shows the numbers of the pages
     where things are mentioned in the book.

[in'dignənt]
indignant   annoyed or angry about something you
     think is wrong

['indigou]
indigo   a purplish-blue colour; a dye of that colour

['in'do:z]
indoors   inside a building; the opposite of outdoors

['indəstri]
industry   hard work. The same word also means
     making things in factories.

['infənt]
infant   a baby; a young child

[in'fə:məri]
infirmary   another name for a hospital

[in'flaməbl]
inflammable   easily set on fire

[in'fo:m]
inform   to tell or give information

[infə'meiʃən]
information   facts told to someone or given in a
     book; knowledge

[in'fjuərieit]
infuriate   to make very angry

[in'habit]
inhabit   to live in or occupy

[i'niʃəl]
initial   the first letter of a word or name

[in'dʒekʃən]
injection   a prick, usually in the arm with a hollow
     needle. Through the needle a liquid medicine is
     pushed into your bloodstream to make you
     better, or to stop you from getting an illness.

['indʒə]
injure   to harm or hurt

['indʒəri]
injury   a hurt or wound

[iŋk]
ink   a coloured liquid used with a pen for writing

[in]
inn a small hotel where travellers can stay, and where they can buy food and drink

['inəsnt]
innocent without guilt

[in'kwaiə]
inquire to ask. This word can also be spelled enquire.

[in'kwaiəri]
inquiry a question; a seeking of information. This word can also be spelled enquiry.

[in'kwizətiv]
inquisitive eager to find out about something; curious; nosey

['insekt]
insect a very small animal with six legs. Ants, bees and beetles are insects.

['in'said]
inside within; not outside

[in'sist]
insist to demand; to say or ask over and over again

[in'spekt]
inspect to look carefully at something; to examine

[in'spektə]
inspector someone who examines things to make sure everything is all right. The same word also means a policeman who is in charge of other policemen.

[in'stɔːlmənt]
instalment one of the parts of a serial story or film: one part of the money owed for something you pay for bit by bit

['instəntli]
instantly at once; without delay

[in'sted]
instead in place of

['instiŋkt]
instinct an ability to do things without being taught. Baby ducks are able to swim by instinct.

[in'strʌkt]
instruct to teach or inform someone

['instrəmənt]
instrument a tool. The same word also means something which makes music.

[in'sʌlt]
insult   to say something rude or hurtful

[in'telidʒənt]
intelligent   brainy; clever at learning

[in'tend]
intend   to mean to do something, as when you
intend to pay someone back

[in'tens]
intense   very great

['intrəst]
interest   a wish to know more about something

['intrəstiŋ]
interesting   attracting or holding your interest

[intə'fiə]
interfere   to meddle; to hinder; to try to stop
something from going on

[intə'rʌpt]
interrupt   to break in on something which is
happening, like starting to speak when someone
is already speaking

['intəvəl]
interval   a period of time between two events, such
as a ten-minute interval between two acts in a
play

['intəvju:]
interview   a talk with someone, often broadcast or
reported in a newspaper

[intrə'dju:s]
introduce   to tell people each other's names when
they meet for the first time. The same word
also means to bring a new idea into what you
are talking about or doing.

[in'veid]
invade   to go into a place by force, as when
an army invades the enemy's country
in wartime

['invəlid]
invalid   a person who is ill

[in'vent]
invent   to think up, or make something which is
completely new and has never been thought of
or made before

[in'vizəbl]
invisible   not able to be seen

[in'vait]
invite   to ask someone to come to your home or to
   go somewhere with you

['aiəris]
iris   the coloured part of the eye. The same word
   also means a garden plant with large flowers
   and sword-shaped leaves.

['aiən]
iron   a strong grey metal. The same word also
   means a tool that takes the wrinkles out of
   clothes.

['iriteit]
irritate   to annoy or make angry. The same word
   ·   also means to itch.

['ailənd]
island   a piece of land with water all around it

[ail]
isle   another word for island

['iʃu:]
issue   a result; a problem. The same word also
   means to send or give something out.

[i'taliks]
italics   a kind of lettering that slants to the right, *as
   these words do*

[itʃ]
itch   a tickling feeling on your skin which makes
   you want to scratch

['aivi]
ivy   an evergreen climbing plant

[dʒab]
jab   to poke or stab at something suddenly

['dʒakɔ:l]
jackal   a wild animal that looks like a dog

['dʒakdɔ:]
jackdaw   a black bird, like a small crow

['dʒakit]
jacket   a short coat. The same word means a loose
   paper cover on a book.

['dʒagid]
jagged   having sharp and rough edges

['dʒagjuə]
jaguar a fierce wild animal, rather like a leopard

[dʒeil]
jail another word for prison. Sometimes the word is spelled gaol.

[dʒam]
jam fruit cooked together with sugar until it is thick and soft

[dʒa:]
jar a pottery or glass container with a wide opening

[dʒɔ:]
jaw one of the two large bones your teeth grow in

[dʒaz]
jazz a kind of lively dance music

['dʒeləs]
jealous wishing you had something someone else has; full of envy

[dʒi:nz]
jeans trousers made of a strong cotton cloth

[dʒi:p]
jeep a small open motor vehicle used by the army

[dʒiə]
jeer to make fun of someone in an unkind way

['dʒeli]
jelly a transparent wobbly food, usually fruit-flavoured

[dʒə:k]
jerk a short sudden movement

['dʒə:zi]
jersey a tight-fitting knitted pullover with sleeves

[dʒest]
jest to say something to make people laugh; to joke

[dʒet]
jet a rush of liquid or gas through a small opening in a pipe or hose. The same word also means a kind of aeroplane without propellers.

['dʒeti]
jetty a small pier

['dʒu:əl]
jewel a valuable stone, like a diamond or emerald

['dʒuːəlri]
jewellery   necklaces, bracelets, rings, brooches and other ornaments made of jewels and precious metals, such as gold and silver

[dʒib]
jib   to refuse to do something. The same word also means the small triangular sail at the front of a sailboat.

[dʒig]
jig   a jolly dance

['dʒigsɔː]
jigsaw   a fine saw that can cut wood or cardboard into small curved and straight pieces

['dʒigsɔː'pʌzl]
jigsaw puzzle   a puzzle made of odd-shaped pieces cut by a jigsaw. You have to put them together to make a picture.

['dʒiŋgl]
jingle   a clinking tinkling sound made by coins or bells

[dʒob]
job   work done, usually for money

['dʒoki]
jockey   a boy or man who rides a horse in a race

[dʒog]
jog   to move along more quickly than walking, but not so fast as running. The same word also means to give a little push, as when you jog someone's elbow.

[dʒoin]
join   to put together or fasten. The same word also means to become a member of a group, such as a club or a choir.

['dʒoinə]
joiner   a carpenter who makes furniture and other woodwork

[dʒoint]
joint   the place where two parts of something grow or are joined together

[dʒouk]
joke   something a person says or does to make you laugh

['dʒɒli]
jolly   cheerful; full of fun

[dʒəult]
jolt   to move forward in jerky movements. The same word also means a bump or shaking-up.

['dʒɒsl]
jostle   to push or knock against someone, usually in a crowd

['dʒə:nl]
journal   another word for a magazine or newspaper. The same word also means a diary.

['dʒə:ni]
journey   a trip. When you travel from one place to another you make a journey.

['dʒəuviəl]
jovial   cheerful; jolly

[dʒɔi]
joy   a feeling of great happiness

[dʒʌdʒ]
judge   the person in authority in a court of law who decides how someone who has done wrong should be punished

[dʒʌg]
jug   a container with a handle, used for pouring milk and other liquids

['dʒʌglə]
juggler   someone who is very clever at balancing things and keeping them moving in the air

[dʒu:s]
juice   liquid in oranges, lemons, tomatoes and other fruit and vegetables

['dʒu:kboks]
juke-box   an instrument that plays records when you put money in it

['dʒʌmbl]
jumble   a mixture of odd things

[dʒʌmp]
jump   to spring up off the ground

['dʒʌmpə]
jumper   a loose-fitting knitted pullover with sleeves, worn mostly by girls and women

['dʒʌŋkʃən]
junction   a place where railway lines or roads meet

['dʒʌŋgl]
jungle   a forest in hot countries where plants and

trees grow so thickly that it is hard to find your way through

['dʒuːnjə]
junior   someone who is younger or less important than others

[dʒʌŋk]
junk   something of no use or value; rubbish. The same word also means a Chinese sailing ship.

[dʒʌt]
jut   to stick out

[kə'laidəskoup]
kaleidoscope   a toy shaped like a tube, with small pieces of coloured glass which change patterns when you turn the tube round

[kaŋgə'ruː]
kangaroo   an animal which can jump a long way. It has a pocket for its babies.

[kiːl]
keel   a heavy piece of wood or metal that goes along the bottom of a boat or ship from one end to the other

[kiːn]
keen   very interested in something. The same word also means sharp; cutting.

[kiːp]
keep   to hold on to something and not give it away. The same word also means the strongest, inside part of a castle.

['kiːpə]
keeper   someone who looks after or guards something, like a gamekeeper or a keeper at the zoo

['kenl]
kennel   a small house or shelter for a dog

[kəːb]
kerb   the edge of a pavement

['kəːnl]
kernel   the inside part of a nut that can usually be eaten

['ketl]
kettle   a metal container used for boiling water. It has a lid, a handle and a spout.

[ki:]
key a small piece of metal, specially shaped so that it will open a lock. The same word also means a lever on a piano or typewriter.

['ki:bo:d]
keyboard the keys of a piano, organ or typewriter, arranged in order

['ki:houl]
keyhole a hole specially shaped so you can put a key in it

[kik]
kick to hit something or someone with your foot

[kid]
kid a young goat. The same word also means a child.

['kidnap]
kidnap to take someone away by force

[kil]
kill to cause someone or something to die

['kiləgram]
kilogramme a unit of weight, equal to 1,000 grammes

[ki'lomitə]
kilometre a unit of length, equal to 1,000 metres

[kilt]
kilt a short pleated skirt with a tartan pattern

[ki'mounou]
kimono a loose garment, usually fastened with a sash

[kaind]
kind friendly; good to other people. The same word also means sort or type.

['kindəga:tn]
kindergarten a school or class for very young children

[kiŋ]
king a man who rules a country usually because his family did so before him

['kiŋdəm]
kingdom   a country ruled by a king or queen

['ki:osk]
kiosk   a small open-fronted hut where you can buy
        sweets, newspapers and tobacco. The same
        word also means a public telephone box.

['kipə]
kipper   a herring that has been salted and then dried
        in a special kind of smoke

[kis]
kiss   to touch with your lips someone you like

[kit]
kit   all the gear needed; a complete outfit

['kitʃən]
kitchen   a room where cooking is done

[kait]
kite   a toy made of paper or cloth on light wood. It
        can be flown on the end of a string when it is
        windy. The same word means a bird of prey.

['kitn]
kitten   a young cat

['napsak]
knapsack   a bag for food and clothes that you carry
        on your back

[neiv]
knave   a man who is not honest

[ni:]
knee   the joint in the middle of your leg

[ni:l]
kneel   to get down on your knees

['nikəz]
knickers   short underpants worn by girls and women

[naif]
knife   a thin sharp piece of metal with a handle,
        used for cutting

[nait]
knight   a nobleman. In the old days, he used to
        dress in armour and fight for his king.

[nit]
knit   to weave wool into clothing with long needles

[nob]
knob   a round handle, like a door knob

[nok]
knock   to hit something hard or to bump into
        something

['nokə]

knocker   a thick piece of metal fastened to a door
    by a hinge. When you lift it and then let it
    drop, it makes a loud noise.

[not]

knot   the place where two pieces of string or ribbon
    have been tied together

[nou]

know   to understand and be sure about something
    you have read or seen

['nolidʒ]

knowledge   what you have learned and understand
    about things

['nʌkl]

knuckle   a finger joint

['leibl]

label   a small piece of paper or cardboard with
    writing or printing on it. You stick labels on
    such things as jars, boxes or luggage, so that
    you know what is inside.

[lə'borətəri]

laboratory   a room or building where scientific tests
    are carried out

['leibə]

labour   hard work

[leis]

lace   a string used to fasten shoes. The same word
    also means material with a pretty pattern of
    holes.

[lak]

lack   to be in need of something you haven't got. If
    you are hungry, you lack food.

[lad]

lad   a boy

['ladə]

ladder   a set of wooden or metal rungs between two
    long pieces of wood or metal, used for climbing
    up or down

['leidl]

ladle   a spoon shaped like a small cup with a long
    straight handle, used for serving soup or other
    liquids

['leidi]

lady   another word for a woman

['leidibə:d]
ladybird   a tiny flying beetle, usually red with
   black spots

[lag]
lag   to follow along slowly behind others
[leə]
lair   a wild beast's den
[leik]
lake   a very large pool of water with land all
   around it
[lam]
lamb   a young sheep
[leim]
lame   not able to walk easily because you have hurt
   your leg or your foot
[lamp]
lamp   a light, usually in a glass container, like an
   electric light bulb
[la:ns]
lance   a long spear. The same word also means to
   cut open a boil so that the fluid can drain away.
[land]
land   the parts of the earth that are not covered by
   water. The same word also means to come
   down from the air on to land or water.
['landiŋ]
landing   coming back to land from the sea or air.
   The same word also means the floor at the top
   of the stairs.
['landleidi]
landlady   a woman who owns a house or flat where
   other people pay to live
['landlo:d]
landlord   a man who owns a house or flat where
   other people pay to live
[lein]
lane   a little road, usually in the country
['laŋgwidʒ]
language   human speech or writing. The same word
   also means the speech used in different
   countries, such as the English language and the
   French language.

['lantən]
lantern a metal and glass container for a candle or oil light. You can carry it about.

[lap]
lap the top part of your legs when you are sitting down. The same word also means once around a racetrack.

[la:tʃ]
larch a tree which has cones and long thin leaves like needles

[la:d]
lard fat from pigs, used in cooking

['la:də]
larder a room or cupboard where food is kept

[la:dʒ]
large very big

[la:k]
lark a small songbird. The same word also means a frolic.

[laʃ]
lash to hit someone with a whip: to tie up firmly

[las]
lass a girl

[la'su:]
lasso a long rope with a sliding loop at the end. It is used to catch wild horses and cattle.

[la:st]
last coming at the end; after all others

[latʃ]
latch a wood or metal fastening for a door or gate

[leit]
late behind time; not early

[leið]
lathe a machine for cutting and shaping pieces of wood and metal while they are being turned round

['la:ðə]
lather a foam made by using soap and water together

[la:f]
laugh   to make a noise to show you feel happy or
think something is funny

[lo:ntʃ]
launch   to start something on its way, such as
launching a ship into the water, or a rocket into
the air. The same word also means a large open
motorboat.

['lo:ndri]
laundry   a place where dirty clothes are washed

['lavətəri]
lavatory   a place where there is a washbasin or a
water-closet (W.C.), sometimes both together

['lavində]
lavender   a plant with lavender or purple flowers
that are dried and used to make linen and
clothing smell sweet

[lo:]
law   rules made by the government of a country

[lo:n]
lawn   a smooth flat area of grass which is cut and
looked after carefully

['lo:nmouə]
lawnmower   a machine that is used to cut the grass
on a lawn

[lei]
lay   to put something down

['leiə]
layer   a flat covering or thickness. You put jam and
cream between two layers of sponge cake.

['leizi]
lazy   not wanting to work or make any effort

[li:d]
lead (*rhymes with seed*)   to be first, before everyone
else

[led]
lead (*rhymes with bed*)   a heavy soft grey metal

['li:də]
leader   someone who is in front or at the head of a
group of people

[li:f]
leaf   the flat, green part of a plant or tree

[li:k]
leak   the accidental escape of liquid or gas from a
hole or crack in a pipe or container

[li:n]
lean   thin; without fat. The same word also means
        to rest against something, so that you are not
        standing up straight.

[li:p]
leap   to jump high in the air

['li:pjə:]
leap year   a year with 366 days, having 29 days in
        February. It comes every four years.

[lə:n]
learn   to find out about things or how to do
        something

[li:st]
least   the smallest in size or importance

['leðə]
leather   the skin of animals, used to make things
        like shoes and gloves

[li:v]
leave   to go away from somewhere. The same word
        also means to let something stay where it is.

['lektʃə]
lecture   a talk given to an audience or a class at
        school

[ledʒ]
ledge   a narrow shelf

[li:k]
leek   a vegetable with long green leaves and a thick
        white stem, tasting something like an onion

[liə]
leer   to smile at someone in a nasty way

[left]
left   the opposite side to right. You have a right
        hand and a left hand.

[leg]
leg   the part of your body which joins on to your
        foot. You have two legs. The same word also
        means one of the pieces of wood that hold up a
        table or chair.

['ledʒənd]
legend   a story from long ago which may or may not
        be true

['legiŋz]
leggings   a covering of cloth or leather for your legs
        in cold weather

['li:dʒən]
legion   a large group of soldiers: a large number

['lemən]
lemon   a sour yellow fruit

[lemə'neid]
lemonade   a drink made from lemon juice and sugar

[lend]
lend   to let someone have something of yours which he will give back to you

[leŋθ]
length   how long something is

['leŋθən]
lengthen   to make longer

[lenz]
lens   a curved piece of glass used in eye glasses or in instruments such as telescopes and cameras

['lepəd]
leopard   a dangerous wild animal that looks like a large cat with spots

['lesn]
lesson   something to be learned

[let]
let   to agree that someone may do something; to give permission

['letə]
letter   how a sound looks when it is written down. Our alphabet has 26 letters. The same word also means a written message that is put in an envelope.

['letis]
lettuce   a garden plant with large green leaves which you can eat without cooking

['levl]
level   another word for flat; with no bumps

['li:və]
lever   a bar pushed down at one end so that it lifts something on the other end

['laiə]
liar   someone who tells lies

['libəti]
liberty   freedom to do as you think is right

['laibrəri]
library   a room or building full of books

['laisəns]
licence   a special piece of printed paper that you must have before you can do certain things. You need a licence to own a gun, to drive a car, or to have a television set.

[lik]
lick   to touch something with your tongue, like a lollipop or an ice cream

[lid]
lid   the top which can be taken off something, such as a box or saucepan

[lai]
lie   to say something that you know is not true. The same word also means to rest flat.

[laif]
life   the time between your birth and your death

['laifbout]
lifeboat   a special boat kept ready to rescue people who have been shipwrecked

[lift]
lift   to move or raise something up. The same word also means a large metal box or cage that carries people up and down in a tall building.

[lait]
light   not heavy. The same word also means something which shines brightly so that you can see in the dark.

['laitn]
lighten   to make less heavy or less dark

['laitə]
lighter   something used to produce fire, like a cigarette lighter or a firelighter

['laithaus]
lighthouse   a tower with a strong light to guide ships at sea in the dark

['laitli]
lightly   gently; not heavily

['laitniŋ]
lightning   a sudden bright flash of light in the sky when there is a thunderstorm

['laikəbl]
likable   pleasant; easy to get on with. Sometimes the word is spelled likeable.

[laik]
like to be fond of or be pleased with. The same word also means the same or almost the same.

['laikli]
likely probable; expected to happen

['laiknis]
likeness something that looks the same as the real thing

['lailək]
lilac a large garden bush with sweet-smelling white or purple flowers in the spring

['lili]
lily a tall garden plant with large white or brightly-coloured flowers

[lim]
limb an arm or leg; a branch

[laim]
lime white powder made from limestone, used for making cement. The same word also means a green-coloured sour fruit, something like a small lemon.

['limit]
limit the place where something ends

[limp]
limp without stiffness, like wilted flowers. The same word also means to walk in a lame way.

[lain]
line a thin mark like this _____

['linin]
linen cloth made from the flax plant. The same word also means sheets, pillowcases, towels and other household linen.

['lainə]
liner a large ship that carries people and cargoes long distances

['liŋgə]
linger to hang about; to delay leaving

[liŋk]
link one of the rings in a chain

[li'nouliəm]
linoleum   a stiff shiny floor covering, usually called
        lino for short

[lint]
lint   soft woolly material used to protect sores or
        wounds

['laiən]
lion   a strong and dangerous wild animal, like a very
        big cat

['laiənis]
lioness   a female lion

[lips]
lips   the soft edges of the mouth

['lipstik]
lipstick   a kind of crayon in a case, used by girls
        and women to colour their lips red or pink

['likwid]
liquid   anything which is wet and flows like water

['likəris]
liquorice   black chewy sweets made from sugar
        mixed with the root of a plant

[list]
list   words placed underneath each other in a
        column, like a shopping list or a list of names

['lisn]
listen   to try to hear something

['litrətʃə]
literature   poems, stories and books

['li:tə]
litre   a measurement of capacity

['litə]
litter   rubbish or waste paper left lying about. The
        same word also means all the babies born to a
        mother animal at one time.

['litl]
little   not big; small

[liv]
live (*rhymes with give*)   to have life; to be alive

[laiv]
live (*rhymes with five*)   living; not dead; alive

['laivli]
lively   jolly; active; full of life

['livə]
liver   an inside part of the body

['liviŋrum]
living-room   a room with comfortable furniture
    where the family gathers together to talk, read,
    watch television or entertain visitors

['lizəd]
lizard   a scaly reptile with four legs

['la:mə]
llama   a large animal with a long
    woolly coat, something like
    a camel without any humps

[loud]
load   all that can be carried at one time, like a load
    of bricks or a load of bananas. The same word
    also means to put bullets into a gun, ready for
    shooting.

[louf]
loaf   a large piece of bread with crust all over it

[loun]
loan   something you lend to someone for a while

[louð]
loathe   to hate or despise greatly

[lob]
lob   a stroke in tennis or cricket, when the ball goes
    high in the air

['lobi]
lobby   the entrance hall in a large building

['lobstə]
lobster   a shellfish with
    two large strong claws

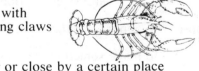

['loukl]
local   nearby; near or close by a certain place

[lok]
lock   a strong fastening for a door or gate that can
    only be opened with a key

[loukə'moutiv]
locomotive   a railway engine

['loukəst]
locust   an insect something like a large grasshopper,
    that destroys crops

[lodʒ]
lodge   a small house at the entrance to a park or at
    the gates of a large house in the country

[ˈlodʒə]

lodger someone who pays to live in someone else's house

[loft]

loft space under the roof which can be used as a store room

[log]

log a thick round piece of wood. The same word also means a ship's diary.

[ˈloitə]

loiter to linger; to dawdle

[lol]

loll to sit or lie about in a lazy way

[ˈlolipop]

lollipop a large sweet on the end of a stick

[loun]

lone the only one

[ˈlounli]

lonely feeling sad because you are alone

[loŋ]

long a big distance from one end to the other

[luk]

look to watch or try to see

[ˈlukiŋglaːs]

looking-glass another word for mirror

[luːm]

loom a machine for weaving thread into cloth

[luːp]

loop a ring of wire, string or ribbon

[luːs]

loose the opposite of tight; not properly fastened

[ˈluːsn]

loosen to make something less tight

[loːd]

lord an important nobleman

[ˈlori]

lorry an open motor vehicle used to carry heavy loads from place to place

[luːz]

lose not to be able to find something

[lot]

lot a large number; a great many

[ˈlouʃən]

lotion a soothing liquid medicine that you put on sore places on your skin

['loutəs]
lotus   a waterlily that grows in some hot countries

[laud]
loud   noisy; easily heard

['laud'spi:kə]
loudspeaker   an instrument that makes sounds
    louder, so that you can hear them from a
    distance

[laundʒ]
lounge   a room with comfortable chairs in a club,
    hotel or house. The same word also means to
    loll or lie about in a lazy way.

['lʌvəbl]
lovable   worth loving

[lʌv]
love   to be very fond of, to like someone or
    something very much

['lʌvli]
lovely   beautiful or pretty; nice

[lou]
low   not high or tall

['loiəl]
loyal   faithful; true to someone

[lʌk]
luck   something that happens by chance. You can
    have good luck or bad luck.

['lʌki]
lucky   having good luck

['lʌgidʒ]
luggage   the cases, trunks or bags you take your
    clothes in when you travel

['lu:kwo:m]
lukewarm   in between warm and cool

['lʌmbə]
lumber   timber. The same word also means
    something big and heavy that you can't use any
    more, like a broken armchair or an old cooker.

[lʌmp]
lump   a piece of something, usually without any
    special shape, like a lump of clay or dough

['lu:nə]
lunar   having to do with the moon

[lʌntʃ]
lunch   the meal eaten at midday. The word is short
    for luncheon.

[lʌndʒ]
lunge to make a sudden thrust or rush at something

[ˈluːpin]
lupin a large garden plant with long spikes of brightly-coloured blossoms

[ləːtʃ]
lurch to jerk forward on to one side

[ləːk]
lurk to hide yourself while you are waiting about for someone or something

[ˈlʌʃəs]
luscious delicious

[ˈlʌkʃəri]
luxury something expensive and pleasant that you would like to have but don't really need: great comfort

[makəˈrouni]
macaroni long stiff tubes of dried wheat paste that become soft when cooked in boiling water. You can buy it in tins, already cooked.

[meis]
mace a long stick with a metal ornament on the top. It was once used as a weapon, but nowadays it is carried in processions in front of the mayor and other important people.

[məˈʃiːn]
machine an instrument, usually made of metal, which does a job of work, like a sewing machine or a washing machine

[məˈʃiːnəri]
machinery the working parts of machines; another name for machines

[ˈmakintoʃ]
mackintosh a raincoat. It is often called mac for short.

[mad]
mad crazy; not right in the head. Someone who is mad does not think properly, because his mind is ill. The same word also means angry.

[magəˈziːn]
magazine a thin book which comes out every week or month. It has different stories and pictures in it each time.

['magət]
maggot a tiny worm or grub that is found in bad
    meat, cheese or fruit
['madʒik]
magic an imaginary power that makes wonderful
    things happen that seem impossible, like
    changing a pumpkin into a beautiful coach
[mə'dʒiʃən]
magician someone who can do magic
['magnit]
magnet a piece of iron or steel that has the power
    to pull other pieces of metal to it
[mag'nifisnt]
magnificent splendid; very grand
['magpai]
magpie a black and white bird of the crow family.
    It is noisy and likes to collect bright shiny
    objects.
[meid]
maid an old-fashioned word for a girl or young
    woman. The same word is also used for a
    woman servant.
[meil]
mail anything that is sent through the post, such
    as letters and parcels
[mein]
main most important; chief
['madʒəsti]
majesty a title given to a king or queen
['meidʒə]
major of great importance. The same word also
    means an officer in the army.
[meik]
make to produce, to build
['meikʌp]
make-up face powder, lipstick and colouring used
    around the eyes
[meil]
male people and animals who can become fathers.
    Boys and men are of the male sex, but girls and
    women are of the female sex.
[mɔ:lt]
malt grain prepared in a special way before it is
    made into beer

['maməl]
mammal   one of any kind of animal whose females
   have milk to feed their babies

['maməθ]
mammoth   huge; enormous. The same word also
   means a huge hairy elephant that lived millions
   of years ago.

[man]
man   a male human being when he is grown up

['manidʒ]
manage   to look after or be responsible for
   something, such as a business or a household

['manidʒə]
manager   a person who is in charge of something,
   such as a business, a football club or a factory

[mein]
mane   the long hair some animals have on their
   necks. Horses have manes and so do lions.

['meindʒə]
manger   a feeding box for animals, usually in a shed
   or stable

['maŋgl]
mangle   a machine with heavy rollers for squeezing
   water out of washing. The same word also
   means to tear or cut something to pieces in a
   very rough way.

['maŋgəld]
mangold   a root vegetable, rather like a beetroot,
   used for feeding animals

[man'kaind]
mankind   all human beings

['manəz]
manners   how you behave towards other people, the
   way in which you do things. It is good manners
   to say please and thank you, but bad manners
   to snatch things and act in a rude way.

['manə]
manor   the land belonging to a nobleman

['manʃən]
mansion   a very large house

['mantlpi:s]
mantelpiece   a narrow shelf above the fireplace

[mə'njuə]
manure   anything put into the ground to make plants
   and crops grow better

['meni]
many   a lot

[map]
map   a special kind of drawing to show how to find
your way about a place, a country or the
different parts of the world

['ma:bl]
marble   a hard kind of stone that is used in
important buildings. Marble is also carved
into statues and beautiful ornaments. The same
word also means one of the round glass balls
used in the game of marbles.

[ma:tʃ]
march   to walk in step. Soldiers march in time to
music in a parade.

[meə]
mare   a female horse

[ma:dʒə'ri:n]
margarine   a soft yellow food that looks like butter

['ma:dʒin]
margin   a blank edge on the side of a page where
nothing is printed

['marigould]
marigold   a bright yellow or orange garden flower

[mə'ri:n]
marine   to do with the sea. The same word also
means a soldier serving on a ship.

[mariə'net]
marionette   a puppet made to move
by pulling strings

[ma:k]
mark   a spot or line on something

['ma:kit]
market   a place, usually out of doors, where people
meet to buy and sell food and other things

['ma:məleid]
marmalade   a kind of jam made from oranges,
lemons or grapefruit cooked with sugar

[mə'ru:n]
maroon   a dark brownish-red colour

['maridʒ]
marriage   the ceremony by which a man and
woman become husband and wife

['mari]
marry   to become husband and wife

[ma:ʃ]
marsh   a piece of wet swampy land which is unsafe
to walk on because your feet sink down into it

['ma:ʃəl]
marshal   an important officer in the army. In the
United States, the same word also means a
sheriff.

[ma:ʃ'malou]
marshmallow   a soft sticky white or pink sweet

['ma:ʃi]
marshy   wet; swampy

['ma:vəl]
marvel   to wonder; to be amazed

['ma:vələs]
marvellous   wonderful; splendid

[ma:zi'pan]
marzipan   a sweet food made of crushed almonds
and sugar

['maskət]
mascot   a person or animal or charm that is
supposed to bring good luck

['maskjulin]
masculine   like, or to do with, men or boys

[maʃ]
mash   to crush something so that it becomes soft
and smooth, like mashed potatoes

[ma:sk]
mask   a cover to hide the face, sometimes funny,
sometimes pretty and sometimes frightening

[mas]
mass   a lump of something; a large quantity or
number

['masiv]
massive   large and heavy

[ma:st]
mast   a long pole that holds up the sails of a sailing
vessel

['ma:stə]
master   someone who is in control or in command
of other people

[mat]
mat   a piece of thick material on a floor. Small mats
are used on tables under hot plates.

[matʃ]
match a small thin piece of wood or cardboard with a tip that makes fire

[meit]
mate a friend or helper; someone you often play or work with

[mə'tiəriəl]
material what anything is made of

[maθə'matiks]
mathematics the study of numbers, measurements and quantities

['matinei]
matinée (*say matinay*) an afternoon performance of a show

['matris]
mattress the thick soft part of the bed that you lie on

[mouv]
mauve a pale purple colour

[mei]
may the pink or white blossom on a hawthorn tree

['meibi:]
maybe another word for perhaps or possibly

[meə]
mayor a man chosen to be leader of the town council

['meipoul]
maypole a high pole set up on the first day of May. The pole is decorated with flowers and ribbons, and people dance around it.

[meiz]
maze a place with lots of paths that cross and turn into each other so that it is hard to find your way out

['medou]
meadow a field of grass, often made into hay and used to feed animals

[mi:l]
meal food eaten at certain times of the day. Breakfast, lunch, tea, dinner and supper are all meals.

[miːn]
mean　selfish and unkind. The same word is also used for explaining things, such as that the word *mean* means selfish and unkind.

['miːniŋ]
meaning　the sense or explanation of something said or written

['miːn'wail]
meanwhile　the time between two events or happenings

['miːzlz]
measles　an illness. You have a high fever and are covered in small itchy red spots.

['meʒə]
measure　to find out the size or amount of anything

['meʒəmənt]
measurement　the size or amount of something

[miːt]
meat　the parts of animals that are cooked and eaten

[mi'kanikəl]
mechanical　machine-like. A mechanical toy is worked by machinery, not by a person.

['medl]
medal　a piece of metal like a coin or cross hanging on a ribbon. It is given as a reward for being very brave or very skilful.

['medl]
meddle　to interfere with what someone else is trying to do

['medisin]
medicine　something that you eat or drink or rub on yourself to make you feel better when you are ill

['miːdjəm]
medium　middle-sized

[miːk]
meek　gentle and patient; not likely to fight back or lose your temper easily

[miːt]
meet　to come together with someone or something

['miːtiŋ]
meeting　coming together for a purpose

[melt]
melt　to turn to liquid when heated. Butter melts in warm weather and so does ice.

['membə]
member   someone who belongs to a team or club or
    some other group of people

['meməri]
memory   the part of your mind that remembers
    things

[men]
men   more than one man

[mend]
mend   to put something right; to repair it when it is
    torn or broken

['mentl]
mental   to do with the mind; worked out in your
    head and not written out

['menʃən]
mention   to speak briefly about something

['menjuː]
menu   a piece of card or paper with a list of what
    there is to eat in a restaurant or café

['məːsi]
mercy   pity; forgiveness

[məˈraŋ]
meringue (*say merang*)   a white crisp food made
    from white of egg and sugar, whipped stiff and
    then baked in an oven

['merit]
merit   to deserve something, such as a reward or
    punishment

['məːmeid]
mermaid   an imaginary sea creature, supposed to be
    half woman and half fish, with a fish tail instead
    of legs

['meri]
merry   happy; enjoying yourself

['merigəraund]
merry-go-round   another word for roundabout

[mes]
mess   an untidy muddle; confusion

['mesidʒ]
message   something you want a person who is not
with you to know, so you write it down or ask
another person to tell him

['mesindʒə]
messenger   someone who carries a message

['metl]
metal   hard materials like iron and steel. Cars and
aeroplanes are mostly made of metal.

['miːtiə]
meteor   a piece of rock travelling in space, often
called a shooting star

['miːtə]
meter   an instrument for measuring a quantity of
something, such as gas, water or electricity

['meθəd]
method   a way of doing something

['miːtə]
metre   a measure of length equal to 100 centimetres

[mjuː]
mew   the crying sound made by a cat or kitten

[mais]
mice   more than one mouse

['maikrəfoun]
microphone   an instrument that picks up sounds for
radio, television or tape recorders

['maikrəskoup]
microscope   an instrument with a tube that you look
through, which makes very tiny things look
much larger

['mid'dei]
midday   the middle of the day between morning and
afternoon

['midl]
middle   halfway; in the centre

['midʒit]
midget   a person who is very small, even when
grown up

['midnait]
midnight   12 o'clock at night, the middle of the night

[midst]
midst   another word for middle, when you mean in
the middle of a crowd of people

['maiti]
mighty   another word for powerful or strong

[maild]
mild   not strong or severe

[mail]
mile   a measure of distance equal to 1,760 yards

[milk]
milk   the white liquid that is used to feed babies.
Most people drink cow's milk.

['milkmən]
milkman   a man who sells milk. or brings milk to
your house

[mil]
mill   a machine for grinding things like grain,
coffee beans and pepper into very small pieces.
The same word also means a building or
factory where cloth or steel is made.

['milimi:tə]
millimetre   a thousandth part of a metre

['miljən]
million   a thousand times a thousand; 1,000,000

[miljə'neə]
millionaire   a very rich man who has a million
pounds or more

['mimik]
mimic   to imitate or copy someone else, usually in a
mocking way

[mins]
mince   to chop or grind something, usually meat,
into very small pieces

['minsmi:t]
mincemeat   a mixture of chopped-up fruit, nuts,
raisins and other things, cooked in pastry,
usually at Christmas time

[maind]
mind   what you think with. The same word also
means to be careful and think what you are
doing.

[main]
mine   a large deep hole in the ground where men
dig for coal. diamonds. gold or other minerals.
The same word also means belonging to me.

['mainə]
miner   a man who works in a mine

['minərəl]
mineral   any substance in the earth that can be dug
out and used, such as coal, metal, rock

['miŋgl]
mingle   to mix with or go about with, as when you
mingle with the crowd at a football match

['minitʃə]
miniature   a small copy of anything

['mainə]
minor   not important. The same word also means a
person who is not yet an adult.

[mint]
mint   a place where coins are made. The same word
also means a small garden plant used for
flavouring sauces and sweets.

['minit]
minute   One minute is 60 seconds. It takes
60 minutes to make an hour.

['mirəkl]
miracle   something wonderful or fortunate that you
would not expect to happen

[mi'ra:ʒ]
mirage   something you imagine you can see that is
not really there, as when hot and thirsty
travellers in the desert think they see
water ahead

['mirə]
mirror   a piece of glass with something behind it so
that you can see yourself instead of seeing
through the glass

[misbi'heiv]
misbehave   to behave badly or in a rude way

['mistʃif]
mischief   harm or damage; naughtiness

['maizə]
miser   someone who hoards all his money and lives
in a very poor way

['mizərəbl]
miserable   feeling very sad and unhappy

['mizəri]
misery   unhappiness; sorrow

[mis'fo:tʃən]
misfortune   bad luck; a calamity

[mis]
miss   to fail to hit, catch or find something

[mist]
mist   very low cloud

[mis'teik]
mistake   something wrong, like a mistake in your
   sums

['misltou]
mistletoe   an evergreen plant with pearly-looking
   berries, which grows on the branches of trees.
   It is used for decoration at Christmas.

[mis'trʌst]
mistrust   not to trust or not to believe someone

[misʌndə'stand]
misunderstand   not to understand; to mistake the
   meaning of something

[mait]
mite   anything very small. In the old days there was
   a very small coin called a mite. The same word
   also means a kind of tiny insect.

['mitnz]
mittens   coverings for the hands, like gloves, but
   without places for the fingers

[miks]
mix   to put different things together

['mikstʃə]
mixture   two or more things put together

[moun]
moan   a long low sound made by someone in pain
   or sorrow

[mout]
moat   a big ditch, usually filled with water. In olden
   times, castles had deep moats around them so
   that enemies could not get across.

[mok]
mock   to make fun of someone

['modl]
model   a copy of something like a boat or aeroplane,
   usually smaller than the real thing. The same
   word also means someone who shows off
   clothes or someone who stays quite still so that
   artists can paint or draw pictures of them.

['modərət]
moderate   fair; between bad and good

['modən]
modern   nowadays; at this time, not old-fashioned

[moist]
moist   damp; slightly wet

['moistʃə]
moisture   dampness; slight wetness

[moul]
mole   a small animal with sharp claws, tiny eyes and dark thick fur. It digs long tunnels in the ground. The same word also means a small, dark spot on the skin.

['moumənt]
moment   a very short time

['monək]
monarch   a king, queen, emperor or empress

['monəstəri]
monastery   a building where monks live

['mʌni]
money   coins and paper banknotes

['mʌŋgrəl]
mongrel   a dog which is a mixture of different types

['monitə]
monitor   a pupil in a school who is given a special job to help the teacher

[mʌŋk]
monk   a member of a religious group living in a monastery

['mʌŋki]
monkey   a small lively animal with a long tail. Monkeys live in hot countries, and are very good at climbing trees and swinging from branch to branch.

['monstə]
monster   an enormous, horrible creature; a plant or animal of unusual or frightening appearance

[mʌnθ]
month   about 4 weeks. There are 12 months in a year.

['mɔnjəmənt]
monument   a statue or building that is put up to
    make people remember someone or some event

[mu:d]
mood   how you feel in your mind. You can be in a
    good mood when you are happy, or in a bad
    mood when something has made you cross or
    unhappy.

[mu:n]
moon   the largest and brightest light we can see in
    the sky at night

[mɔ:]
moor   a large open piece of land where nothing
    much grows except heather. The same word
    also means to fasten a boat or ship to the land.

[mɔp]
mop   pieces of sponge or thick cotton fastened on a
    long stick, used to clean floors or wash dishes

['mɔ:niŋ]
morning   the time between dawn and midday

['mɔ:tə]
mortar   a mixture of cement, sand and water used
    in building to make bricks stick together

[mə'zeiik]
mosaic   a pattern or picture made by arranging lots
    of small pieces of coloured glass or stones

[mɔs'ki:tou]
mosquito   a small flying insect that bites

[mɔs]
moss   a very small green plant that looks like velvet.
    It grows close to the ground in damp places,
    especially in the woods.

[mɔθ]
moth   an insect rather like a butterfly, except that it
    only flies at night. The grubs of some small
    moths eat holes in your clothes.

['mʌðə]
mother   a woman who has a family

['moutə]
motor   a machine which makes something work or
    move

['moutəbaik]
motorbike   a kind of heavy bicycle
    with a motor

['moutəwei]
motorway   a special road for fast traffic

['motou]
motto   a short saying which gives a rule for
   behaviour, such as *Be prepared*

[mould]
mould   a container into which you pour liquid that
   will get hard, and will have the shape of the
   container when you turn it out. The same word
   also means a green or grey furry covering that
   grows on stale bread or cheese.

[maund]
mound   a heap of stones or earth; a small rounded
   hill

[maunt]
mount   another word for mountain. The same word
   also means to get up on something, like a horse
   or a bicycle.

['mauntən]
mountain   a very high hill

[maus]
mouse   a little animal with a long tail and sharp
   teeth

[məs'ta:ʃ]
moustache (*say mustash*)   the hair that grows above
   a man's upper lip

[mauθ]
mouth   the opening in your face which you use for
   speaking and eating

[mu:v]
move   to go, or make something go, from one place
   to another

['mu:vmənt]
movement   the act of moving

[mou]
mow (*rhymes with go*)   to cut grass or hay

[mʌtʃ]
much   a lot

[mʌk]
muck   damp dirt or rubbish; manure

[mʌd]
mud   soft wet earth

['mʌdl]
muddle   to make a mess of things; to do things in a
   confused way

['mʌdgaːd]
mudguard   a piece of metal over the wheels of a car or bicycle to stop the mud from splashing up

[mʌf]
muff   a tube-shaped piece of fur or warm material. You put your hands in through the openings to keep them warm.

['mʌfin]
muffin   a soft cake, toasted and eaten with butter

['mʌflə]
muffler   a woolly scarf

[mʌg]
mug   a large heavy cup with straight sides

['mʌlbəri]
mulberry   a tree with berries something like raspberries. Mulberry leaves are the main food of silkworms.

[mjuːl]
mule   an animal whose parents are a donkey and a horse

['mʌltiplai]
multiply   to increase or make something a number of times larger

['mʌmbl]
mumble   to speak with your mouth nearly closed so that your words are not heard clearly

[mʌmps]
mumps   a very uncomfortable illness. You have a fever, your neck swells up, and it hurts to swallow.

[mʌntʃ]
munch   to chew with a crunching sound

[mju'nisəpəl]
municipal   having to do with a city

['məːdə]
murder   to kill someone against the law of a country, not by accident or in wartime

['məːdərə]
murderer   someone who kills another person against the law

['məːmə]
murmur   a gentle soft sound that goes on and on

['mʌsl]
muscle   the fleshy parts of the body that tighten and loosen to make it move

[mju'ziəm]
museum   a place where interesting collections of things are set out for people to look at

['mʌʃrum]
mushroom   a small plant shaped like an umbrella. It can be cooked and eaten.

['mju:zik]
music   pleasing sounds that you sing or play on a musical instrument

[mʌst]
must   to have to do something, such as going to school every day

['mʌstəd]
mustard   a kind of browny-yellow paste, eaten with meat. It has a very strong flavour and makes your tongue feel hot.

['mju:təni]
mutiny   a refusal by soldiers, sailors or airmen to obey their officers

['mʌtə]
mutter   to speak so softly that it is hard to understand the words

['mʌtn]
mutton   the meat from sheep

['mʌzl]
muzzle   the jaws and nose of an animal. The same word also means a sort of cage or arrangement of straps fastened on an animal's nose and mouth to keep it from biting.

[mai'self]
myself   me and no one else

['mistəri]
mystery   something strange that has happened, but that cannot be explained or easily understood

[miθ]
myth   an old, old story which explains how something began or happened. The same word also means an imaginary person or event.

[nag]
nag   to keep on scolding or finding fault

[neil]
nail   the hard part at the end of a finger or toe.
The same word also means a thin sharp piece
of metal used to join pieces of wood.

['neikid]
naked   without clothes or covering

[neim]
name   what a person or thing is called

['nanigout]
nanny-goat   a female goat

[nap]
nap   a short sleep

['napkin]
napkin   a square piece of cloth or paper used to
wipe your mouth and fingers when you are
eating

[na:'sisəs]
narcissus   a spring flower, white or yellow, that
smells very sweet

['narou]
narrow   slim; thin; not wide

[nəs'tə:ʃəm]
nasturtium   a plant with lots of round leaves and
orange, red and yellow coloured flowers

['na:sti]
nasty   not nice; not pleasant

['neiʃən]
nation   all the people living in one country under
one government

['naʃənl]
national   belonging to one nation or country

['neitiv]
native   a person born in a particular place or
country

['natʃərəl]
natural   not man-made

['neitʃə]
nature   everything in the world that is not man-made

['no:ti]
naughty   not doing what you should; behaving badly

['navigeit]
navigate   to steer or guide a ship or aeroplane

['neivi]
navy   a nation's warships and the sailors who run
them

[niə]
near   close to; not far away

['niəli]
nearly   very closely; almost; not far from

[ni:t]
neat   tidy; in good order

['nesisəri]
necessary   having to be done; needed

[nek]
neck   the part of your body between your head and
your shoulders

['neklis]
necklace   a string of beads or thin chain worn
round the neck

['nektə]
nectar   a sweet juice found in some flower blossoms

[ni:d]
need   to have to have something. You need clothes
to keep you warm.

['ni:dl]
needle   a long, thin pointed piece of metal used for
sewing. There are also special needles for
knitting.

['negətiv]
negative   meaning or saying *no*

[ni'glekt]
neglect   to forget or be careless about looking after
something

[nei]
neigh   the cry a horse makes, usually when it is
frightened or excited

['neibə]
neighbour   a person who lives near you

['naiðə]
neither   not one or the other

['nefju:]
nephew   the son of a brother or sister

[nə:v]
nerve   one of the small thread-like parts of your
body that carries messages to and from the
brain so that you can move and feel. The same
word also means courage and daring.

['nə:vəs]
nervous   jumpy; easily frightened

[nest]
nest a bird's home, where the eggs are laid and
   hatched out

[net]
net pieces of string knotted together so that there
   are more holes than string

['netbo:l]
netball a game played by two teams. A large ball is
   thrown into a small net on a pole.

['netl]
nettle a weed with prickly hairs that sting if they
   touch your skin

['nevə]
never not ever; not at any time

[nju:]
new only just made; not old; not seen before

['nju:bo:n]
newborn just born

[nju:z]
news things that have just happened

['nju:speipə]
newspaper a printed daily or weekly paper that tells
   you about things that have just happened

[nju:t]
newt a small animal like a lizard that can live on
   land as well as in water

[nekst]
next the nearest; the one after

[nib]
nib the metal point of a pen

['nibl]
nibble to eat with tiny bites

[nais]
nice kind; friendly; pretty; pleasant

[nik]
nick a little cut in something

['nikl]
nickel a silvery-grey metal

['nikneim]
nickname a name you give to someone for fun, to
   describe what he is like, such as *shorty* for
   someone who is not very tall

[niːs]
niece   the daughter of a brother or sister

[nai]
nigh   another word for near

[nait]
night   the time between sunset and sunrise, when the sky is dark

['naitdres]
nightdress   a garment worn in bed by girls and women

['naitgaun]
nightgown   another word for nightdress

['naitiŋgeil]
nightingale   a small brown bird whose song is even more beautiful at night than in the daytime

['nimbl]
nimble   quick or clever in moving or climbing

[nip]
nip   to pinch or bite off a little bit of something

[nou]
no   the opposite of yes. The same word also means not any.

['noubl]
noble   great; grand

['noublmən]
nobleman   a man of high rank

['noubədi]
nobody   no one; no person

[nod]
nod   to bend your head forward and back to show you agree. The same word also means to let your head fall forward when you are sleepy.

[noiz]
noise   a sound, sometimes very loud

['noumad]
nomad   one of a group of people who have no permanent home, but who roam about looking for food for themselves and their animals

[nʌn]
none   not one; not any

['nonsəns]
nonsense   talk which means nothing

[nuːn]
noon   12 o'clock in the day; midday

[nu:s]
noose a loop in a rope, with a slip-knot that can be
tightened by pulling it

[ˈnoːməl]
normal ordinary; usual

[noːθ]
north the direction which is the opposite of south,
on your left as you face the rising sun

[nouz]
nose the part of your face with which you smell,
and through which you breathe

[ˈnouzi]
nosey wanting to know all about other people's
belongings and activities

[ˈnostrəl]
nostril one of the two openings in your nose

[nout]
note a short letter. The same word also means a
sound in music or a piece of paper money.

[ˈnoutbuk]
notebook a little book in which you write things
down that you don't want to forget

[ˈnʌθiŋ]
nothing not anything

[ˈnoutis]
notice to see something. The same word also means
a printed piece of paper announcing something.

[noːt]
nought nothing; zero

[ˈnʌriʃ]
nourish to feed

[ˈnovəl]
novel new and different. The same word also means
a long story about imaginary people.

[ˈnovəlti]
novelty something new and different

[nau]
now at this time

[ˈnouweə]
nowhere not anywhere or any place

[ˈnozl]
nozzle a spout at the end of a pipe or hose

[njuːd]
nude naked; without clothing

[nʌdʒ]
nudge   to poke or push someone gently with your elbow

['njuːsns]
nuisance   something or someone who gets in the way of what others want to do

[nʌm]
numb   not able to feel, as when your fingers are numb with cold

['nʌmbə]
number   a word which says how many. One (1), two (2), three (3), and four (4) are numbers.

['njuːmərəl]
numeral   a figure, a number such as 1, 2 or 3

['njuːmərəs]
numerous   very many

[nʌn]
nun   a female member of a religious group living in a convent

[nəːs]
nurse   someone who helps the doctor to look after people who are ill

['nəːsəri]
nursery   a room or building where very young children sleep or play

[nʌt]
nut   a fruit or seed with a hard shell. The same word also means a piece of metal with a hole through it that you screw on to the end of a bolt.

['nʌtmeg]
nutmeg   a hard spicy seed used to flavour food

['nailən]
nylon   a man-made material used for making clothing, brushes and other useful things

[ouk]
oak   a kind of tree that can grow very big and lives to a very old age. It has acorns as its fruit.

[oː]
oar   a long piece of wood with one flat end, used to row a boat

[ou'eisis]
oasis   a place in a desert where plants and trees grow because there is water

[ouθ]
oath   a solemn promise that you will speak the truth
or keep your word

[outs]
oats   a kind of grain used mostly to feed animals.
Oats are also ground up and cooked with
water to make porridge.

[ə'biːdjəns]
obedience   doing as you are told

[ə'bei]
obey   to do as you are told

['obdʒikt], [əb'dʒekt]
object   a thing; something you can see or handle.
The same word also means to disagree with
someone else's idea.

[ə'blaidʒ]
oblige   to force someone to do something. The
same word also means to do someone a favour.

['obloŋ]
oblong   a squared shape with four straight sides.
Two opposite sides are of equal length and the
other sides are also equal but longer or shorter
than the first two.

[əb'zəːv]
observe   to watch carefully; to notice

['obstəkl]
obstacle   anything that stands in the way so that you
cannot go forward

['obstənət]
obstinate   wanting your own way; stubborn

[əb'tein]
obtain   another word for get

[ə'keiʒən]
occasion   a particular event or happening

[okju'peiʃən]
occupation   the kind of work that you do

['okjupai]
occupy   to live in, as when a family occupies a
house. The same word also means to go
into enemy land in wartime and take over
towns and cities.

[ə'kəː]
occur   to happen

['ouʃən]
ocean   a very big sea

[ə'klok]
o'clock   the time by the clock

['oktəpəs]
octopus   a sea creature with eight arms covered with suckers

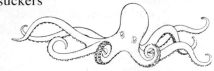

[od]
odd   strange; queer. The same word also means not even in number (1, 3, 5, 7, 9 are odd numbers).

['oudə]
odour   smell

[ə'fens]
offence   a crime. The same word also means something that hurts someone's feelings or makes him angry.

[ə'fend]
offend   to do something wrong; to displease; to make someone angry

[ə'fensiv]
offensive   causing hurt; unpleasant

['ofə]
offer   to say you will do or give something

['ofis]
office   a building or room where people work with business papers

['ofisə]
officer   someone who commands others, as in the army, navy or air force

['ofn]
often   many times; happening over and over again

[oil]
oil   a thick greasy liquid which can come from animals or plants, or from under the ground

['ointmənt]
ointment   a soothing paste you put on sores or cuts

['ou'kei]
O.K.   all right

[ould]
old   having been alive or on earth for a long time

['ouldən]
olden   long ago, as when we say in olden days or in olden times

['ouldə]
older   having lived longer than someone else, or existed longer than something else

['ould'faʃənd]
old-fashioned   of times long ago; not modern

['omlit]
omelette   eggs beaten up, fried until the mixture is almost solid, and then folded over

[ə'mit]
omit   to leave out; not to do something

[wʌns]
once   for one time only; at a time long ago

['ʌnjən]
onion   a bulb-like vegetable with a strong smell and flavour

['ounli]
only   single; one and no more

['oupən]
open   not shut; able to let things through

['oupniŋ]
opening   an open place; a hole or space

[opə'reiʃən]
operation   something that is done, especially something done by doctors in a hospital to make people well again

[ə'pinjən]
opinion   what you think about something

[opə'tju:nəti]
opportunity   a chance to do something

['opəzit]
opposite   as different as possible from something else; across from

['optikəl]
optical   having to do with eyes or with seeing

['orindʒ]
orange   a sweet fruit. The same word also means the colour of the fruit.

['o:raŋ'u:tan]
orangutan   a large reddish-brown ape that lives in jungles

['ɔ:bit]
orbit the path in which something moves around another thing in space

['ɔ:tʃəd]
orchard a lot of fruit trees growing together

['ɔ:də]
order a command. The same word also means to ask for something to be done, such as for something to be sent to you from a shop.

['ɔ:dənəri]
ordinary usual; not special or different

[ɔ:]
ore rock or mineral from which we get metal

['ɔ:gən]
organ a large musical instrument with a keyboard and pipes that the sounds come from

[ɔ:gənai'zeiʃən]
organization a group of people or of nations who get together to work for a particular purpose; such as the World Health Organization

['ɔ:gənaiz]
organize to get a group of people together for a particular purpose: to plan and arrange something

['ɔ:nəmənt]
ornament anything used to make something look prettier, such as jewellery or a vase

['ɔ:fən]
orphan a child whose mother and father are both dead

['ostritʃ]
ostrich a very large bird which has long legs but which cannot fly because its wings are too small

['ʌðəwaiz]
otherwise if not; if things are different

['otə]
otter a furry web-footed swimming animal rather like a large weasel

[ɔ:t]
ought must; should

[auns]
ounce a measurement of weight. There are 16
  ounces in a pound.

['autbə:st]
outburst a sudden bursting out, such as cheering
  when a goal is scored at a football match

['autfit]
outfit a set of clothing or equipment

['autiŋ]
outing a pleasure trip or walk

['autlo:]
outlaw a person who fights against the law and is
  told that he cannot be protected by the law.
  Robin Hood and his men were outlaws.

['autlain]
outline a line drawn to show the shape of
  something round the outside edge. The same
  word also means the main ideas of a story or a
  plan.

['aut'said]
outside the opposite of inside; out of doors

['ouvəl]
oval egg-shaped. A rugby football is oval.

['ʌvn]
oven the inside part of a stove where you bake
  things

['ouvəro:l]
overall a piece of clothing worn over other clothes
  to keep them clean

['ouvəkout]
overcoat an outdoor coat worn over all your other
  clothes

[ouvə'kʌm]
overcome to get the better of someone or
  something; to defeat

[ouvə'flou]
overflow to spill over the top of a container because
  it is too full

[ouvə'haŋ]
overhang to hang out over; to stick out over

[ouvə'teik]
overtake to catch up with and go in front of
  someone or something

[ouvə'θrou]
overthrow to destroy or defeat completely

[ou]
owe   to need to pay for something you have bought
[aul]
owl   a bird with big eyes and a sharp curved beak.
Owls fly at night and sleep through the day.
[oun]
own   to have something that belongs to you
['oistə]
oyster   a shellfish with a very hard flat shell in two
parts
['oksən]
oxen   bulls and cows
[peis]
pace   a step or the length of a step, as when you say
something is six paces away
[pak]
pack   to put things into a container. You pack
clothes into a trunk or suitcase when you go
away. The same word also means a bundle of
things carried on your back.
['pakidʒ]
package   a parcel or bundle
['pakit]
packet   a small parcel or package
[pad]
pad   a lot of sheets of paper glued or sewn together
at the top. The same word also means a piece
of thick, soft material, usually to protect a part
of your body from harm.
['padl]
paddle   to walk around in water up to your ankles.
The same word also means a pole with a broad
part at the end, which you use to move a canoe
through the water.
[peidʒ]
page   one side of a sheet of paper in a book,
newspaper, magazine or notebook. The same
word also means a young boy who attends a
bride at her wedding, or who runs errands in a
hotel.
['padʒənt]
pageant   a show in costume, usually about things
that happened long ago
[peil]
pail   another word for bucket

[pein]
pain the feeling when something hurts you

[peint]
paint to colour something with a brush and coloured liquid called paint

['peintiŋ]
painting a coloured picture painted on paper or canvas

[peə]
pair two things which are meant to be used together, like a pair of shoes

['palis]
palace the house where a king or queen lives

[peil]
pale not having much colour or brightness; looking washed out

['peiliŋ]
paling one of the pieces of wood in a special kind of fence

[pa:m]
palm the inside of your hand between your fingers and your wrist. The same word also means a tall tree with large fan-shaped leaves at the top. It grows in hot countries.

[pan]
pan a metal container with a handle, used for cooking

['pankeik]
pancake a thin round cake eaten hot. You cook it in a frying pan.

['pandə]
panda a large black and white wild animal, something like a bear. Some pandas are much smaller and look rather like a large cat with a bushy tail and a pointed nose.

['panik]
panic sudden fear or terror that keeps people from thinking reasonably

['panzi]
pansy a small garden plant with velvety, brightly coloured flowers

[pant]
pant to gasp for breath

['panθə]
panther a kind of leopard

['pantəmaim]
pantomime a musical play for children, usually a
fairy tale. The same word also means a play in
which the actors do not speak.

['pantri]
pantry a small room or cupboard where food is
kept

[pants]
pants trousers

['peipə]
paper the material used to write on or wrap
parcels in

['parəbl]
parable a fable or story that is meant to show you
how to behave towards others

['parəʃu:t]
parachute a large piece of strong cloth which is
fastened to a man who is going to jump from
an aeroplane. It opens like an umbrella, and
brings him safely and slowly to the ground.

[pə'reid]
parade a lot of people walking or marching
together, sometimes in costume

['parəfin]
paraffin a kind of oil that is burned in stoves and
lamps

['parəlel]
parallel going in the same direction the same
distance apart and never meeting, like a pair of
railway lines

['pa:sl]
parcel a bundle of things, usually tied up in paper

['pa:tʃmənt]
parchment the skin of a goat, sheep or other animal,
cleaned and dried. In olden days, before
paper was invented, it was used to write on.

['pa:dn]
pardon   to forgive

['peərənt]
parent   a mother or a father

['pariʃ]
parish   a part of a county with its own church

[pa:k]
park   an open space with grass and trees and
playgrounds for children. The same word also
means to stop a car and leave it at the side
of the street or in a parking space.

['pa:ləmənt]
parliament   a group of men and women who are
chosen to make the laws for the people in a
country

['pa:lə]
parlour   another word for living-room

['parət]
parrot   a brightly-coloured bird often kept as a pet
in a cage. Some parrots can imitate talking.

['pa:snip]
parsnip   a vegetable with a thick whitish root
shaped rather like a carrot

[pa:t]
part   a piece of something. The same word also
means to leave someone.

['pa:tikl]
particle   a tiny bit or piece of something

[pə'tikjulə]
particular   single or special. The same word also
means fussy or very careful.

['pa:tnə]
partner   a person who shares equally, or who plays
or works with another person

['pa:tridʒ]
partridge   a plump wild bird rather like a small
pheasant

['pa:ti]
party   a lot of people all together having a good
time

[pa:s]
pass   to move ahead of something in front of you.
The same word also means to hand something
to someone.

['pasidʒ]
passage a long narrow part inside a building, with
doors opening at the sides and end of it

['pasindʒə]
passenger someone who rides in a vehicle but who
is not the driver

['paːspoːt]
passport special papers from the government
that help you to travel in other countries

[peist]
paste a thick white liquid, used to stick paper and
other things together. The same word also
means a thick food which is spread on bread
or toast for flavour.

['paːstaim]
pastime a game or hobby that you like to do to pass
the time

['peistri]
pastry a mixture of flour and water and fat which
is rolled flat before it is baked

['paːstʃə]
pasture a field where sheep and cattle are
allowed to eat the grass

[pat]
pat to hit something very lightly

[patʃ]
patch a small piece of cloth used to cover a hole in
clothes. The same word also means a small
piece of ground.

[peit]
pate the top of the head

['peitənt]
patent a government paper that keeps other people
from using an invention without permission

[paːθ]
path a narrow way along which people may
travel, usually on foot

['peiʃəns]
patience the ability to wait for something without
making a fuss

['peiʃənt]
patient able to wait for something without making a
fuss; taking a lot of trouble to get something
right. The same word also means a sick person
who is being looked after by a doctor.

['patə]
patter   to tap lightly and quickly. Rain patters on the roof.

['patən]
pattern   curved or straight lines repeated many times over, as on a patterned carpet or wallpaper. The same word also means a model or plan to help you make something, like a dress pattern.

[po:z]
pause   to stop what you are doing for a moment

['peivmənt]
pavement   a hard path at the side of the street for people to walk safely

[pə'viljən]
pavilion   a large tent or a wooden building, usually for the players on a sports ground

[po:]
paw   the foot of a four-legged animal which has claws

[pei]
pay   to give money for something you have bought or for work someone has done

[pi:]
pea   one of the round green seeds which are used as food. Peas grow in pods on a climbing plant.

[pi:s]
peace   a time when no one is fighting

[pi:tʃ]
peach   a juicy round fruit with a velvety skin and a stone-like seed

['pi:kok]
peacock   a large bird with beautifully-coloured feathers. He can spread his tail out like a large fan.

[pi:k]
peak   the topmost point. The same word also means the brim of a cap that sticks out in front.

[pi:l]
peal   a loud sound, as of bells ringing, or of thunder

['pi:nʌt]
peanut a nut which grows underground in a pod.
Sometimes peanuts are called monkey nuts
because monkeys are very fond of them.

[peə]
pear a juicy fruit rather like an apple, only softer
and rather cone-shaped

[pə:l]
pearl a small creamy-white jewel, used for
necklaces and other jewellery. Pearls grow
inside some oyster shells.

['pebl]
pebble a small smooth roundish piece of stone

[pek]
peck to pick up food in the beak with short jerky
movements. Hens peck at their food.

[pi'kju:ljə]
peculiar odd; strange; unusual

['pedl]
pedal a foot lever to make something work.
Bicycles have pedals and so have pianos.

[pə'destriən]
pedestrian someone who is walking

[pi:l]
peel the skin of fruit or vegetables. You can peel
bark off trees and sometimes pieces of your
skin when you have been sunburned.

[pi:p]
peep to take a quick look

[piə]
peer a nobleman, usually with the rank of Lord.
The same word also means to look very closely.

[peg]
peg a strong clip or pin used to hang things up —
like washing on a line, or to fasten things down
— like a tent rope

[pi:ki'ni:z]
pekinese a small, fluffy dog with almost no nose

['pelikən]
pelican a big water-bird which has a large pouch
under the lower part of its beak. It can scoop
up fish in its pouch, and store them there until
it wants to eat.

['pelit]
pellet a tiny ball of something, such as paper, clay
or metal

[pelt]
pelt the skin or hide of an animal. The same
word also means to throw something, such as
snowballs, or to pour down, like heavy rain.

[pen]
pen a tool used for writing with ink

['penlti]
penalty a punishment for breaking a rule

[pens]
pence more than one penny

['pensl]
pencil a thin tool for writing and drawing. It is
made of wood with a stick of black or coloured
material in the middle.

['pendjuləm]
pendulum a weight on the end of a rod that swings
from side to side as in a clock

['peŋgwin]
penguin a web-footed swimming bird that lives near
the South Pole. It has short legs and wings
but cannot fly.

['pennaif]
penknife a small knife that you can carry in your
pocket

['peni]
penny a piece of money

['pi:pl]
people men, women, boys and girls

['pepə]
pepper a spicy powder used to flavour food. It
tastes hot, and can make you sneeze if you
breathe it in. The same word also means a
bright green or red vegetable that grows in hot
countries.

['pepəmint]
peppermint   a green plant used for flavouring
sauces, drinks and sweets

[pə:tʃ]
perch   something a bird sits or stands on, like a
stick or twig

[pə'kʌʃən]
percussion   all those musical instruments, such as a
drum or cymbals, that are banged or struck

['pə:fikt]
perfect   without any faults or mistakes

[pə'fo:m]
perform   to do or act: to play a part on the stage or
to play a musical instrument

[pə'fo:məns]
performance   an act: a play or other entertainment

['pə:fju:m]
perfume   a sweet smell; a liquid having a sweet
smell

[pə'haps]
perhaps   possibly; maybe

['peril]
peril   great danger

[pə'rimətə]
perimeter   the outside measurement of a figure or
area

['piəriəd]
period   a length of time

['periskoup]
periscope   a tube containing mirrors used in
submarines or underground so that people can
see what is going on above them

['periʃ]
perish   to die or be destroyed

['pə:mənənt]
permanent   long-lasting, not ever changing. A perm,
a short word for permanent wave, keeps hair
curly for a long time.

[pə'miʃən]
permission   freedom given to do something, as when
you are given permission to stay up especially
late to watch television

[pə'mit]
permit   to allow; to give permission

[pə'sist]
persist   to keep on trying to do something or asking
for something

['pə:sn]
person   a man, woman or child

['pə:sənl]
personal   belonging to one person

[pə'spaiə]
perspire   to give off sweat from your skin when you
are very hot

[pə'sweid]
persuade   to talk someone into doing something,
even if he doesn't want to

[pest]
pest   something or someone that makes
difficulties for others; a nuisance

[pet]
pet   an animal that is kept at home; not wild.
Dogs and cats are pets.

['petl]
petal   the part of a flower that grows out from the
middle

['petrəl]
petrel   a small seabird with long wings

['petrəl]
petrol   short for petroleum; a kind of liquid oil used
to make motor engines work

['petikout]
petticoat   a skirt worn under dresses by girls and
women

['peti]
petty   small; unimportant

[pju:]
pew   a long wooden bench with a back, for people
to sit on in church

['feznt]
pheasant   a bird, usually wild, with beautiful long
tail feathers

[foun]
phone   short for telephone

['foutəgra:f]
photograph   a picture taken with a camera

[freiz]
phrase   a group of words, usually part of a sentence

['fizikəl]
physical to do with nature or with the body.
Physical Education (P.E.) exercises your
muscles.

[pi'anou]
piano a large musical instrument with a keyboard

[pik]
pick to choose; to gather. The same word also
means a sharp tool used to break rock or hard
ground.

['pikl]
pickle to keep in vinegar cooked vegetables like
beetroot and cucumbers

['piknik]
picnic an outing when you take food to eat out of
doors

['piktʃə]
picture a drawing, painting or photograph

[pai]
pie food made of pastry outside, and filled with
fruit or meat

[pi:s]
piece a part or bit of something, but not all of it,
like a piece of pie. The word also means one of
something, like a piece of paper.

[piə]
pier a platform of stone, wood or metal, that
reaches out over the water so that ships and
boats can stop at the end of it

[piəs]
pierce to make a hole with something sharp

[pig]
pig a fat farm animal with a curly tail

['pidʒən]
pigeon a plump bird with short legs, that makes a
cooing sound. Some pigeons are kept as pets
and some are used to carry messages or for
racing.

['pigmi]
pigmy one of a tribe of very small people who live
in the jungles of some hot countries. The word
can also be spelled pygmy.

['pigstai]
pigsty a place where pigs are kept

['pigteil]
pigtail a braid or plait of hair hanging from the
back of the head

[paik]
pike a large greedy freshwater fish. The same word
also means a weapon like a spear, used in the
old days.

[pail]
pile a lot of things on top of each other, like a pile
of books, or a pile of old junk

['pilgrim]
pilgrim someone who travels a long way to visit a
holy place

[pil]
pill medicine like a little ball or pellet, that must
be swallowed

['pilə]
pillar a large post of stone or wood, used to hold
up part of a building

['piljən]
pillion a seat on a motor cycle, behind the driver

['pilou]
pillow a bag filled with feathers or some soft
material, where you lay your head in bed

['piləkeis]
pillowcase a covering for a pillow. The word
pillowslip has the same meaning.

['pailət]
pilot a man who steers a ship into harbour or who
controls an aeroplane

['pimpl]
pimple a small pointed swelling on the skin

[pin]
pin a thin pointed piece of metal used for fastening
or holding things together

['pinəfoː]
pinafore an overall to keep your clothes clean; a
sleeveless dress worn over a blouse or jumper

['pinsəz]
pincers   a small tool used for holding things steady
   or pulling nails out of wood

[pintʃ]
pinch   to squeeze something tightly, usually
   between finger and thumb

[pain]
pine   an evergreen tree with cones and leaves like
   needles

['painapl]
pineapple   a sweet-tasting fruit that looks something
   like a large pine cone. It grows in hot countries.

[piŋk]
pink   a very pale red colour. The same word also
   means a garden flower with a sweet spicy smell.

[paint]
pint   a measure for liquid

[pip]
pip   a fruit seed

[paip]
pipe   any tube, usually of metal, through which a
   liquid (such as water) or gas flows. The same
   word also means a small bowl on the end of a
   tube, used for smoking tobacco.

['paiərət]
pirate   someone who robs ships at sea

['pistl]
pistol   a small hand gun that can be carried in the
   pocket

[pit]
pit   a hole in the ground

[pitʃ]
pitch   to throw or fall forward: to set something up,
   such as a tent or a stall in a market. The same
   word also means the highness or lowness of
   musical notes.

['pitʃə]
pitcher   a person who throws a ball in some games.
   The same word also means a large jug for
   holding or pouring liquids.

['pitʃfoːk]
pitchfork   a tool used for lifting hay

['piti]
pity   a feeling of sadness you have because someone
else is ill or unhappy

['pivət]
pivot   the pin or centre on which something turns

['piksi]
pixie   a kind of fairy

['plakaːd]
placard   a written or printed poster or notice

[pleis]
place   somewhere where something is

[pleig]
plague   a terrible illness that spreads from person
to person very quickly

[pleis]
plaice   a flat sea fish that is good to eat

[plad]
plaid (*rhymes with sad*)   a piece of woollen cloth
with a checked or tartan pattern

[plein]
plain   ordinary; not fancy or decorated. The same
word also means a large flat part of the country.

[plat]
plait (*rhymes with mat*)   several pieces of ribbon,
straw or hair twisted under and over each
other, like a rope

[plan]
plan   to think out how a thing can be done before
you do it. The same word also means a model
or drawing showing the shape and design of
something, like a building or a town.

[plein]
plane   a carpenter's tool used to make wood smooth.
It is also a short word for aeroplane.

['planit]
planet   anything in the sky which, like the earth,
goes round the sun

[plaŋk]
plank   a long flat heavy piece of wood, thicker than
     a board

[pla:nt]
plant   anything that grows up from the earth, like
     grass or flowers

['pla:stə]
plaster   a mixture of water, sand and lime, which
     hardens when it is put on walls and ceilings.
     The same word also means a piece of sticky
     tape that holds a bandage in place.

['plastik]
plastic   material that can be moulded into different
     shapes when it is soft. Later it becomes hard.
     Lots of things are made of plastic, such as
     combs, cups and buckets.

['plastisi:n]
plasticine   a soft clay-like substance that doesn't
     ever get hard. It is used for modelling.

[pleit]
plate   a round flat dish for food

['platfo:m]
platform   the raised part of a hall or theatre for
     the speakers or actors. The same word also
     means the part of a railway station beside the
     tracks, where you get on to a train.

[plei]
play   to have fun: to take part in a game: to perform
     on a musical instrument. The same word also
     means a show acted on a stage, usually without
     music.

['pleigraund]
playground   a special place at school or in a park
     where children can play

['pleimeit]
playmate   someone you play with

['pleitaim]
playtime   a period of time for playing, not working
     or studying

['pleznt]
pleasant   nice; agreeable; enjoyable

[pli:z]
please   to make someone feel happy. You also use
     this word when you are being polite in asking
     someone to do something.

['pleʒə]
pleasure a feeling of being glad and happy when you are enjoying yourself

[pli:t]
pleat a fold in cloth, pressed or stitched down to keep it in place

['plenti]
plenty more than enough; all that is needed

['plaiəz]
pliers a tool, like small pincers, used to twist or bend wire

['plimsəlz]
plimsolls canvas shoes with rubber soles

[plod]
plod to walk heavily and slowly

[plot]
plot a small piece of land. The same word also means the main happenings in a play or story. Sometimes it means a wicked or evil plan, like the Gunpowder Plot.

[plau]
plough a farm tool pulled along by horses or a tractor. It cuts into the ground and turns it over.

[plʌk]
pluck courage; bravery. The same word also means to pull at the strings of a musical instrument, such as the guitar.

[plʌg]
plug a piece of metal or rubber made to fit a hole so the water doesn't run out. An electric plug fits into a socket to obtain electric power.

[plʌm]
plum a juicy fruit with a stone in the middle

['plʌmə]
plumber a man who connects up or mends water pipes

[plu:m]
plume a large curly feather, sometimes worn as an ornament on a hat

[plʌmp]
plump rather fat and well-rounded

[plʌndʒ]
plunge to throw yourself into water; to rush into something

['pluərəl]
plural more than one. The plural of cat is cats.

[plʌs]
plus the sign + which shows that numbers are to be added

['plaiwud]
plywood very thin layers of wood glued together

[nju'mouniə]
pneumonia (*say newmonia*) a painful illness of the lungs

[poutʃ]
poach to cook foods, such as eggs without their shells, or fish, in very hot water. The same word also means to catch animals or fish on someone else's land without his permission.

['pokit]
pocket a little bag sewn into clothes to put things in

[pod]
pod the outside covering of seeds

['pouim]
poem a piece of writing, like a song without music, that shows your thoughts and imaginings

['pouit]
poet someone who writes poems

['pouitri]
poetry the art of writing poetry. The same word also means poems as in *a book of poetry*.

[point]
point the sharp end of something, like a pin or a pencil

['pointid]
pointed sharp; with a point; like the end of a pin

['poizn]
poison something swallowed or injected that can make you very ill or even kill you

[pouk]
poke to jab or push anything suddenly

['poukə]
poker a metal rod used for stirring a fire. The same word is the name of a card game.

['poulə]
polar having to do with the North and South Poles. Polar bears live near the North Pole.

[poul]
pole a long rounded piece of wood or metal, used

to hold something up, such as a flag. The same word also means the north or south ends of the world's axis.

[pə'li:s]
police   a group of men and women whose job is to see that the laws of the country are obeyed. If you see someone breaking the law, you can ask the police to do something about it.

['poliʃ]
polish   to make something shiny by rubbing it hard, usually with special powder, paste or liquid

[pə'lait]
polite   having good manners

['polən]
pollen   yellow powder in the middle of flowers

['pontʃou]
poncho   an outer garment like a blanket with a hole in the middle for the head to go through

[pond]
pond   a small lake

['pouni]
pony   a little horse

['pu:dl]
poodle   a kind of dog with very curly hair

[pu:l]
pool   a small area of water, sometimes no bigger than a puddle

[puə]
poor   having little money or few belongings. The same word also means not good, like poor soil where nothing grows very well.

[pop]
pop   a sharp quick exploding sound. The same word can be short for popular. Then it means music or art that most people like.

['popko:n]
popcorn   a special kind of corn that makes a popping sound and bursts open when it is heated

['poplə]
poplar   a tall, straight, narrow tree

['popi]
poppy   a plant, usually with bright red flowers, often seen growing wild in the fields in summer

['popjulə]
popular liked by most people

[popju'leiʃən]
population the people, or the number of people living in any country, city, town or village

[po:tʃ]
porch a covered entrance to a building

['po:kjupain]
porcupine a wild animal with a coat of quills mixed with hairs

[po:k]
pork pigmeat

['po:pəs]
porpoise a sea animal, rather like a small whale with a blunt snout

['poridʒ]
porridge a cooked breakfast food made from ground-up oats

[po:t]
port a harbour, or a town with a harbour

['po:tə]
porter a man who carries your luggage. The same word also means someone who lets people in or out of a door or a gate at the entrance to a building.

['po:ʃən]
portion a part; a helping of food

['po:trit]
portrait a painting or drawing of a person

['pozətiv]
positive meaning yes: absolutely sure

[pə'zes]
possess to own or to have

['posəbl]
possible able to be done

[poust]
post a long piece of wood or metal, fastened in the ground so that it stands up straight. The same word also means letters and parcels sent and delivered; another word for mail.

['pouska:d]
postcard   a piece of thin cardboard on which you can write to your friends. Most postcards have a picture on the back.

['poustə]
poster   a large notice or picture that tells you about something that is going to happen. Some posters show you pictures of things you can buy, like food or clothes.

['pousmən]
postman   a man who collects and delivers the post

['poustofis]
post office   the place where you buy stamps and licences. It is also the place where all letters and parcels are sorted before they are delivered.

[pous'poun]
postpone   to put off to another time

['pouzi]
posy   a small bunch of flowers

[pot]
pot   any deep dish for cooking. The same word also means plastic or clay containers for plants.

[pə'teitou]
potato   a vegetable that grows under the ground

['potə]
potter   someone who makes pots and other things out of clay. The same word also means to do things in a rather lazy way.

['potəri]
pottery   crockery, ornaments and other things made out of baked clay

[pautʃ]
pouch   a small bag

[pu:f]
pouffe   a large floor cushion to sit on, or to put your feet on

[pauns]
pounce   to spring or jump down on something suddenly

[paund]
pound   a measure of weight: a piece of paper money. The same word also means to hit something with very heavy blows, like pounding on a locked door.

[pɔ:]
pour to make liquid run out of a container by
tipping it forward

[paut]
pout to close your lips and push them out to show
that you are not pleased

['paudə]
powder very tiny dustlike bits of something. Flour
and cocoa are powders.

['pauə]
power ability to do something; strength

['praktikəl]
practical useful

['praktis]
practice something done over and over until you
are good at it, like throwing a ball, or playing a
musical instrument

['praktis]
practise to do something often, so that you become
good at it

['preəri]
prairie a large area of flat grassy land with very
few trees

[preiz]
praise to say very nice things about someone or
something

[pram]
pram a four-wheeled vehicle for babies and
very young children, pushed by hand. The
word is short for perambulator.

[prei]
pray to ask God for help; to request humbly

[preə]
prayer the act of praying

[pri:tʃ]
preach to speak to others about being good, usually
in church

['preʃəs]
precious very valuable; worth a lot of money

['presipis]
precipice a steep cliff

['prefəs]
preface   a short beginning to a book to explain
what it is about

[pri'fə:]
prefer   to like one thing better than another

['pri:fiks]
prefix   a syllable at the beginning of a word which
changes its meaning. If you put *un* before the
word *pleasant* it changes the meaning to *not
pleasant.*

['pregnənt]
pregnant   carrying a baby or babies not yet born

[pri'peə]
prepare   to make or get something ready

['preznt]
present   something that is given to you. The same
word also means at this time; now.

['prezidənt]
president   the chief person in the government of a
country that hasn't a king or queen. The same
word can also mean the most important man
in a club or business.

[pres]
press   to push against or push down. The same
word also means all newspapers and magazines
and the people who write what is printed in
them.

['preʃə]
pressure   force or weight pushing against something

[pri'tend]
pretend   to make believe

['priti]
pretty   lovely; beautiful

[pri'vent]
prevent   to stop something from happening

['pri:viəs]
previous   happening or occurring before some
other event

[prei]
prey   a bird or animal that is hunted for food by
another bird or animal

[prais]
price   how much money you have to pay for
something

[prik]
prick to make a tiny hole with something sharp.
You must be careful not to prick your finger
with a needle when you are sewing.

['prikl]
prickle a sharp point growing on the stem of a
plant or on an animal. The thorns on a
rosebush are prickles, and so are the stiff hairs
on a hedgehog.

[praid]
pride a high opinion of how clever you are and
how nice you look. Sometimes it means a
feeling of pleasure about something you have
done well.

[priːst]
priest a man in charge of a church who leads the
prayers there

['praiməri]
primary first of all

['primrouz]
primrose a small pale yellow wildflower that is one
of the earliest to bloom in spring

[prins]
prince the son of a king or queen

[prin'ses]
princess the daughter of a king or queen

[print]
print to press words and pictures on paper with a
heavy machine

['prizn]
prison a place where people who do things against
the law have to stay for a period of time

['priznə]
prisoner someone who has been captured in war
or who is locked up in a prison because he
has done something wrong

['praivət]
private belonging to one person or group of people.
The same word also means a soldier in
the army.

[praiz]
prize a reward for doing something well

['probəbl]
probable likely to happen

['probləm]
problem   a question that is difficult to answer or
decide

[prə'si:d]
proceed   to go ahead; to go on

[prə'seʃən]
procession   a large number of people or vehicles
moving along in a line

[prod]
prod   to poke

[prə'dju:s]
produce   to make; to cause; to bring into being

[prə'dju:sə]
producer   someone who produces something,
especially a film or play

[prə'feʃən]
profession   a kind of work that needs special study
and training, such as the nursing profession or
the teaching profession

['profit]
profit   gain; the money left over after you have
paid all your expenses

['prougram]
programme   a printed paper giving information
about a performance

['prougres]
progress   movement forward or onward;
improvement

[prə'hibit]
prohibit   to forbid or prevent

[promə'na:d]
promenade   a public footpath in a park or at the
seaside where you walk for pleasure

['promis]
promise   to say that you will or will not do
something, without fail

[prompt]
prompt   quick; at once; with no delay

[proŋ]
prong   one of the sharp spikes on a fork

[prə'nauns]
pronounce   to speak or sound out words

[pru:f]
proof   a way of showing that what is said is true

[prop]
prop a long piece of wood or metal that is put under something to keep it from falling down

[prə'pel]
propel to drive forward

[prə'pelə]
propeller the part of a ship or aeroplane that drives it forward

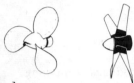

['propə]
proper right; as it should be

['propəli]
properly in the right way

['propəti]
property something that belongs to someone

['profəsi]
prophecy what someone says will happen in the future

['profəsai]
prophesy to say what will happen in the future

[prə'pouz]
propose to suggest something, such as a plan of action or way of going about things

['prosikju:t]
prosecute to speak against someone in a court of law because he is supposed to have done something wrong

[prə'tekt]
protect to guard or defend

[prə'test]
protest to object to something; to disagree

[praud]
proud having a feeling of pride; pleased that you are good at something

[pru:v]
prove to show that what is said is true

['provə:b]
proverb a well-known short saying which is often used to show you how you should act, like *Least said soonest mended*

[prə'vaid]
provide   to supply; to give what is needed

[praul]
prowl   to move about silently and secretly

[prai]
pry   to peer into or try to find out about things that do not concern you

[pʌb]
pub   a place where beer and other drinks are sold. The word is short for public house.

['pʌblik]
public   open to or belonging to everyone; the opposite of private

['pudiŋ]
pudding   any soft, sweet food eaten at the end of a meal. Some puddings are made with meat, and eaten as the main part of a meal.

['pʌdl]
puddle   a small pool of water, usually left in the road after it has been raining

[pʌf]
puff   to blow air or smoke out of the mouth. The same word also means a soft piece of material used to put powder on the skin.

['pʌfin]
puffin   a sea bird with a short thick beak

[pul]
pull   to get hold of something and bring it towards you

['puli]
pulley   a wheel with a hollow rim. You put a rope around the rim and pull on it to lift heavy things.

['pulouvə]
pullover   a knitted garment with sleeves

[pʌmp]
pump   a machine used to get water from a well. The same word also means the machine you use to put air into tyres.

['pʌmpkin]
pumpkin   a large yellow- or orange-coloured fruit that grows on a vine on the ground

[pʌntʃ]
punch   to hit hard, usually with your fists

['pʌŋktʃuəl]
punctual   on time; not late

['pʌŋktʃueit]
punctuate   to divide writing into phrases or
      sentences by using special marks, such as a
      full-stop (.), question mark (?) or comma (,)

['pʌŋktʃə]
puncture   to make a hole in something

['pʌniʃ]
punish   to make someone suffer or pay for doing
      something wrong

['pʌniʃmənt]
punishment   something that makes a person suffer
      or pay for wrong-doing

[pʌnt]
punt   a small flat-bottomed boat that is square at
      both ends

['pju:pl]
pupil   a person who is taught by a teacher. The
      same word also means the round dark circle in
      the middle of your eye through which you see.

['pʌpit]
puppet   a doll which can be moved by pulling
      strings or putting your hand inside it

['pʌpi]
puppy   a young dog

['pə:tʃəs]
purchase   to buy something

[pjuə]
pure   clean; without fault

[pə:l]
purl   a knitting stitch, the opposite to plain stitch

['pə:pl]
purple   a colour made by mixing red and blue

['pə:pəs]
purpose   something you plan to do

[pə:]
purr   the sound a cat makes when it is happy

[pə:s]
purse   a small bag to keep money in

[pə'sju:]
pursue   to go after, to follow

[puʃ]
push to move something away from you without lifting it

['puʃtʃeə]
pushchair a small chair on wheels, for a young child to ride in

[put]
put to place something

['pʌzl]
puzzle a kind of game or question. You have to think very hard to get the answer.

['pigmi]
pygmy one of a tribe of very small people who live in the jungles of some hot countries. The word can also be spelled pigmy.

[pəˈdʒɑːməz]
pyjamas a sleeping suit

['pailən]
pylon a metal tower or mast that holds up electric cables

['pirəmid]
pyramid a solid shape with flat triangular sides, usually on a square base

['paiθən]
python a large dangerous snake that can kill people by squeezing them in its coils

[kwak]
quack the noise a duck makes

[kweil]
quail a wild bird like a small partridge. The same word also means to lose courage.

[kwẹint]
quaint old-fashioned; a little odd

[kwẹik]
quake to tremble, shake or quiver

['kwoləti]
quality how good or bad something is. Clothes of good quality usually cost more but will last longer than clothes of poor quality.

['kwontəti]
quantity   the size, number or amount of things

['kworəl]
quarrel   to argue or disagree with someone in an
     angry way

['kwori]
quarry   a place where stone for building is dug out.
     The same word also means an animal that is
     being hunted.

[kwo:t]
quart   a measure of liquid equal to two pints

['kwo:tə]
quarter   one-fourth of anything, a fourth part

[ki:]
quay (*say kee*)   a landing place for boats or ships

[kwi:n]
queen   a woman who is the ruler of a country, or
     the wife of a king

[kwiə]
queer   odd; strange; not ordinary

[kwentʃ]
quench   to put an end to something, as when you
     quench your thirst by having a drink, or when
     you quench a fire by putting water on it

['kwiəri]
query   a question

['kwestʃən]
question   something someone wants to know

[kju:]
queue (*say kew*)   a line of people waiting their turn.
     The same word also means a pigtail at the back
     of the head.

[kwik]
quick   fast; in a very short time

['kwaiət]
quiet   not making a noise; silent; at rest

[kwil]
quill   the hard stiff part of a feather: one of the
     sharp spines on some animals, such as
     hedgehogs

[kwilt]
quilt   a thick padded bedcover

[kwit]
quit   to leave: to go away

['kwivə]
quiver   to tremble or shiver

[kwiz]
quiz   a lot of questions to find out how much
someone knows

[koit]
quoit   a heavy flat ring
which you try to throw
on to a peg

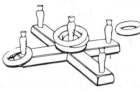

['rabit]
rabbit   a small furry animal with long ears. Some
rabbits are kept in hutches as pets, but wild
rabbits dig holes in the ground to live in.

[reis]
race   to move very quickly to get to a place before
someone else does. The same word also means
a large group of people having a similar
appearance, especially the same skin
colour. Europeans, Africans and Chinese all
belong to different races.

['reistrak]
racetrack   the path or course where a race is run

[rak]
rack   a framework to keep things on, such as a hat
rack

['rakit]
racket   a bat with a network of strings used in
playing tennis and other games. Sometimes the
word is spelled racquet. The same word also
means a loud noise.

['reidiənt]
radiant   bright; sending out rays of heat or light.
The same word also means showing joy.

['reidieit]
radiate   to send out rays of heat or light: to
spread out in many directions from a centre

['reidieitə]
radiator   a set of pipes or other apparatus used to
heat a room by electricity, hot water or steam.
The same word also means the part of a car
that holds water to keep the engine from
getting too hot.

['reidiou]
radio   an instrument that brings broadcast music
        and other people's voices through the air
        from far away

['radiʃ]
radish   the small red and white root of a plant,
        used in salads

['reidiəs]
radius   a straight line from the centre of a circle
        to its outer edge

['rafiə]
raffia   strips of palm leaves used to make things
        such as mats and baskets

[ra:ft]
raft   floating logs or boards fastened together

[rag]
rag   a piece of cloth that is old and often full
        of holes

[reidʒ]
rage   great anger; fury

[reid]
raid   a quick surprise attack

[reil]
rail   a wooden or metal bar used as part of a fence:
        a long metal bar which is used to make a
        railway track

['reiliŋ]
railing   a fence of posts and rails

['reilwei]
railway   very long parallel bars of metal that make
        a road or track for trains to run on

[rein]
rain   drops of water that fall out of the clouds

['reinbou]
rainbow   a beautifully-coloured arch that you can
        see in the sky when the sun shines through
        rain

['reinkout]
raincoat   a coat made of rubber or some other
        material that doesn't let the rain through

['reinfo:l]
rainfall   the amount of rain that falls in a certain
        period of time

[reiz]
raise   to lift up. The same word means to collect,

as when you raise money for charity. It also means to grow or breed something. like plants or animals.

['reizn]
raisin a dried grape used in cakes and puddings

[reik]
rake a garden tool with a long handle and metal teeth

[ram]
ram a male sheep. The same word also means to push hard or crash into something.

['rambl]
ramble to stroll about for pleasure. The same word also means a long walk in the country.

[ra:ntʃ]
ranch a very big farm where large numbers of cattle, horses or sheep are raised

['reindʒə]
ranger a man who is paid to look after a forest or large area of land

[raŋk]
rank the position of a soldier, sailor or airman in the armed forces. The same word also means a row or line of things or people.

['ransak]
ransack to search through something in a rather rough and untidy way

['ransəm]
ransom a sum of money paid for the safe return of someone who has been captured or kidnapped

[rap]
rap to hit sharply

['rapid]
rapid quick; speedy

['rapidz]
rapids a rocky, steep part of a river where the water flows very quickly

['reipiə]
rapier a long thin sword

[reə]
rare unusual; valuable

['ra:skəl]
rascal a dishonest person; one who makes mischief or who cannot be trusted

[ra∫]
rash an outbreak of red spots on the skin. The
same word also means acting hastily, without
careful thought.

['ra:zbəri]
raspberry a small soft red fruit with lots of seeds

[rat]
rat an animal like a large mouse, with long sharp
teeth

[reit]
rate how fast something happens. The same word
also means how much you pay for something.

['ra:ðə]
rather somewhat; to some extent

['ra∫ən]
ration a share or portion. When there is not enough
food to go round, everyone is allowed the same
ration, so that everyone has a fair share.

['ratl]
rattle the noise you hear when you shake hard
things together

['ratlsneik]
rattlesnake a poisonous snake with rattling bony
rings on its tail

[ro:]
raw not cooked

[rei]
ray a thin line of light, like a sunbeam

['reion]
rayon a man-made silky material. Dresses, blouses,
ties and other clothes are often made of rayon.

['reizə]
razor a very sharp instrument, used to shave hair
off

[ri:t∫]
reach to stretch out far enough to touch or get hold
of something. The same word also means to get
to a place; to arrive.

[ri:d]
read to understand printed or written words

['redi]
ready able to do something at once; prepared

[riəl]
real true; not made up or imaginary

['riəlaiz]
realize to understand clearly

['riəli]
really without question; in fact

[ri:p]
reap to cut and gather in crops of grain

[riə]
rear the back part

['ri:zn]
reason why something is done or said; an
    explanation

['ri:znəbl]
reasonable sensible; fair; good enough

[rə'bel]
rebel to go against someone in authority

[rə'si:t]
receipt a written or printed note that proves you
    have paid for something

[rə'si:v]
receive to take something that is given or sent to
    you

['ri:snt]
recent happening a short time ago

[rə'ses]
recess a place set back in a wall. The same
    word also means a short rest from work
    or lessons.

['resəpi]
recipe (*say ressipee*) information that tells you how
    to cook something and what to put in it

[rə'sait]
recite to say something aloud that you have learned
    by heart, like reciting a poem

['reklis]
reckless careless; not thinking or caring about what
    could happen

['rekən]
reckon to count or add up. The same word
    sometimes means to suppose or consider.

['rekəgnaiz]
recognize to know something because you have
    seen it before

['reko:d]

record   a disc played on a gramophone. The same word means a written account of something that has happened and also the best someone has ever done, like the fastest time for a race.

[rə'ko:də]

recorder   an instrument you blow into to make musical sounds

['reko:dpleiə]

record-player   an instrument for playing gramophone records; the usual word for a gramophone worked by electricity

[rə'kʌvə]

recover   to find or get something back, which you have lost. The same word also means to get better after being ill.

[rekri'eiʃən]

recreation   something people like to do in their spare time, such as sport or gardening

['rektaŋgl]

rectangle   a shape with four sides and four right angles

[rə'kə:]

recur   to happen again

[red]

red   a bright colour. Fire engines are usually red.

[rə'dju:s]

reduce   to make something smaller or less in quantity

[ri:d]

reed   a tall stiff grass that grows in or near water. Reeds are usually hollow.

[ri:f]

reef   a line of rocks lying just under the water, so that the waves break over it

[ri:k]

reek   to smell very strongly and usually unpleasantly

[ri:l]

reel   a lively dance. The same word also means a circular piece of wood or metal on which wire, thread or string is wound.

[rə'fə:]
refer to mention or speak of: to look up
information in a book

[refə'ri:]
referee someone who has to see that rules are
obeyed in games and sports

[rə'flekt]
reflect to throw back light or heat from a shiny
surface

[rə'freʃmənt]
refreshment a light snack or a drink that makes
you feel better when you are tired

[rə'fridʒəreitə]
refrigerator a cold box or room where food is
stored to keep it fresh

['refju:dʒ]
refuge a shelter

[rə'fju:z]
refuse to say you will not do something you are
asked to do

[rə'ga:d]
regard to look at. The same word also means
to think well or affectionately of someone.

['redʒistə]
register a written list of names or things kept for a
special purpose

[rə'gret]
regret to feel sorry about something

['regjulə]
regular usual; always happening at the same
time

[rə'hə:s]
rehearse to practise for a performance

[rein]
reign the period of time that a king or queen
rules

['reindiə]
reindeer a kind of large deer that lives in very cold
places

[reinz]
reins leather straps used to guide a horse

[rə'dʒois]
rejoice to feel full of joy; very happy

[rə'leiʃən]
relation someone who is connected with your
      family, like a cousin or an aunt

['relətiv]
relative another word for relation

[rə'laks]
relax to rest and take it easy

[rə'li:s]
release to let go; to set free

[rə'lent]
relent to become less angry with someone; to
      forgive

[rə'laiəbl]
reliable able to be trusted

[rə'li:v]
relieve to give help; to reduce a pain or worry.
      The same word also means to take over work
      or duty from someone else.

[rə'lidʒən]
religion a belief in God or gods

[rə'lidʒəs]
religious believing in and worshipping God or gods

[rə'lai]
rely to trust or depend on

[rə'mein]
remain to stay behind or to be left

[rə'meində]
remainder the part left over; the rest of

[rə'ma:k]
remark something someone says

[rə'membə]
remember to keep something in your mind always
      or bring something back into your mind; the
      opposite of forget

[rə'maind]
remind to make someone remember something

[rə'mu:v]
remove to take away or take off

[rent]
rent the money you pay for the use of something
      you do not own, such as a house or machine

[rə'peə]
repair to mend; to put right

[rə'piːt]
repeat to say or do over again

[rə'pent]
repent to be sorry for something you have said or
    done; to regret

[rə'pleis]
replace to put back

[rə'plai]
reply to answer

[rə'poːt]
report to write or tell about something that has
    happened. The same word also means the noise
    when a gun is fired.

[repri'zent]
represent to speak or act for someone or something
    else

[rə'proutʃ]
reproach to scold or blame someone for what he
    has done

['reptail]
reptile a crawling or creeping cold-blooded scaly
    animal, such as a snake or a crocodile

[rə'kwest]
request to ask someone to do something; to ask for
    something

[rə'kwaiə]
require to need

['reskjuː]
rescue to save, to take someone away from danger

[rə'zembl]
resemble to look like someone or something else

['rezəvwaː]
reservoir a man-made lake for storing water

[rə'zist]
resist to struggle or fight against someone who is
    trying to make you do something you
    don't want to do

[rə'zolv]
resolve to make up your mind; to decide to do
    something

[rə'spekt]
respect to admire or have a very good opinion of
    someone

[rəs'ponsəbl]
responsible looking after the safe keeping of
    someone or something

[rest]
rest to stop working or playing and be quiet

['restəront]
restaurant a place where you can buy and
    eat food

[rə'zʌlt]
result whatever happens at the end of some action.
    For example, if you go out without your coat
    you may catch cold as a result.

[rə'tri:t]
retreat to go back or run away from danger

[rə'tə:n]
return to come back again or give something back

[rə'vi:l]
reveal to show something that is hidden or secret

[rə'vendʒ]
revenge to get your own back on someone who
    has hurt or injured you

[rə'və:s]
reverse the opposite; the other way

[rə'voult]
revolt to rebel against authority

[revə'lu:ʃən]
revolution the overthrowing of a government by
    rebels who want another kind of government

[rə'volv]
revolve to turn around in a circle

[rə'volvə]
revolver a kind of pistol

[rə'wo:d]
reward something you get in return for something
    you have done, such as a prize for winning a
    race

[rai'nosərəs]
rhinoceros a large wild animal with a very thick
    skin and one or two horns on its snout

[roudə'dendrən]
rhododendron   an evergreen shrub with large
    leaves and large, beautifully coloured flowers

['ru:ba:b]
rhubarb   a plant with thick red stalks that taste
    good when they are cooked with sugar

[raim]
rhyme (*say rime*)   words that have the same sound
    at the end, like *blue*, *zoo* and *shoe*

['riðəm]
rhythm (*say rithm*)   a regular pattern or beat of
    music that you can keep time to

[rib]
rib   one of the rounded bones between your
    shoulders and your waist

['ribən]
ribbon   a narrow piece of silky or velvety cloth
    used to make your hair or your clothes look
    pretty

[rais]
rice   the seeds of a food plant that grows in hot
    countries. Rice grains are hard, but become
    soft when they are cooked.

[ritʃ]
rich   having lots of money

[rik]
rick   a stack or pile of hay

[rid]
rid   to remove entirely

['ridl]
riddle   a special kind of question. You have to be
    clever and try to guess the answer.

[raid]
ride   to be carried on a vehicle or an animal

['raidə]
rider   someone who rides

[ridʒ]
ridge   a long narrow top of a hill between valleys; a
    narrow raised strip of something

['ridikju:l]
ridicule   to make fun of or laugh at someone

[ri'dikjuləs]
ridiculous   silly; foolish; laughable

['raifl]
rifle   a long gun

[rait]
right   the opposite of left and the opposite of
wrong. The same word also means the correct
and proper thing to say or do.

['raitaŋgl]
right angle   an angle of 90 degrees. The corners
of a square are all right angles.

[rim]
rim   the outside edge of something round, like the
rim of a wheel

[riŋ]
ring   a circle. Some rings are made of gold or silver
and pretty stones, to be worn on your fingers.
The same word also means the sound of a bell.

['riŋmaːstə]
ring-master   a man who announces the acts in a
circus

[riŋk]
rink   a large circle or square of ice that you can
skate on

[rins]
rinse   to take soap away by washing in clear water

['raiət]
riot   a noisy disturbance by a lot of people, often
dangerous and violent

[rip]
rip   to tear something

[raip]
ripe   ready to eat

['ripl]
ripple   a small wave or movement on the surface of
water

[raiz]
rise   to move upwards; to go higher

[risk]
risk   a chance that you may lose something or be
harmed in some way

['rivə]
river   a large amount of water that flows across the
land into a lake or sea

[roud]
road   a hard level surface with no trees or buildings
in the way, so that vehicles can get from one
place to another

[roum]
roam   to wander about

[ro:]
roar   a loud deep noise made by big animals like lions and tigers when they are angry

[roust]
roast   to cook meat in an oven

[rob]
rob   to take something that is not yours; to steal by force

['robə]
robber   someone who steals by force

[roub]
robe   a long garment that covers you down to your ankles

['robin]
robin   a small wild bird with a red breast and brown and grey feathers

[rok]
rock   a large piece of stone. The same word also means to move back and forth or from side to side.

['rokit]
rocket   a kind of firework. The same word also means a machine that is shot up into space, sometimes carrying astronauts.

[rod]
rod   a long thin stick or bar, usually of wood or metal

[roug]
rogue   a person who is dishonest; a cheat

[roul]
roll   to move along by turning over and over. The same word also means a kind of bread.

['roulə]
roller   a machine which rolls to move along, or to make things flat and smooth. The same word also means a hair curler.

['rouləskeits]
roller-skates   skates with wheels

['roulinpin]
rolling-pin   a tube-shaped piece of wood or metal used to flatten dough or pastry before it is cooked

['rompəz]
rompers   a child's overall with short trousers
     pulled together above the knees by elastic

[ru:f]
roof   the covering on top of a building or car

[ruk]
rook   a black bird like a crow. It has a hoarse
     loud cry.

[ru:m]
room   a part of the inside of a house such as a
     bedroom or kitchen

['ru:stə]
rooster   an adult male chicken; a cock

[ru:t]
root   the part of a plant or tree that grows
     underground

[roup]
rope   very thick string. It is used to tie heavy
     things together.

[rouz]
rose   a beautiful sweet-smelling flower with a
     prickly stem

['rouzi]
rosy   pinky-red colour

[rot]
rot   to go bad or decay

['rotn]
rotten   bad, spoiled. Apples go rotten if they are
     kept too long.

[rʌf]
rough   not smooth; bumpy

[raund]
round   curved like a circle

['raundəbaut]
roundabout   a machine at the fair which you can
     ride on as it goes round and round. The same
     word also means a circle where roads meet.

[rauz]
rouse   to awaken or to stir up somebody's feelings

[ru:t]
route (*say root*)   the exact way you go to get from
one place to another

[rouv]
rove   to roam or wander about

['rouvə]
rover   someone who doesn't stay in one home for
very long, but wanders from place to place

[rou]
row (*rhymes with no*)   a line of things or people.
The same word also means to move a boat
through water, using oars.

[rau]
row (*rhymes with now*)   a noisy quarrel or fight

['roiəl]
royal   to do with a king or queen

[rʌb]
rub   to move something against something else,
such as rubbing polish on furniture with a cloth

['rʌbə]
rubber   a material that stretches or bounces. The
same word also means something that takes
away pencil marks.

['rʌbiʃ]
rubbish   something worn out or of no value that
you throw away. The same word also means
nonsense.

['ru:bi]
ruby   a jewel, deep red in colour

['rʌdə]
rudder   a piece of wood or metal at the back of
a boat or aeroplane, used for steering

[ru:d]
rude   the opposite of polite; bad-mannered. The
same word sometimes means rough.

[rʌg]
rug   a small floor mat or carpet. The same word
also means a kind of blanket used when
travelling.

['rʌgid]
rugged   rough and strong

['ruin]
ruin   to spoil or destroy; to make something
useless. The same word also means an old
building that is falling down.

[ru:l]
rule what you must or must not do. You must
obey the rules at school. The same word also
means a ruler for measuring.

['ru:lə]
ruler a straight piece of wood used for measuring
things. The same word also means a man or
woman who is the head of a country.

[rʌm]
rum a strong drink made from sugar cane

['rʌmbl]
rumble a low-pitched, deep rolling sound, like
far-away thunder

['ru:mə]
rumour something said about a person or events
that may or may not be true

['rʌmpəs]
rumpus a disturbance

[rʌn]
run to move quickly on your feet

[rʌŋ]
rung a piece of metal or wood used as a step
in a ladder

['ruərəl]
rural to do with the country; the opposite of
urban

[rʌʃ]
rush to hurry; to move quickly to get somewhere
on time. The same word also means a tall
kind of grass growing near water.

[rʌsk]
rusk a kind of dry, very crisp toast or biscuit

[rʌst]
rust a reddish-brown coating that appears on
things made of iron or steel after they have
been in water or out in damp air for some time

['rʌsl]
rustle a soft whispering sound, such as is made by
dry leaves rubbing together

[rʌt]
rut a deep track made by a wheel in soft ground

[rai]
rye a kind of grain

[sak]
sack a large bag made of cloth paper or plastic

['seikrid]
sacred holy

[sad]
sad not happy; feeling sorry

['sadl]
saddle a leather seat for a rider, which is fastened
    on to a horse's back or a bicycle

[sə'fa:ri]
safari an expedition in Africa in search of wild
    animals

[seif]
safe not able to hurt you; out of danger. The same
    word also means a very strong metal box used
    to lock money and valuable things away safely.

['seifti]
safety freedom from harm or danger

[sag]
sag to sink down or bend in the middle; to hang
    limply or droop

['sa:gə]
saga a long story about people and legends of olden
    days; a long story about a family and their
    family before them

[seil]
sail a piece of canvas fastened to a ship's mast.
    Sails catch the wind so that the ship is moved
    along.

['seilə]
sailor a man who works on a ship

[seint]
saint a very good and holy person

['saləd]
salad a mixture of cold vegetables, such as lettuce,
    tomatoes and beetroot. Often cold meat, fish
    or eggs are added to salads, and some
    salads have fruit in them.

['saləri]
salary money paid regularly, usually every month,
    for work done

[seil]
sale the exchange of something for money. The
same word also means a period when shops
sell some of their goods more cheaply.

[sə'laivə]
saliva the liquid that keeps the inside of your
mouth moist

['samən]
salmon a large fish with silvery scales and pink
flesh

[sɔ:lt]
salt a white powder we get from the earth and from
sea water. It is used in cooking or at meals to
make food taste better.

[sə'lu:t]
salute to greet someone, usually by raising your
right hand to your forehead

[seim]
same not different; like something else

['sa:mpl]
sample one of, or a small part of something that
shows what the rest of it is like

[sand]
sand small grains of rock which we find in large
quantities at the seaside or in the desert

['sandl]
sandal a light shoe, held on the foot by straps

['sanwidʒ]
sandwich two pieces of bread with meat or some
other food between them

[sap]
sap the juice in plants and trees

[sa:'di:n]
sardine a small fish, usually sold in tins

['sa:ri]
sari a long piece of cloth wrapped around the body
and hanging loose over the shoulder, worn by
girls and women in India

[saʃ]
sash a strip of ribbon or cloth worn round the waist
or over the shoulder. The same word also
means the frame of a window that slides up and
down.

['satʃəl]
satchel a bag, used for carrying school books

['satəlait]
satellite   a planet that revolves around another larger
      planet, as the moon revolves around the earth

['satin]
satin   a soft shiny material

[satis'faktəri]
satisfactory   good enough; pleasing

['satisfai]
satisfy   to do all you can to please someone, or to
      fill a need

[so:s]
sauce   liquid poured over food to give it more
      flavour. Mint sauce is used with roast lamb.

['so:spən]
saucepan   a cooking pot with a lid and a handle

['so:sə]
saucer   a small curved plate put under a cup

['so:si]
saucy   cheeky; a bit impudent

['sosidʒ]
sausage   a meat mixture chopped up very small and
      put into a thin bag made of animal skin

['savidʒ]
savage   fierce and cruel; wild

[seiv]
save   to keep something to use later on. The same
      word also means to help someone who is in
      danger.

[so:]
saw   a metal tool with pointed teeth on one edge,
      used for cutting wood

['so:dʌst]
sawdust   powder from wood that has been sawn

[sei]
say   to speak; to tell something

['seiiŋ]
saying   a thing that is often said. like *A stitch in
      time saves nine.*

[skab]
scab   the dry crust on a sore place or wound when
      it begins to heal

['skabəd]
scabbard   a case or holder for a sword; a sheath

[sko:ld]
scald   to burn yourself with a very hot liquid or
steam

[skeil]
scale   one of the small horny flakes that cover the
skin of snakes and fishes. The same word also
means a set of notes in music.

[skeilz]
scales   a weighing machine

[ska:]
scar   the mark left on your skin after a sore or
wound has healed

[skeəs]
scarce   not enough; difficult to find

['skeəsli]
scarcely   hardly; not quite

['skeəsəti]
scarcity   a very small supply of something, so that
there is not enough to go round

['skeəkrou]
scarecrow   something, usually like the dummy
figure of a man, which is put in a field to
frighten the birds away from the crops

[skeəd]
scared   afraid

[ska:f]
scarf   a long thick piece of material you wear to
keep your neck warm

['ska:lit]
scarlet   bright red

['skatə]
scatter   to throw things around in all directions, like
scattering bread crumbs on the ground for birds
to eat

[si:n]
scene   a view: the place where something happens:
part of a play

['si:nəri]
scenery   what you see when you look around you,
such as hills and fields and trees in the country.
The same word also means the painted curtains
and other things used on a stage to make it
look like a real place.

[sent]
scent   a smell. The same word also means a liquid
with a sweet pleasant smell; a perfume.

['septə]
sceptre   a rod or staff, usually of gold or silver, carried by a king or queen at ceremonies

['skolə]
scholar   a person who studies; a pupil or student

['skoləʃip]
scholarship   knowledge or learning. The same word also means a sum of money given to a student each year because of his good work, so that he can afford to go on studying.

[sku:l]
school   a place where people go to learn

['sku:nə]
schooner   a large sailing ship

['saiəns]
science   knowledge got by careful study and testing of things, often to do with nature. Chemistry is a natural science.

[saiən'tifik]
scientific   to do with science. When you study chemistry you do scientific experiments.

['saiəntist]
scientist   someone who finds out why things happen on earth and in space

['sizəz]
scissors   a cutting tool like two knives fastened together in the middle

[skould]
scold   to speak crossly to someone about something he has done

[sku:p]
scoop   a tool shaped like a deep shovel, that is used to dig up earth or sand. Small scoops are used to measure out dry foods, such as sugar, shelled nuts and flour.

[sku:t]
scoot   to move away quickly

['sku:tə]
scooter   a small two-wheeled vehicle, moved by pushing with one foot or by an engine

[sko:tʃ]
scorch   to burn slightly; to dry up with heat.
Anything that has been scorched turns a
yellowy-brown colour.

[sko:]
score   the number of points, goals or marks you
get in a game or examination

[sko:n]
scorn   to think that something or someone is not
worth bothering about, or no good

[skaut]
scout   someone sent to spy on the enemy: a member
of the Boy Scouts

[skaul]
scowl   to frown

['skrambl]
scramble   to climb up on rough ground, usually
using your hands and feet

[skrap]
scrap   a small piece of something. The same word
also means to quarrel or fight.

[skreip]
scrape   to rub against something with a rough or
sharp edge

[skratʃ]
scratch   a mark made with something sharp. The
same word also means to scrape with
fingernails or claws.

[skro:l]
scrawl   to write in an untidy way that is not easy
to read

[skri:m]
scream   a very loud high-pitched cry of surprise,
pain or fear

[skri:tʃ]
screech   a piercing scream

[skri:n]
screen   a light-weight wall that you can move
about. The same word also means what a
television or cinema picture is shown on.

[skru:]
screw   a special kind of thick nail with grooves.
You turn it round and round with a tool called
a screwdriver to make it go into wood.

['skribl]
scribble   to write in a careless and untidy way

[skript]
script   handwriting, or printing that looks like
   handwriting

[skrʌb]
scrub   to rub something, usually with a brush, to get
   it clean

['skʌləri]
scullery   a small room next to the kitchen, where
   rough kitchen work is done

['skʌlptʃə]
sculpture   the art of carving stone and wood, or
   modelling clay or metal into statues and
   beautiful designs

['skʌri]
scurry   to hurry along in a bustling way

[si:]
sea   the salty water that covers parts of the earth
   where there is no land

['si:gʌl]
seagull   a sea bird, usually coloured grey and white.
   It makes a loud screeching sound.

['si:hɔ:s]
seahorse   a pretty little sea animal with no legs.
   Its body ends in a curly tail to help it swim
   along in an upright position.

[si:l]
seal   a fish-eating animal that can also live on land.
   The same word also means to close or fasten
   something, so that it cannot be opened without
   breaking the fastening.

['si:laiən]
sea lion   a large kind of seal. The male makes a
   roaring noise, like a lion.

[si:m]
seam   a line where two pieces of material are
   joined together by sewing

['si:plein]
seaplane   an aeroplane that can take off from or land
　　on the sea

[sə:tʃ]
search   to look everywhere for something
['sə:tʃlait]
searchlight   a very powerful beam of light that
　　shows things clearly in the dark
['si:ʃel]
seashell   the hard covering on some kinds of fish
　　and sea animals
['si:said]
seaside   a place by the sea, where you can go for
　　your holidays
['si:zn]
season   spring, summer, autumn and winter are the
　　four seasons of the year. The same word also
　　means to add things like salt and pepper to
　　food to improve the flavour.
[si:t]
seat   a piece of furniture for sitting on
['si:wi:d]
seaweed   plants that grow in the sea
['sekənd]
second   next after first. The same word also means
　　a measurement of time. There are 60 seconds
　　in a minute.
['sekəndəri]
secondary   next after primary; second in importance
['si:krit]
secret   something known only to you or to a very
　　few other people
['sekrətri]
secretary   someone who writes or types business
　　letters in an office
['sekʃən]
section   a part or a piece of something
[si'kjuə]
secure   safe; fastened tightly
[si:]
see   to use your eyes to look at something

[si:d]
seed   the part of the plant from which new plants
    grow

[si:k]
seek   to look for

['si:so:]
see-saw   a strong board fastened in the middle to a
    heavy piece of wood or metal. Two people can
    sit on it, one on each end, and go up and down
    in turn.

[si:z]
seize   to grasp and hold on to

['seldəm]
seldom   not often

[si'lekt]
select   to choose

[self]
self   your own person

['selfiʃ]
selfish   thinking only of yourself, and not caring
    much about other people's wishes

[sel]
sell   to give something in exchange for money

['semisə:kl]
semi-circle   a half circle

[semə'li:nə]
semolina   small hard particles of wheat, usually
    cooked in a pudding

[send]
send   to make a person or thing go somewhere

['si:njə]
senior   someone who is older or more important
    than others

[sen'seiʃən]
sensation   a feeling

[sens]
sense   good or right knowledge. The same word
    also means being able to tell what things are
    like by tasting, smelling, touching, seeing or
    hearing.

['senslis]
senseless   foolish; without good sense. The same
    word also means not to be conscious of what
    is going on around you.

['sensəbl]
sensible wise; having good sense

['sentəns]
sentence a number of words that make a complete
     thought when put together. The same word
     also means a punishment for breaking the law.

['sentri]
sentry a soldier who keeps guard

['seprət]
separate not joined together; divided

['si:kwin]
sequin a small round shiny ornament sewn on
     clothing to make it sparkle

['sa:dʒənt]
sergeant an officer in the army or police

['siəriəl]
serial a story or film that appears in parts and not
     all at one time

['siəri:z]
series a number of things or events following one
     another in regular order

['siəriəs]
serious not foolish or making fun; deeply
     thoughtful. The same word also means causing
     worry, as when someone has a serious illness.

['sə:pənt]
serpent another word for snake

['sə:vənt]
servant someone who is paid to work in someone
     else's house

[sə:v]
serve to work for someone; to hand out food at
     meals; to sell things over the counter in a shop

[sə:vi'et]
serviette another word for table napkin

[se'ti:]
settee a long seat with a back and arms, with room
     for several people to sit

['setl]
settle to agree upon something, such as settling on
     a day to go out with someone

['sevrəl]
several more than two of something; a few

[sə'viə]
severe very serious: not merciful

[sou]
sew to join cloth together with a needle and thread

[seks]
sex either of the two groups, male and female,
that animals and humans are divided into

['ʃabi]
shabby nearly worn out; almost ragged. The same
word also means not fair or kind, as when
someone plays a shabby trick on you.

[ʃeid]
shade to keep the light away from something

['ʃadou]
shadow a dark shape that appears on the ground
when an object gets in the way of light

['ʃagi]
shaggy covered with rough long hair or fur,
usually untidy

[ʃeik]
shake to move something quickly up and down or
from side to side

['ʃalou]
shallow the opposite of deep; not very far to the
bottom

[ʃeim]
shame a feeling of unhappiness because you have
hurt someone or done something you know is
wrong

['ʃeimful]
shameful wrong; mean

[ʃam'pu:]
shampoo to wash your hair

['ʃamrok]
shamrock a kind of clover plant with tiny leaves
divided into three sections

[ʃeip]
shape what something is like if you draw a line
around the outside of it. A ball is shaped like
a circle.

[ʃeə]
share to give part of something to someone else

[ʃa:k]
shark a large dangerous sea fish, which has very
sharp teeth

[ʃɑːp]
sharp   having an edge that can cut or a point that can make holes

['ʃatə]
shatter   to break something into many pieces

[ʃeiv]
shave   to cut off hair with a razor

[ʃɔːl]
shawl   a square piece of cloth folded and worn around the head and shoulders by girls and women

[ʃiːf]
sheaf   a bundle (of corn) or a bunch (of papers)

[ʃiəz]
shears   large scissors, used for cutting things like hedges or sheep's wool

[ʃiːθ]
sheath   a scabbard; a cover for the blade of a sword or knife

[ʃed]
shed   a hut made of wood or metal, often used to keep tools in

[ʃiːp]
sheep   an animal covered with thick wool

[ʃiːt]
sheet   a large piece of cloth used on a bed. The same word also means a single piece of paper, glass or metal.

[ʃelf]
shelf   a board fastened to a wall. You can keep books and other things on it.

[ʃel]
shell   the hard covering on a nut or egg. Some fish, animals and insects also have shells.

['ʃeltə]
shelter   a place where you are safe from danger or from bad weather

['ʃepəd]
shepherd   a man who looks after sheep

['ʃerif]
sheriff   the chief government officer in a county or district

[ʃiːld]
shield   something you hide behind or hold up to protect yourself from attack

[ʃift]
shift to move something, usually something
heavy. The same word also means a group
of people working together for a number of
hours, such as a night shift.

['ʃiliŋ]
shilling a silver-coloured coin, worth five pence

['ʃimə]
shimmer to shine with a soft trembling light

[ʃain]
shine to give out bright light. Silver and gold are
shiny; a torch shines in the dark.

['ʃiŋgl]
shingle the small rounded stones that are found at
the edge of the sea. The same word also means
one of the flat pieces of wood used like slates
to cover a roof.

[ʃip]
ship a very large boat that goes across the ocean

['ʃiprek]
shipwreck a ship that has been sunk or destroyed,
usually by a storm at sea

[ʃə:t]
shirt a piece of clothing worn on the upper part of
the body by men and boys

['ʃivə]
shiver to shake because you are cold

[ʃok]
shock a nasty surprise

[ʃu:]
shoe a covering for your foot

[ʃu:t]
shoot to send a bullet from a gun, or an arrow
from a bow

[ʃop]
shop a place where you can buy things

[ʃo:]
shore land at the edge of a lake or the sea

[ʃo:t]
short not very long; not very tall

['ʃo:thand]
shorthand a quick way of writing down what is
said

[ʃot]
shot small bullets for a shotgun

['ʃəuldə]
shoulder   the joint between your arm and body
[ʃaut]
shout   to speak or call out very loudly
[ʃʌv]
shove   to push roughly
['ʃʌvl]
shovel   a tool like a spade, but wider
[ʃou]
show   to point out; to guide. The same word also
        means a spectacle.
['ʃauə]
shower   a sudden brief fall of rain, sleet or snow.
        The same word also means a bath in which
        you stand up and water sprays all over you.
[ʃred]
shred   a scrap or strip torn off something
[ʃri:k]
shriek   a high-pitched scream; a shrill laugh
[ʃril]
shrill   high-pitched and piercing to the ears
[ʃrimp]
shrimp   a small grey shellfish that turns pink when
        cooked

[ʃriŋk]
shrink   to become less or smaller. Some kinds of
        cloth shrink when they have been washed.
['ʃrivl]
shrivel   to dry up and become smaller. A raisin is
        a shrivelled grape.
[ʃrʌb]
shrub   a small woody plant that doesn't grow very
        tall; a bush
['ʃʌdə]
shudder   to shiver or tremble with fear or disgust
['ʃʌfl]
shuffle   to move your feet along without lifting
        them. The same word also means to mix a pack
        of cards before playing a game.
[ʃʌnt]
shunt   to move railway carriages and wagons
        from one track to another

[ʃʌt]
shut   closed, not open

['ʃʌtə]
shutter   a wooden cover for a window, used to keep
heat and light out in daytime, and to keep
burglars out at night

['ʃʌtlkok]
shuttlecock   a toy made of feathers stuck in
a cork, used in the game of badminton

[ʃai]
shy   not wanting to be with lots of other people

[sik]
sick   ill, not well

['saidbo:d]
sideboard   a large, heavy piece of furniture like a
cupboard, where dishes, table linen and cutlery
are kept

[si:dʒ]
siege   an attempt to capture a town or fort by
surrounding it, so that help cannot reach it

[siv]
sieve   a container with many small holes, used to
separate large and small lumps of soil, grain
or food

[sift]
sift   to separate grains or powder from larger lumps
by means of a sieve

[sai]
sigh   to breathe out heavily when you are tired or
sad

[sait]
sight   the ability to see

[sain]
sign   a movement to show what you mean, like
nodding your head to mean *yes*. The same
word also means a mark or notice that tells
you something, like a traffic sign.

['signəl]
signal   a message sent by signs

['sailənt]
silent   not making a sound

[silk]
silk   very fine smooth cloth made from threads that
silkworms spin

['silkwə:m]
silkworm   a caterpillar that spins silk threads

[sil]
sill   the wooden or stone ledge at the bottom of a
door or window

['sili]
silly   not clever; not thinking carefully

['silvə]
silver   a shiny greyish-white metal. Money, knives,
forks and spoons are sometimes made of silver.
The same word also means the colour of the
metal.

['simələ]
similar   like, or almost like something else

['simpl]
simple   easy, not difficult. The same word also
means foolish, not very clever.

[sins]
since   from a certain time until now, as when you
say you have had nothing to eat since breakfast

[sin'siə]
sincere   honest; meaning what you say

[siŋ]
sing   to make music with your voice

[sindʒ]
singe (*say sinj*)   to burn slightly, to scorch

['siŋgl]
single   only one. The same word also means not
married.

['siŋgjulə]
singular   one only, not plural. The same word also
means unusual, extraordinary.

[siŋk]
sink   a place in the kitchen where there is running
water for washing dishes and preparing
vegetables. The same word also means to
go under the water.

[sip]
sip   to drink something a little bit at a time

['saiərən]
siren   a hooter or whistle that makes a loud, wailing
noise

['sistə]
sister   a daughter of the same parents

[sit]
sit   to be on a chair or seat

[sait]
site   an area of ground where a building is, or will
be built

[sitju'eiʃən]
situation   the place or position of something. The
same word also means a job.

[saiz]
size   the amount of space something takes up

[skeit]
skate   a metal blade or wheels fastened on a shoe,
so that you can move quickly and smoothly on
ice or a flat surface. The same word also means
a large flat fish with very wide fins.

['skelitn]
skeleton   all the bones inside your body

[sketʃ]
sketch   a rough quick drawing

[ski:]
ski (*say skee*)   to move quickly over hard snow
on two long pieces of wood called skis, which
are fastened to your boots

[skid]
skid   to slide sideways, as a car sometimes does on
wet or icy roads

['skilful]
skilful   clever; able to do something well

[skil]
skill   cleverness; the ability to do something well

[skim]
skim   to glide quickly over the surface of something.
The same word also means to take the cream
off the top of the milk.

[skin]
skin   the outside covering of your body

[skip]
skip   to jump up and down on one leg at a time, often over a rope. The same word also means to leave out something, like skipping dull parts of a book.

['skipə]
skipper   the captain of a ship

[skə:t]
skirt   a garment that hangs down from the waist; the part of a dress that hangs down from the waist

['skitl]
skittle   one of the nine bottle-shaped pieces of wood in the game of skittles

[skʌl]
skull   the bony part of your head

[skʌŋk]
skunk   a small black animal with white stripes and a bushy tail. It gives out a very bad-smelling liquid when it is in danger.

[skai]
sky   the air above you that you see when you look up out of doors

['skaila:k]
skylark   a lark, a small bird which sings when it is flying very high up in the air

['skaiskreipə]
skyscraper   a very tall building

[slab]
slab   a thick slice

[slak]
slack   loose; not tightly stretched. The same word also means not busy.

[slam]
slam   to shut or bang something with a loud noise

['sla:ntiŋ]
slanting   not straight up and down; sloping, like this line /

[slap]
slap   to hit with the palm of the hand

[slaʃ]
slash   to make long cuts in something, sometimes violently

[sleit]
slate   a kind of stone used for roofs

['slɔːtə]
slaughter   killing of animals, usually for food: a
    terrible killing of one person or great numbers
    of people

[sleiv]
slave   someone who is not free because he is owned
    by another person and has to work for him

[slei]
slay   to kill

[sled]
sled   a vehicle with metal or wooden runners, that
    moves easily over snow-covered ground

[sledʒ]
sledge   a sled

[sliːk]
sleek   smooth and shiny, like the coat of a horse
    which has been well fed and cared for

[sliːp]
sleep   You sleep when you are not awake.

[sliːt]
sleet   rain mixed with snow or hail

[sliːv]
sleeve   the part of your clothes that covers your
    arm

['sliːvlis]
sleeveless   without sleeves

[slei]
sleigh   a large sled, usually pulled by horses

['slendə]
slender   slim; narrow; not looking strong or heavy

[slais]
slice   a flat piece cut from something, like a slice of
    bread or cake

[slaid]
slide   to move smoothly down or along on
    something

[slait]
slight   small in quantity or importance; slim or
    slender

['slaitli]
slightly   by a small amount

[slim]
slim   thin; narrow; not fat

[slaim]
slime   thin slippery mud or dirt

[sliŋ]
sling   a piece of leather used for throwing stones:
a piece of cloth tied around your neck and
shoulder to hold up a broken or injured arm

[slip]
slip   to slide when you don't mean to. The same
word also means to move away quickly and
quietly.

['slipə]
slipper   a soft shoe you wear indoors

['slipəri]
slippery   smooth on the surface so that you slip in
walking, as on ice or thin mud

[slit]
slit   a long thin cut

[slop]
slop   to spill

[sloup]
slope   ground that goes upwards or downwards;
slanting; not straight

[slot]
slot   a narrow opening, usually in a machine, for
something like a coin to fit in

[slautʃ]
slouch   to walk or move in a lazy droopy way, not
holding yourself up straight

[slou]
slow   the opposite of fast. To be slow is to take a
long time to do something.

[slʌdʒ]
sludge   nasty soft mud

[slʌg]
slug   a large kind of snail without a shell

[slʌʃ]
slush   melting snow; soft mud

[slai]
sly   cunning; artful

[smak]
smack   to hit with the open hand; to slap

[smo:l]
small   another word for little; the opposite of large

[sma:t]
smart   clever; quick to learn: well dressed, stylish

[smaʃ]
smash   to break something into pieces, usually with a crashing noise

[smiə]
smear   to spread or rub something greasy or sticky so as to leave a dirty mark

[smel]
smell   what your nose tells you about something

[smail]
smile   to look happy

[smiθ]
smith   a man who makes things out of metal, like a silversmith or blacksmith

[smok]
smock   a loose garment, usually worn over other clothes to keep them clean

[smouk]
smoke   the cloud of tiny particles that comes from something burning

[smu:ð]
smooth   without any bumps; the opposite of rough

['smʌðə]
smother   to cover completely: to stop someone breathing by covering his mouth and nose

['smouldə]
smoulder   to burn slowly without much flame

[smʌdʒ]
smudge   a stain, a smear of dirt

['smʌgl]
smuggle   to bring something secretly into one country from another without paying tax

[snak]
snack   a small quick meal, like a sandwich or biscuits and cheese

[sneil]
snail   a small animal that moves very slowly. It has a shell on its back.

[sneik]
snake   a crawling animal with a long body and no
legs. Some snakes are dangerous because
they have a poisonous bite.

[snap]
snap   to break with a sudden sharp noise. The
same word also means a card game for
children.

[sna:l]
snarl   to make a growling noise, with the teeth
showing. The same word also means a knot
or tangle.

[snatʃ]
snatch   to grab something quickly

[sni:k]
sneak   to tell tales about someone behind his
back: to creep along quietly

[sniə]
sneer   to smile in a scornful or mocking way

[sni:z]
sneeze   to make a sudden blowing noise through
your nose because it tickles

[snif]
sniff   to take in a noisy breath through your nose

[snip]
snip   to cut a little piece off something, usually with
scissors

['snu:kə]
snooker   a game played with coloured balls on a
special table

[sno:]
snore   to make a loud breathing noise through your
mouth when you are asleep

['sno:kəl]
snorkel   a tube with one end sticking out
of the water so that swimmers can stay
under and still keep breathing air

[snaut]
snout   the sticking-out nose and mouth of
some animals such as pigs and porpoises

[snou]
snow   drops of water that become frozen in the air
in winter. The pieces that float down through
the air are called snowflakes.

['snoubo:l]
snowball a ball of snow pressed together

['snoudrop]
snowdrop a little white flower which appears in
very early spring

['snouman]
snowman a man made out of snow

['snouʃu:]
snowshoe one of a pair of frames strung with thin
strips of leather. People wear snowshoes to
keep their feet from sinking into deep soft
snow.

[snʌg]
snug cosy and warm

[souk]
soak to make something or someone very wet

[soup]
soap something you use with water to make things
clean

[so:]
soar to fly high into the air

[sob]
sob to weep noisily

[sok]
sock something you put on to cover your feet and
ankles before you put on your shoes

['sokit]
socket a hollow place that you fit something into,
like a socket for an electric bulb

['soufə]
sofa another word for couch

[soft]
soft not hard, rough or loud

['sogi]
soggy damp and heavy; very wet

[soil]
soil loose earth. The same word also means to
make something dirty.

['soulə]
solar having to do with the sun

['souldʒə]
soldier a man in the army

[soul]
sole the bottom of your foot or your shoe. The
same word also means a kind of flat fish.

['soləm]
solemn   serious; very earnest

['solid]
solid   hard and firm all through, not hollow or liquid

['solitəri]
solitary   alone; by yourself

[solv]
solve   to find the answer to something puzzling or difficult

[sʌm]
some   a few; not all

['sʌmbədi]
somebody   a person who is not named

['sʌmwʌn]
someone   another word for somebody

['sʌməsoːlt]
somersault   to go head over heels

['sʌmθiŋ]
something   a thing not named

['sʌmtaim]
sometime   at a time not known

['sʌmtaimz]
sometimes   not all the time; now and then

['sʌmwot]
somewhat   rather; a little

['sʌmweə]
somewhere   at an unknown place

[sʌn]
son   a male child of a father or mother

[soŋ]
song   words and music together, which you sing. The same word also means the musical notes sung by birds.

['sonik]
sonic   having to do with sound waves, as in sonic boom

[suːn]
soon   in a short time

[sut]
soot   a soft black powdery stuff which comes from burning wood or coal. It sticks to the inside of the chimney.

[suːð]
soothe   to calm someone down; to comfort

[sɔ:]
sore painful when touched

['sorou]
sorrow unhappiness; sadness

['sori]
sorry feeling unhappy about something you have
    done, or something that has happened

[sɔ:t]
sort to put together things that belong together

[soul]
soul the invisible part of a person which is
    believed to live on after death

[saund]
sound anything that can be heard

[su:p]
soup a liquid food made by boiling meat,
    vegetables or other foods together in water

['sauə]
sour not sweet tasting. Lemons taste sour.

[sɔ:s]
source the beginning or starting place of something,
    like a stream or river

[sauθ]
south the direction opposite to north, on your
    right as you face the rising sun

[sau'westə]
sou'wester a waterproof hat which covers the back
    of the neck. The same word also means a wind
    blowing from the south-west.

[sou]
sow (*rhymes with no*) to scatter seed over the
    ground or plant it in the ground

[sau]
sow (*rhymes with now*) a female pig

[speis]
space a place with nothing in it. The same word is
    often used to mean the sky higher than
    aeroplanes can fly, where there is not even any
    air.

['speiʃʃip]
spaceship a special machine moved by rocket
    motors that can go far
    up into space to
    the moon and beyond

[speid]
spade   a tool used for digging in the ground

[spə'ɡeti]
spaghetti   long tubes of dried wheat paste, like macaroni only much longer and thinner

[span]
span   the distance between the tip of your thumb and little finger when your hand is stretched out. The same word also means the length of anything from end to end.

['spaŋɡl]
spangle   a thin piece of shiny metal sewn on to a garment. Lots of spangles sewn on to a dress make it glitter and sparkle.

['spanjəl]
spaniel   a kind of dog with a silky coat and long floppy ears

[spaŋk]
spank   to smack with your open hand

['spanə]
spanner   a tool for tightening or loosening nuts and bolts

[speə]
spare   to let something go. The same word also means extra. If you have two copies of the same book, one of them is a spare copy.

[spa:k]
spark   a tiny bit of something burning, that flies out of the fire

['spa:kl]
sparkle   to give off bright flashes of light; to glitter. Snow sparkles in the sunlight.

['spa:klə]
sparkler   a firework which gives off silver or coloured sparks when you light it

['sparou]
sparrow   a small brown and grey bird

[spi:k]
speak   to say something

[spiə]
spear   a pole with a metal point on the end. It is used as a weapon.

['speʃəl]
special   not like anything else; made for one use only

['spesimən]
specimen   one of something; a sample
[spek]
speck   a small spot or dirty mark; a tiny piece
['spekld]
speckled   marked with lots of small spots
['spektəkl]
spectacle   something interesting which makes people
    want to look at it
['spektəklz]
spectacles   another word for the glasses people wear
    to help them to see better
[spek'teitə]
spectator   someone who looks on or watches others
    doing something
[spi:tʃ]
speech   the act of speaking. The same word also
    means a talk or lecture.
[spi:d]
speed   quickness, swiftness
[spel]
spell   to put letters together in the right order to
    make up a certain word. The same word also
    means magic words which are supposed to
    make something happen.
[spend]
spend   to pay out money
[spais]
spice   dried or powdered flavourings for food,
    usually tasting and smelling strongly
['spaidə]
spider   a small animal with eight legs. It spins a web
    to catch insects.

[spaik]
spike   a long sharp point. The same word also
    means an ear of grain or a tall cluster of
    flowers on a stem.
[spil]
spill   to let something, such as powder or liquid
    accidentally run out from a container
[spin]
spin   to go round and round. The same word also
    means to make thread out of raw wool, cotton
    or flax.

['spinidʒ]
spinach   a dark green leafy vegetable
['spindl]
spindle   a thin rod on which thread is twisted in
    spinning
[spain]
spine   the backbone of a person or animal. The
    same word also means a thorn, or one of the
    thin, stiff prickles growing on some
    animals, such as hedgehogs.
['spinstə]
spinster   an unmarried woman
['spaiərəl]
spiral   something that winds upwards, going round
    and round in continuous curves
['spaiə]
spire   the long pointed top of a church steeple
['spirit]
spirit   another word for soul; a ghost
[spit]
spit   to throw out something from your mouth
[spait]
spite   a wish to be cruel to someone or to hurt
    his feelings
['spaitful]
spiteful   saying and doing cruel things to someone
    you don't like
[splaʃ]
splash   the noise of something heavy falling into
    liquid. The same word also means to throw
    liquid about.
['splaʃdaun]
splashdown   the landing of a space capsule in the
    ocean
['splendid]
splendid   wonderful; very rich and grand; very good
['splintə]
splinter   a tiny thin piece of wood, glass or metal,
    which has broken off from a larger piece
[split]
split   to break or cut something from end to end
[spoil]
spoil   to damage something or make it of no use.
    The same word also means to give a child his
    own way too much.

[spʌndʒ]
sponge   the soft, yellowish skeleton of a sea
animal, which becomes much softer when it
soaks up water. It is used for washing
yourself. The same word also means a kind of
soft cake.

[spu:l]
spool   a reel on which you wind things like thread,
ribbon, or film

[spu:n]
spoon   a tool used in cooking and eating food

[spo:t]
sport   a game, usually played outdoors. Football
and cricket are sports.

[spot]
spot   a small mark

[spaut]
spout   a small tube or pipe through which liquid is
poured, like the spout of a teapot

[sprein]
sprain   to twist a joint or muscle so badly that it
swells

[spro:l]
sprawl   to sit or lie in a relaxed position, with your
arms and legs spread out

[sprei]
spray   to send out fine drops of liquid

[spred]
spread   to cover a surface, like spreading butter on
bread

[spriŋ]
spring   to move quickly and suddenly. The same
word also means a piece of metal which can
be pressed down but jumps back into position
when you let it go. The word also means the
season after winter, when plants begin to grow.

['spriŋkl]
sprinkle   to scatter small drops of water or bits of
something, like sugar or sawdust

[spraut]
sprout   to begin to grow. The same word also
means a green vegetable like a tiny cabbage.
Its full name is a brussels sprout.

[spə:t]
spurt   to squirt out suddenly; a rush of liquid

[spai]
spy   someone who secretly watches what other
people are doing, especially during a war when
he is paid to get information about the enemy

[skweə]
square   a rectangle whose four sides are equal in
length

[skwoʃ]
squash   to crush or squeeze something out of shape.
The same word also means a bottled drink
made of fruit, sugar and water.

[skwo:]
squaw   an American Indian woman

[skwi:k]
squeak   a small high sound. A mouse squeaks and
so does a rusty door hinge.

[skwi:l]
squeal   a long high piercing sound made by some
animals

[skwi:z]
squeeze   to press hard; to crush; to hug

['skwirəl]
squirrel   a small red or grey animal with a long
bushy tail

[skwə:t]
squirt   to force liquid out of an opening in a sudden
stream; to spurt

[stab]
stab   to pierce or cut with a pointed weapon

['steibl]
stable   a building where horses are kept

[stak]
stack   a large heap

['steidiəm]
stadium   an open-air sports ground with rows of
seats all round

[sta:f]
staff   a group of people working together, like
people in an office, or teachers in a school. The
same word also means a pole or stick carried in
the hand.

[stag]
stag a male deer

[steidʒ]
stage the platform in a theatre or hall where
people act, sing, or speak

['steidʒkoutʃ]
stage coach a horse-drawn coach which travelled
across the country in olden days, stopping at
certain places to let people off or on

['stagə]
stagger to walk unsteadily, lurching and stumbling

[stein]
stain a dirty mark

['steəkeis]
staircase a number of stairs, usually with a side-rail
to keep you from falling

[steəz]
stairs a set of steps in a building for walking up or
down

[steik]
stake a strong pointed stick or post

[steil]
stale not fresh; dry and without much taste
because of being kept too long

[stoːk]
stalk another word for stem. The same word also
means to creep quietly after an animal that you
are hunting.

[stoːl]
stall a kind of table on which things for sale are
shown at a market. The same word also
means a place for one animal in a cattle shed or
stable.

['staljən]
stallion a male horse

['stamə]
stammer to repeat the beginning of a word
several times before going on to say the whole
word: to speak in jerks and pauses

[stamp]
stamp a little piece of coloured paper you stick on
a letter or parcel, which pays for sending it by
post. The same word also means to hit the
floor hard with the sole of your foot.

[stand]
stand to be on your feet; not sitting. The same
word also means rows of raised seats for
people watching an outdoor game.

['standəd]
standard a flag. The same word also means a grade.

[sta:]
star a tiny light which shines in the night sky. The
same word also means someone who is
famous and popular, like a film star.

[steə]
stare to look at something or someone for a long
time without looking away

['sta:fiʃ]
starfish a flat sea animal with five arms like the
points of a star

['sta:liŋ]
starling a wild bird with glossy, dark greenish-
purple feathers, speckled with white

[sta:t]
start to begin: to move suddenly

['sta:tl]
startle to make a person or animal start with
sudden fear or surprise

[sta:'veiʃən]
starvation suffering or death caused by lack of food

[sta:v]
starve to be in great need of food; to die, of hunger

['steitmənt]
statement something said or told

['steiʃən]
station the place where a train stops to let people
on or off. The same word also means a
building for policemen or firemen.

['steiʃənəri]
stationary not moving; standing still

['steiʃənəri]
stationery   writing paper and envelopes

['statʃuː]
statue   the figure of a person or animal which is
carved from stone or wood. Sometimes statues
are made of metal or some other material.

[stei]
stay   to be in one place and not leave

['stedəli]
steadily   in a steady, firm way

['stedi]
steady   standing firm; moving without jerking or
shaking. The same word also means loyal and
faithful.

[steik]
steak   a thick slice of meat or fish

[stiːl]
steal   to take something which belongs to someone
else

[stiːm]
steam   the cloud-like gas that water turns into when
it boils

[stiːl]
steel   a very strong metal made from iron

[stiːp]
steep   rising nearly straight up from the ground, like
a steep hill

['stiːpl]
steeple   a high pointed tower on a church

[stiə]
steer   to guide a vehicle or ship to the right or left.
The same word also means a young bull.

['stelə]
stellar   having to do with the stars

[stem]
stem   the thin part of a plant that holds up the
flowers or leaves

[step]
step   to put one foot in front of the other when
walking. The same word also means one stair
in a staircase.

[stə:n]
stern severe; strict; grim. The same word also
  means the back part of a ship or boat.

[stjuː]
stew to cook food, especially meat with vegetables,
  by boiling it slowly

[stik]
stick a long thin piece of wood: anything shaped
  like a stick, such as a stick of wax or gum

['stiklbak]
stickleback a small river-fish with prickles or
  spines on its back

['stiki]
sticky clinging or holding on, as when something
  like glue or honey sticks to your fingers

[stif]
stiff firm; hard; not easily bent or moved

[stail]
stile a little set of steps fixed to a fence or a wall to
  help you climb over

[stil]
still not moving; calm

[stilt]
stilt one of a pair of tall poles with foot rests

[stiŋ]
sting the sharp part of an insect, like a pin, which
  can hurt you

[stəː]
stir to move; to shake up or mix

['stirəp]
stirrup a metal ring hanging down each side of a
  saddle. It is flat at the bottom so that you can
  put your foot in it when you ride a horse.

[stitʃ]
stitch a loop of thread that has been sewn. The
  same word also means a sudden sharp pain in
  your side, usually caused by running.

[stok]
stock supplies of food and other goods stored by
  shop-keepers. The same word also means a
  sweet-smelling garden flower.

['stokiŋ]
stocking a kind of sock that covers the whole of
  your leg. Stockings are usually made of nylon,
  wool or silk.

[stouk]
stoke   to put fuel on the fire to make it hotter

[stoul]
stole   a long, narrow piece of material, often made of fur or silk, worn over the shoulders and hanging down

['stʌmək]
stomach   a kind of pocket in the middle of your body, which holds food after it has been swallowed

[stoun]
stone   a small piece of rock. The same word also means the hard seed inside some fruit like plums and cherries.

[stu:l]
stool   a little seat with no back or arms

[stu:p]
stoop   to bend the upper part of your body downwards

[stop]
stop   to end or leave off what you are doing

['stopə]
stopper   something you put in the neck of a bottle to close the opening

[sto:]
store   to keep something until it is needed. The same word also means a shop.

[sto:k]
stork   a large bird with very long legs and a long beak

[sto:m]
storm   a sudden outburst of bad weather with heavy rain, snow or hail, and sometimes thunder and lightning

['sto:ri]
story   an adventure told or written. It can be a true story, or made up like a fairy tale.

[stouv]
stove   something which makes heat for us to cook food or warm the room

[streit]
straight   not crooked or curved. This is a straight line _____

['streitn]
straighten to make straight; to put things neat and tidy

[strein]
strain to make every effort; to put all your strength into doing something

['streinə]
strainer a kind of bowl with holes in it, usually made of metal or plastic. You put vegetables or other food in it to let the water out.

[streindʒ]
strange unusual; out of place

['streindʒə]
stranger someone you do not know

['straŋgl]
strangle to kill a person or animal by squeezing its throat; to choke

[strap]
strap a long thin piece of leather, usually with a buckle, to fasten something

[strɔ:]
straw dry stiff yellow stalks that farm animals like to sleep on

['strɔ:bəri]
strawberry a small soft red fruit with a lot of seeds

[strei]
stray to wander away or go in the wrong direction by mistake

[stri:k]
streak a stripe or long narrow mark

[stri:m]
stream a small river

['stri:mə]
streamer a long thin flag, or a paper decoration for parties

[stri:t]
street a road with houses or other buildings on both sides of it

[streŋθ]
strength how strong or powerful something is

[stretʃ]
stretch to make longer or wider by pulling

[strikt]
strict insisting on complete obedience without exception; severe; stern

[straid]

stride   to walk with long steps

[straik]

strike   to hit someone or something as hard as you can. The same word also means to stop work because the workers want more money or because they think something at work needs putting right.

[striŋ]

string   a long piece of thick thread for tying up things: one of the parts of a musical instrument, such as a violin or guitar

[strip]

strip   a long narrow piece of something. The same word also means to take off all your clothes.

[straip]

stripe   a long narrow line or mark of colour, usually in material. Flags often have different coloured stripes on them.

[strouk]

stroke   to rub gently, as you would stroke a cat. The same word also means a blow, or the sound of a clock striking.

[stroul]

stroll   to walk slowly, in no hurry to get anywhere

[stroŋ]

strong   not weak or easily broken: able to lift heavy things

['strʌktʃə]

structure   something constructed. like a dam or a building: the way things are built up or arranged

['strʌgl]

struggle   to make a great effort; to fight to get free

['stʌbən]

stubborn   not willing to give way to others; obstinate

[stʌd]

stud   a kind of fastening for a shirt

['stju:dənt]

student   someone who studies, usually at a college or university

['stju:diou]

studio   the workshop of an artist: a place where films are made: a room from which radio or television programmes are broadcast

['stʌdi]
study　to learn; to examine something closely

[stʌf]
stuff　the material something is made of. The same
　　word also means to pack tightly.

['stʌfi]
stuffy　without enough fresh air

['stʌmbl]
stumble　to trip over something or lose your footing

[stʌmp]
stump　the part of a tree trunk that is left after the
　　tree has been cut down

[stʌn]
stun　to knock someone senseless; to amaze or
　　surprise greatly

['stju:pid]
stupid　foolish; silly; slow to think

['stə:di]
sturdy　strong; healthy

['stʌtə]
stutter　to speak with difficulty because you find it
　　hard to get words out easily; to stammer

[stai]
sty　a place where pigs are kept. The same word
　　also means a small swelling on the eyelid, often
　　spelled stye.

[stail]
style　the way something is done, such as old-style
　　dancing, the newest style of clothes, or good
　　style in writing

['sʌbdʒikt]
subject　a person who is ruled by the head of a
　　country. The same word also means what is
　　being talked or written about—for example,
　　The subject of the talk was sport.

[sʌbmə'ri:n]
submarine　a special kind of ship that can go along
　　under water

['sʌbstəns]
substance　anything solid that you can handle or
　　feel: the main part of something

[səb'trakt]
subtract to take away a number or a quantity from a larger number or quantity

['sʌbwei]
subway an underground passage for pedestrians: an underground electric train

[sək'si:d]
succeed to do what you set out to do. The same word also means to come after, or to follow in order, as when a prince becomes king by succeeding his father.

[sək'ses]
success a satisfactory ending to something you set out to do, like success in passing an examination or winning a race

[sʌk]
suck to draw liquid into your mouth; to keep something in your mouth without chewing it

['sʌdn]
sudden happening all at once

['sʌdnli]
suddenly unexpectedly; all at once

[sʌdz]
suds soapy bubbles

[sweid]
suede a soft leather which doesn't shine

['suit]
suet a kind of hard fat taken from sheep and cattle and used in cooking

['sʌfə]
suffer to feel pain; to put up with

[sə'fiʃənt]
sufficient enough

['ʃugə]
sugar a white substance used in food and drinks to make them taste sweet

['ʃugəkein]
sugar cane a plant with sweet-tasting stems from which sugar is made

[sə'dʒest]
suggest to tell others about an idea or plan that you think would be good

[su:t]
suit a set of clothes, such as a coat and trousers, which are meant to be worn together

['su:təbl]
suitable fitting in well; proper; right

['su:tkeis]
suitcase a flat case for carrying clothes when you are going away

[swi:t]
suite a set of rooms at an hotel or large house. The same word also means a set of furniture for a room.

[sʌlk]
sulk to show you are angry and bad-tempered by not speaking and not being friendly

[səl'ta:nə]
sultana a small light-coloured raisin

[sʌm]
sum the total number when two or more things are added together

['sʌməraiz]
summarize to go over the main points of what you have been saying or writing

['sʌmə]
summer the warmest season of the year, between spring and autumn

['sʌmit]
summit the highest point of something, such as the summit of a mountain

[sʌn]
sun the round bright ball seen in the sky during the day. It sends out light and heat.

['sʌnbə:n]
sunburn burning or reddening of the skin when you have been too long in the hot sun

['sʌndaiəl]
sundial an instrument that shows the time of day by the position of the sun's shadow on a dial

['sʌni]
sunny full of sunshine

['sʌnraiz]
sunrise the time when the sun comes up: the actual rising of the sun

['sʌnset]
sunset the time when the sun goes down: the actual setting of the sun

['sʌnʃain]
sunshine the light from the sun

['sʌp]
sup to eat supper: to take spoonfuls of soup or liquid into your mouth

['su:pəma:kit]
supermarket a large shop where you can buy all kinds of food and some other things as well. You help yourself and pay when you go out.

['su:pə'sonik]
supersonic moving faster than sound travels in air

['sʌpə]
supper the last meal before you go to bed

[sə'plai]
supply to provide; to give something that is needed

[sə'pɔ:t]
support to hold something up; to bear the weight of something

[sə'pouz]
suppose to imagine; to pretend

[ʃuə]
sure knowing you are right

['ʃuəli]
surely without question or doubt

['sə:fis]
surface the outside of anything; the top of a lake or the sea or the earth

['sə:dʒən]
surgeon a doctor who cures patients by cutting out or repairing diseased parts of the body

['sə:dʒəri]
surgery a doctor's office where you can visit him. The same word also means curing illness by cutting out or repairing the diseased part.

['sə:li]
surly bad-tempered; not friendly

['sə:neim]
surname your last name; the family name

[sə'praiz]
surprise something you don't expect

[sə'rendə]
surrender to give up

[sə'raund]
surround to be all around; on all sides of something

[sə'vei]
survey to take a careful look over something or some place

[səs'pekt]
suspect to have a feeling in your mind that something is wrong or that someone is not telling the truth

['swolou]
swallow to let food or drink go down your throat. The same word also means a pretty dark blue and white bird with a forked tail.

[swomp]
swamp wet, marshy ground. The same word also means to put too much water in something.

[swon]
swan a large water-bird with a very long neck. It is usually white.

[swo:m]
swarm a large number of insects, animals or people moving together

[swei]
sway to swing or move from side to side

[sweə]
swear to make a very solemn promise. The same word also means to use bad language.

[swet]
sweat the moisture that comes from your skin when you are hot

['swetə]
sweater a heavy knitted jersey

[swi:p]
sweep to use a brush or broom to clean the floor. The same word also means a man who sweeps chimneys.

[swi:t]
sweet tasting of sugar; not sour

['swi:tha:t]
sweetheart someone you love and hope to marry

[swel]
swell to grow larger or louder

[swə:v]
swerve to turn aside quickly, as when you swerve so as not to bump into something when you are running

[swift]
swift fast; quick; rapid. The same word also means a bird with long pointed wings that can fly very fast.

[swil]
swill to drink in large amounts. The same word also means pigs' food.

[swim]
swim to move along in the water using your arms and legs

[swiŋ]
swing a seat hanging from ropes or chains. The same word also means to move in the air, back and forth, or from side to side.

[swaip]
swipe to hit hard and rather wildly

[swə:l]
swirl to move about quickly with a circling movement, as when dried leaves are blown about by the wind

[switʃ]
switch a little lever which turns on electricity

['swoulən]
swollen made bigger by swelling

[swop]
swop to exchange something for something else

[so:d]
sword a very long knife with a special handle, used for fighting or for carrying in some ceremonies

['siləbl]
syllable a group of sounds that make a word or part of a word. The words *boy* and *girl* each have one syllable, the words *women* and *children* have two syllables.

['simpəθi]
sympathy a feeling of kindness and pity towards someone who is sad or ill

['sirəp]
syrup a thick sweet liquid made by boiling sugar with water or fruit juice

['sistəm]
system a group of things working together

[tab]
tab a small flap or loop, usually on a piece of clothing

['teibl]
table a piece of furniture with legs and a flat top. The same word also means a set of facts or figures arranged in columns.

['teiblkloθ]
tablecloth a large piece of material used to cover a table

['tablit]
tablet a small, flat piece of something, like stone, soap and some kinds of medicine

[tak]
tack a short nail with a wide flat head. The same word also means to sew something together with long loose stitches.

['takl]
tackle to use all your strength to try to do something. The same word also means the equipment for doing something, such as fishing tackle.

['tadpoul]
tadpole a frog when it is very young, before its legs develop

['tafitə]
taffeta a kind of stiff shiny cloth used for making dresses

[tag]
tag a label. The same word also means a children's game in which one person chases and tries to touch another.

[teil]
tail the part that comes out at the end of anything, like the tail of an animal, a kite or an aeroplane

['teilə]
tailor a man who makes clothes, such as suits, overcoats, skirts and trousers

[teik]
take to get hold of: to carry away

[teil]
tale another word for a story

[to:k]
talk to speak or say something

['to:kətiv]
talkative fond of talking, talking too much

[to:l]
tall very high

[tambə'ri:n]
tambourine a small thin drum which you tap with your hand. It has small metal discs around the edge which make a tinkling sound when you shake it.

[teim]
tame not wild; able to live with human beings as pets, like tame rabbits

['tampə]
tamper to meddle or interfere with something

[tan]
tan the brown colour of your skin when you have been out in the sun for a long time. The same word also means to make animal hide into leather.

[tandʒə'ri:n]
tangerine a kind of small sweet orange with a loose skin that comes off easily

['taŋgld]
tangled all twisted up in knots, like hair that has not been combed

[taŋk]
tank a special heavy car made of iron and steel, with big guns in it. The same word also means a large metal or glass container for water and other liquids.

['taŋkə]
tanker a ship that carries oil or other liquids

[tap]
tap to hit something lightly. The same word also means a kind of handle that you turn off and on to control the flow of something from a pipe, like gas and water.

[teip]
tape a narrow strip of something such as strong cloth, plastic or sticky paper used to tie or fasten things together

['teipriko:də]
tape recorder a machine that takes down and plays back sounds on a special kind of tape

[ta:]
tar a thick sticky black liquid which comes from wood and coal. Tar is used in making roads.

['ta:di]
tardy late; slow

['ta:git]
target something you aim at in shooting

['ta:mak]
tarmac a kind of surface found on most roads, made with tar. The word is short for tarmacadam.

[ta:t]
tart a piece of pastry with jam or fruit in it

['ta:tən]
tartan a woollen material, especially worn in Scotland. It has a coloured check pattern, and some Scottish families have their own special colours and patterns.

[ta:sk]
task a job; an amount of work that you have to do

['tasəl]
tassel a number of threads all tied in a knot at the top. Tassels are used to decorate clothing or furniture.

[teist]
taste to put a bit of food in your mouth or sip a drink to see if you like it or not

[taks]
tax money paid to the government to help them pay for things everyone uses. such as roads. bridges, schools, hospitals and medicine

['taksi]
taxi a car that you pay to ride in

[ti:]
tea a hot drink made by pouring boiling water on to the dried leaves of the tea plant

[ti:tʃ]
teach to show someone how to do something; to give lessons

['ti:kouzi]
tea cosy a warm cover which you put over a teapot to keep the tea hot

['ti:tʃə]
teacher someone who helps you to learn things

[ti:m]
team a group of people all helping each other in a
job or game

['ti:pot]
teapot a special pot to make tea in. It has a handle
and a spout.

[teə]
tear (*rhymes with spare*) to pull apart; to rip

[tiə]
tear (*rhymes with spear*) one of the drops of water
that come from your eyes when you are sad or
hurt

[ti:z]
tease to annoy someone by making fun of him

['ti:zə]
teaser a tricky question or problem

['ti:set]
tea set cups and saucers. plates and a teapot which
all have the same pattern

[ti:m]
teem to be abundant; to be full to overflowing as
when a river teems with fish

[ti:θ]
teeth more than one tooth

['teləgram]
telegram a short message which you give to the
post office to send by telegraph

['teləgra:f]
telegraph a way to send messages quickly by
electricity

['teləfoun]
telephone an instrument that carries your voice
through electric wires so that you can speak to
someone far away

['teləskoup]
telescope an instrument like a tube that you look
through to see things that are far away, like the
stars

['teləviʒən]
television   an instrument that brings pictures and
     sound through the air from far away

[tel]
tell   to give news or say what you know about
     something

['tempə]
temper   the mood you are in. You can be in a bad
     temper and be cross with everyone, or in a
     good temper when you are nice to be with.

['temprətʃə]
temperature   how hot or cold something is. It is
     measured in degrees.

['tempist]
tempest   a violent storm with a very strong wind

['templ]
temple   a building in which people pray and worship

['tempou]
tempo   how fast or slow a piece of music has to be
     played

[tempt]
tempt   to try to persuade someone to do something
     which he ought not to do

['tendə]
tender   soft; delicate. The same word also means
     gentle and loving.

['tenis]
tennis   a game played by two or four people. They
     use rackets to hit a ball back and forth over a
     net.

[tent]
tent   a shelter made of a thick piece of cloth held
     up by strong sticks. You can camp out of doors
     under it.

['tiːpiː]
tepee   a cone-shaped tent American Indians lived in

['tepid]
tepid   lukewarm

[təːm]
term   a length of time. The school year is divided
     into three terms, with holidays between.

['təːmənəs]
terminus   the place where buses, trains or
     aeroplanes end their journeys

['terəs]
terrace   a raised flat area of earth: a row of houses
joined together

['terəbl]
terrible   dreadful, awful

['teriə]
terrier   a kind of small dog

[tə'rifik]
terrific   fearful, alarming. The same word can also
be used to mean very great.

['terifai]
terrify   to frighten someone very greatly

['terə]
terror   very great fear

[test]
test   an examination to find out how much someone
knows. The same word also means to find out
whether something such as a car or a machine
is working properly.

['teðə]
tether   to tie an animal with a rope or chain so that
it can walk around a bit, but cannot get away

['θaŋkful]
thankful   grateful; pleased

['θaŋkju]
thank you   You say *thank you* when someone has
been kind or has given you something. and you
want to show him you are pleased.

[θatʃ]
thatch   a roof or covering of straw or reeds

['θiətə]
theatre   a building where plays are acted

[θeft]
theft   the act of stealing

[ðəm'selvz]
themselves   those people; they and no one else

['ðeəfo:]
therefore   for that reason

[θə'momitə]
thermometer   an instrument for measuring how hot
or cold something is

[θik]
thick   wide or deep; the opposite of thin

['θikit]
thicket   shrubs and trees growing closely together

[θi:f]
thief   someone who steals

[θai]
thigh   the thick part of your leg above the knee

['θimbl]
thimble   a metal or plastic cover for the top of your finger. It keeps the needle from hurting you when you are sewing.

[θin]
thin   not wide or fat; the opposite of thick

[θiŋ]
thing   an object which is not named

[θiŋk]
think   to use your mind to help you do things better: to have ideas

[θə:d]
third   next after second; one of three

['θə:sti]
thirsty   wanting to drink

['θisl]
thistle   a plant with a prickly stem and leaves. It grows wild and usually has purple flowers.

[θo:n]
thorn   a sharp woody spike or prickle on a bush or shrub

['θʌrə]
thorough   complete; very careful

[ðau]
thou   an old-fashioned word for *you*

[ðou]
though   although

[θo:t]
thought   an idea; something that is in your mind

['θo:tful]
thoughtful   thinking deeply: thinking of what others would like

[θraʃ]
thrash   to beat

[θred]
thread   a very thin, very long piece of material used in sewing

['θretn]
threaten   to warn someone that you are going to punish or harm him

['θri:'wi:lə]
three-wheeler   a vehicle that runs on three wheels

[θreʃ]
thresh   to beat out grain from its covering. Sometimes the word is spelled thrash.

[θril]
thrill   a feeling of excitement

[θrout]
throat   the inside of the front of your neck which contains the gullet and the windpipe

[θrob]
throb   to quiver; to feel your heart beating strongly, as when you have been running very fast

[θroun]
throne   a special chair for a king or queen on ceremonial occasions

['θrotl]
throttle   to choke or strangle. The same word also means the fuel control of a car engine.

[θru:]
through   from one end to the other

[θru'aut]
throughout   in every part

[θrou]
throw   to release something like a ball or a stone out of your hand and into the air with some force

[θrʌʃ]
thrush   a wild song bird with a brown and white speckled breast

[θrʌst]
thrust   to push with great force; to stab

[θʌd]
thud   a heavy bumping sound when something falls to the ground

[θʌm]
thumb the short thick finger on your hand

[θʌmp]
thump to hit with a heavy blow, usually using your
fist

['θʌndə]
thunder the loud noise which you hear during a
storm after a flash of lightning

[ðʌs]
thus therefore; in this way

[tik]
tick a soft clicking noise such as a clock makes.
The same word also means a mark to show
that something is correct, like this ✓.

['tikit]
ticket a small piece of paper or cardboard which
you get when you pay to ride on a public
vehicle, or go to a show

['tikl]
tickle a funny feeling on your skin which makes
you want to scratch. Sometimes it can make
you laugh when someone tickles you.

[taid]
tide the coming in and going out of the sea

['taidi]
tidy neat; in order; not in a mess

[tai]
tie to make a knot with string or ribbon. The same
word also means a narrow piece of cloth worn
around the neck.

['taigə]
tiger a dangerous wild animal like a very large cat.
It has a striped fur, and lives mostly in India.

[tait]
tight close-fitting; closely packed; the opposite of
loose

['taitn]
tighten to make something tight or tighter

[tail]
tile   a flattish piece of baked clay which is used for roofs and sometimes for floors

[til]
till   up to a certain time. The same word also means a special drawer where a shopkeeper keeps his money.

[tilt]
tilt   to lean to one side

['timbə]
timber   wood which is going to be made into something or used for building

[taim]
time   seconds, minutes, hours, days, weeks, months and years

['timid]
timid   easily frightened; the opposite of brave

[tin]
tin   a silvery metal. The same word also means a container made of tin.

['tiŋgl]
tingle   a prickly feeling

['tiŋkə]
tinker   a man who mends pots and pans

['tiŋkl]
tinkle   a small ringing sound

['tinsəl]
tinsel   long strips of silvery sparkling material which are used to decorate Christmas trees

['taini]
tiny   very, very small

[tip]
tip   the thin end of something, usually pointed. The same word also means to overturn or tilt something.

['tiptou]
tiptoe   to walk on the tips of your toes very quietly

['taiə]
tire   to become tired; to bore or make someone tired

['taiəd]
tired   When you are tired you have the feeling that you want to rest or go to sleep.

[tit]
tit   a small prettily-coloured wild bird

['taitl]
title   the name of something, such as a book, a song
or a play. The same word also means a word
in front of someone's name such as Sir, Lord,
Doctor, or Captain.

[toud]
toad   an animal that looks like a frog which has a
rough, lumpy skin. It usually lives on land.

['toudstu:l]
toadstool   a poisonous plant shaped like a mushroom

[toust]
toast   bread which is made brown and crisp by
heating it

[tə'bakou]
tobacco   a plant with large leaves which are dried,
cut up and used for smoking in cigarettes,
cigars or a pipe

[tə'bogən]
toboggan   a long flat sledge, curved up at the front,
usually without runners

[tə'dei]
today   on this day

['todl]
toddle   to walk with short wobbly steps like a very
young child

[tou]
toe   a part of your foot. You have five toes on each
foot.

['tofi]
toffee   a sweet sticky food made from sugar and
butter

[tə'geðə]
together   being with

[toil]
toil   to work very hard, with great effort

['toilit]
toilet   washing, dressing and doing your hair. The
same word also means a lavatory.

[tə'ma:tou]
tomato   a soft round red fruit, often used as a
vegetable or in salads

[tu:m]
tomb   a place where someone is buried, either in the
   ground or in a stone box above the ground

['tomboi]
tomboy   a girl who behaves like a boy and enjoys
   playing boys' games

[tə'morou]
tomorrow   the day after today

[tʌn]
ton   a measurement of weight. One ton is equal to
   2,240 pounds.

[toun]
tone   a sound, usually musical. The word is also
   used to describe the way a person's voice
   sounds, such as a harsh or a sweet tone of
   voice.

[toŋz]
tongs   a tool with two pieces of metal like pincers
   for holding and lifting things

[tʌŋ]
tongue   the thick soft part inside your mouth that
   moves when you talk and with which you taste
   things

[tə'nait]
tonight   this night

['tonsl]
tonsil   one of two little round pieces of flesh at the
   back of your mouth. Sometimes they have to
   be taken out if they become unhealthy.

[tu:]
too   as well; also

[tu:l]
tool   any instrument that helps people to do work.
   Hammers and shovels are tools.

[tu:θ]
tooth   one of the white bones in your mouth that
   you use to bite with

['tu:θeik]
toothache   a pain in your teeth

['tu:θbrʌʃ]
toothbrush   a small long-handled brush which you
   use to clean your teeth

['tu:θpeist]
toothpaste   a paste which you squeeze from a tube
   on to a toothbrush and use to clean your teeth

[top]
top the highest part of something. The same word also means a spinning toy.

['topik]
topic any subject people choose to speak, write or argue about

[to:tʃ]
torch a light which you can carry about, like an electric torch or a stick which is flaming at one end

[to:'pi:dou]
torpedo a long rounded bomb which is fired through or along the surface of water

['torənt]
torrent a very fast-moving stream or river

['to:təs]
tortoise a slow-moving animal with a very thick shell

['to:tʃə]
torture to make someone suffer great pain, usually to make him confess or admit something

[tos]
toss to throw something carelessly into the air

[tot]
tot a small child. The same word also means to add up.

['toutl]
total the sum of; the whole amount

['totə]
totter to walk unsteadily and shakily

[tʌtʃ]
touch to feel something with your fingers or with some part of your body

[tʌf]
tough hard; strong; not easily broken

[tuə]
tour to travel round for pleasure from place to place, ending up where you started from

['tuənəmənt]
tournament a sports competition which several teams try to win, to see which is the best

[tou]
tow (*rhymes with go*)   to pull something along by a
    rope

[tə'wo:dz]
towards   in the direction of

['tauəl]
towel   a piece of thick cloth or paper that you use
    to dry things that are wet

['tauə]
tower   a building or part of a building that is very
    high and narrow

[taun]
town   a lot of houses and buildings together. It is
    larger than a village.

[toi]
toy   something children play with

[treis]
trace   to copy a drawing by putting transparent
    paper over it and going over the lines with a
    pencil

[trak]
track   a rough path through woods or fields. The
    same word means a railway line.

['traktə]
tractor   a heavy motor with wheels that pulls
    something along

[treid]
trade   to buy and sell: to exchange. The same word
    also means a particular kind of business, like
    hairdressing or dressmaking.

['trafik]
traffic   cars, buses and vans moving along the
    streets

['tradʒədi]
tragedy   a disaster; a terribly sad happening

[treil]
trail   footprints or other signs that have been left
    by something or someone moving ahead of you

['treilə]
trailer   any wheeled vehicle drawn behind a motor
    car or lorry

[trein]
train   a lot of carriages pulled along a railway by an
    engine. The same word also means to teach.

['treinə]
trainer someone who teaches a person or animal
to do something well, like swimming or
running in a race

['treitə]
traitor someone who betrays his friends or country

[tram]
tram a kind of bus which runs on rails and works
by electricity

[tramp]
tramp to walk heavily. The same word also means
a person who wanders from place to place,
often sleeping out of doors and begging for
money from other people.

['trampl]
trample to tread heavily on something

['trampəli:n]
trampoline a large piece of canvas fastened
to a frame with springs. You can bounce up
and down and do somersaults on it.

[trans'fə:]
transfer to carry or send something or someone
from one place to another

[trans'fo:m]
transform to change the way something looks, as a
caterpillar is transformed into a butterfly

[trans'leit]
translate to express the meaning of words in one
language in another language

[trans'peərənt]
transparent easily seen through. Window glass is
transparent.

[trans'pla:nt], ['transpla:nt]
transplant to remove a plant from the ground and
plant it somewhere else. The same word also
means a kind of surgery in which a diseased
part of the body is removed and a healthy part
put in its place.

[trans'po:t]
transport to carry something from one place to
another

[trap]
trap a way of catching animals or birds

['trap'do:]
trapdoor a door in the floor or ceiling

[trə'pi:z]
trapeze a kind of swing with only
a thin bar for a seat

['travl]
travel to make a journey; to go from place to place
['trɔːlə]
trawler a special fishing boat that drags a large net
along the bottom of the sea
[trei]
tray a flat piece of wood, metal or plastic, on
which you can carry light things, such as cups
and saucers and food
['tretʃərəs]
treacherous not to be trusted; likely to betray
['tri:kl]
treacle a thick dark sticky food which comes from
sugar cane
[tred]
tread to step or walk
['treʒə]
treasure a collection of money or jewels. The
same word also means anything which is
valuable or much loved.
[tri:t]
treat to act in a certain way towards someone or
something. The same word also means a
special outing or present for which you do not
have to pay.
[tri:]
tree a very large plant with leaves and branches
['trembl]
tremble to shake or shiver
[trə'mendəs]
tremendous very large; enormous; huge
[trentʃ]
trench a deep ditch
['trespəs]
trespass to go on someone else's land or property
without permission
['traiəl]
trial a test to see if something works well: the
judging of a person in a court of law

['traiaŋgl]
triangle an area with three straight sides

[traib]
tribe a group of families who all live together with
one chief who rules them

[trik]
trick something clever. Some people can do magic
tricks and others can do tricks like walking on
a wire, or standing on a horse when it is
running.

['trikl]
trickle to flow in a very small stream

['traisikl]
tricycle a three-wheeled cycle

['traifl]
trifle something small and unimportant. The same
word also means a sweet food made of sponge
cake, cream or custard, and jelly.

['trigə]
trigger the little lever which is pulled to fire a gun

[trim]
trim to make something neat, often by cutting off
rough edges and loose threads. The same word
also means to decorate a piece of clothing by
adding lace, ribbons or some other pretty
trimming.

[trip]
trip a short journey. The same word also means to
stumble or fall as a result of catching your foot
on something.

['troli]
trolley a set of trays on wheels; a small hand-cart

[trot]
trot to run, but not as fast as you can

['trʌbl]
trouble anything which annoys or causes worry or
unhappiness

['trʌblsəm]
troublesome causing trouble or difficulty

[trof]
trough a long narrow container which holds water
or food for animals

['trauzəz]
trousers   a piece of clothing which covers you from
        your waist to your ankles, fitting around
        each leg separately

[traut]
trout   a kind of fish which lives in fresh water and
        is very good to eat

['trauəl]
trowel   a little spade with a curved blade. It is used
        in the garden for turning over earth and digging
        up small plants.

[trʌk]
truck   a big open vehicle for carrying heavy things
        from place to place

[trʌdʒ]
trudge   to walk along wearily, with heavy footsteps

[tru:]
true   real; correct

['trʌmpit]
trumpet   a musical instrument that you blow into

[trʌŋk]
trunk   the thick stem of a tree. The same word
        also means an elephant's nose, or a big box for
        sending clothes in.

[trʌst]
trust   to believe that someone is honest, or that you
        will not be tricked

[tru:θ]
truth   whatever is true and has really happened

[trai]
try   to test to see if something works: to do the
        best you can

['traiiŋ]
trying   annoying; rather naughty

[tʌb]
tub   an open container for washing in or for holding
        liquids

[tju:b]
tube   a long thin hollow piece of metal, wood or
        other material. The same word also means a
        container from which you squeeze out the
        contents. such as toothpaste. Tube is
        also another word for an underground
        railway.

[tʌk]
tuck   to roll or fold up. The same word also means chocolates and sweets.

[tʌft]
tuft   a small bunch of grass, hair or feathers, growing closely together

[tʌg]
tug   to pull hard at someone or something

['tʌgbout]
tugboat   a small but powerful ship which tows larger ships

['tʌgəv'wɔ:]
tug of war   a game in which a team pulls on each end of the same rope. Each team tries to pull the other team over a line.

['tju:lip]
tulip   a brightly-coloured flower with a few large leaves. It grows from a bulb.

['tʌmbl]
tumble   to fall over suddenly

['tʌmblə]
tumbler   a plain drinking glass with no stem

['tʌmi]
tummy   a pet name for stomach

[tju:n]
tune   a lot of musical notes played one after the other to make a pretty sound

['tju:nik]
tunic   a close-fitting jacket worn as part of a uniform. The same word also means a loose-fitting belted garment.

['tju:niŋfɔ:k]
tuning-fork   a metal instrument with two prongs that give out a musical sound when you strike it

['tʌnl]
tunnel   a hole cut right through a hill or under the ground

['tə:bən]
turban   a long piece of cloth wound round the head and worn as a hat

['tə:bain]
turbine   an engine that works by force of water, steam or gas

[tə:f]
turf   the top layer of earth with grass growing on it

['tə:ki]
turkey   a big farmyard bird with
    small wings and a fan-shaped tail

[tə:n]
turn   to move yourself or some object to the left or
    the right or all the way round

['tə:niŋ]
turning   a road branching off a main road to the left
    or right

['tə:nip]
turnip   the large round root of the turnip plant
    which can be cooked and eaten

['tə:nteibl]
turntable   the part of a gramophone or record-player
    which goes round and round when a record is
    played

['tə:pəntain]
turpentine   a kind of oil used in painting. It comes
    from pine trees.

['tʌrit]
turret   a small tower on a building. The same word
    also means a revolving platform on a ship or
    tank that has guns on it.

['tə:tl]
turtle   an animal with a shell, like a tortoise. It has
    paddle-shaped legs and lives in water.

[tʌsk]
tusk   one of the two very long teeth that stick out
    of the mouths of some animals such as
    elephants

[twi:d]
tweed   a thick, rather rough woollen cloth which is
    often used to make suits and overcoats

[twais]
twice   two times

[twig]
twig   a little branch on a tree or bush

['twailait]
twilight   the fading dim light just before the sun sets

[twin]
twin one of two children or animals born at the same time to the same mother

[twain]
twine threads twisted together to make strong string. The same word also means to turn or twist round something.

['twiŋkl]
twinkle to shine and sparkle in flashes, like a star in the sky

[twə:l]
twirl to turn round and round very quickly

[twist]
twist to bend something; to wind one thing around another; to turn sharply

['twitə]
twitter to make a chattering noise, as birds do when a lot of them are together

[taip]
type to print words on paper by using a typewriter. The same word also means something that belongs to or stands for a group of things, like a type of person or type of food.

['taipraitə]
typewriter a machine which prints words on paper. It has keys with letters on them which you press.

['taiərənt]
tyrant a person who rules over people in a cruel way

['taiə]
tyre a rubber ring, usually filled with air on the outer rim of a car or bicycle wheel

['ʌgli]
ugly not pretty or pleasant to look at

[ju:kə'leili]
ukelele a small musical instrument shaped like a guitar

['ʌlsə]
ulcer   an open sore on the skin or inside you

[ʌm'brelə]
umbrella   a round piece of material stretched over thin pieces of metal. It can be opened and held over your head to keep you from getting wet in the rain.

['ʌmpaiə]
umpire   someone who settles arguments and decides whether players have broken the rules in games like cricket and tennis

['ʌŋkl]
uncle   the brother of your mother or father

[ʌn'kʌmfətəbl]
uncomfortable   not at ease; feeling awkward

['ʌndəgraund]
underground   underneath the ground. The same word also means a railway that runs in a tunnel under the ground.

[ʌndə'lain]
underline   to draw a line under a word

[ʌndə'ni:θ]
underneath   in a lower place; under something

[ʌndə'stand]
understand   to know what something means

[ʌn'du:]
undo   to unfasten, untie or open something

[ʌn'dʌn]
undone   unfastened; opened

[ʌn'dres]
undress   to take your clothes off

[ʌniks'pektid]
unexpected   not expected; sudden

[ʌn'hapi]
unhappy   not happy; sad

[ʌn'helθi]
unhealthy   not healthy; sickly

['ju:niko:n]
unicorn   an imaginary animal that looks like a horse with a horn in the middle of its forehead

['ju:nifo:m]
uniform   special clothes worn by those who belong to a group of people such as the army, the navy, or a school

[ʌnim'pɔːtənt]
unimportant   not important

[ʌn'intrəstiŋ]
uninteresting   not interesting

['juːnjən]
union   a joining together. The same word also
    means a group of workers who have joined
    together.

['juːnjən'dʒak]
Union Jack   the national flag of the United
    Kingdom

['juːnit]
unit   a single thing

[juː'nait]
unite   to join together; to do something together as
    a group

[juːni'vəːsəl]
universal   to do with everyone, everywhere

['juːnivəːs]
universe   all things existing on the earth and out in
    space

[juːni'vəːsəti]
university   a place where students who have finished
    school can go for more education

[ʌn'kaind]
unkind   not kind; cruel

[ən'les]
unless   if not; if you do not

[ʌn'laik]
unlike   not like; different

[ʌn'loud]
unload   to take a load from; to take the bullets out
    of a gun

[ʌn'pleznt]
unpleasant   not pleasant; nasty

[ʌn'stedi]
unsteady   not steady; shaky

[ʌnsək'sesful]
unsuccessful   not successful; not able to do
    something you try to do

[ʌn'taidi]
untidy   not neat; not well arranged

[ən'til]
until   up to the time. You are not allowed to
    drive a car until you are old enough.

[ʌn' juːʒuəl]
unusual not usual; out of the ordinary

[ʌn'wel]
unwell ill; not healthy

[ʌn'rap]
unwrap to take the covering off something

[ʌp]
up towards a higher place; the opposite of down

[ə'pon]
upon on top of something

['ʌpəkʌt]
uppercut an upward blow used by a boxer

['ʌproː]
uproar a noisy disturbance; shouting and yelling

[ʌp'set]
upset to knock something over. The same word
also means to be worried or ill.

['ʌpsai'daun]
upside-down turned over, with the top part
underneath

[ʌp'steəz]
upstairs on a floor above the ground floor of a
building

[ʌp'striːm]
upstream towards the upper part of a stream

['ʌpwəd]
upward going up

['ə:bən]
urban having to do with towns or cities and not the
countryside

[ə:dʒ]
urge to try to get someone to do something; to try
to persuade

[juːz]
use to do something with an object made for a
special purpose. You use a knife to cut your
food.

[juːzd]
used something that is not new

['juːsful]
useful something that is likely to be used a lot;
helpful

['juːslis]
useless of no use; of no worth or value

['ju:ʒuəl]
usual   happening more often than not

['ju:ʒuəli]
usually   almost always; more often than not

['veikənt]
vacant   empty; not lived in, like a house that people
    have moved away from

[və'keiʃən]
vacation   a holiday

['vaksineit]
vaccinate (*say vaksinate*)   to give an injection that
    will prevent you from getting some diseases

['vakjuəm]
vacuum   a space with no air in it

[veig]
vague   not very clear or sure

[vein]
vain   thinking how pretty or good-looking you are;
    having a very good opinion of yourself

['valəntain]
valentine   a card or greeting sent to someone you
    love on Saint Valentine's Day, February 14th

['vali]
valley   the low land between two hills or mountains

['valjuəbl]
valuable   worth a lot of money; high-priced:
    important

['valju:]
value   the worth of something; the price or cost of
    something

[van]
van   a closed motor vehicle used for carrying things
    from place to place. The same word also means
    a special railway carriage used for luggage, mail
    and animals.

[vein]
vane   a shaped piece of metal on top of a building,
    that swings to show which way the wind is
    blowing

[vəˈnilə]
vanilla   a food flavouring which comes from the
      dried seed pod of a climbing plant

[ˈvaniʃ]
vanish   to go out of sight very quickly; to disappear

[ˈvanəti]
vanity   too high an opinion of yourself

[ˈveipə]
vapour   mist, steam or smoke floating in the air

[vəˈraiəti]
variety   a collection of many kinds of things: a show
      with different kinds of entertainment

[ˈveəriəs]
various   different; many; several. Ice cream comes
      in various flavours.

[ˈvaːniʃ]
varnish   a clear liquid that you paint on to wood
      and metal to make it look shiny

[vaːz]
vase   a pretty container for putting flowers in

[vaːst]
vast   huge; very big; immense

[viːl]
veal   the meat from a calf

[ˈvedʒitəbl]
vegetable   any plant used for food

[ˈviːikl]
vehicle   any form of transport with wheels

[veil]
veil   a thin piece of netting or material, worn by
      women to hide their faces or to protect them
      from strong wind or sunshine

[vein]
vein   one of the very thin long tubes that carry the
      blood around in your body

[ˈvelvit]
velvet   soft warm material that looks and feels like
      very thin fur

[ˈvendʒəns]
vengeance   revenge

[ˈventileitə]
ventilator   a small opening in a wall to let stale air
      out or fresh air in

[vəˈrandə]
verandah   an open porch with a roof, joined on to a
      house

[vəːs]
verse   poetry; part of a poem

['vesl]
vessel   a ship. The same word also means a
      container, usually for liquid.

[vest]
vest   an undershirt; a waistcoat

[vet]
vet   a person who looks after sick animals. The
      word is short for veterinary surgeon. The same
      word also means to examine something to see
      that it is all right.

[veks]
vex   to annoy someone or make him cross

['vaiədʌkt]
viaduct   a long bridge made to carry a road or
      railway over a valley or low-lying area

['viʃəs]
vicious   wicked; fierce; very spiteful

['viktim]
victim   a person who is hurt in some way or is
      killed by someone else's action

['viktəri]
victory   the winning of a battle or contest

['vidiəteip]
videotape   a special kind of tape that shows pictures
      and gives out sounds when it is played through
      a special machine

[vjuː]
view   what you can see in front of you. When you
      are on top of a hill, you have a good view of
      the countryside around the hill.

['vigə]
vigour   strength

['vaikiŋ]
viking   a pirate from the north in olden times

['vilidʒ]
village   houses and buildings all together, like a
      town but smaller

['vilən]
villain   a bad man; a rogue

[vain]
vine   a plant that climbs up poles or a fence or
      wall or creeps along on the ground. Some vines
      have grapes on them.

['viniɡə]
vinegar   an acid-tasting liquid used in salads and
        pickles

['vaiələnt]
violent   very rough; forceful

['vaiəlit]
violet   a small wild plant with purple or white
        flowers

[vaiə'lin]
violin   a musical instrument with four strings. It is
        held under the chin and played with a special
        stick called a bow.

['vizəbl]
visible   able to be seen

[vizi'biləti]
visibility   the clearness with which things can be
        seen. In a fog or mist the visibility is bad
        because you cannot see far.

['viʒən]
vision   the ability to see; eyesight

['vizit]
visit   to go to see someone at his house

['vitəmin]
vitamin   something in foods that is good for you
        because it keeps you healthy. Milk and oranges
        both have vitamins that you need.

['vivid]
vivid   very bright; brilliant

['viksn]
vixen   a female fox

[və'kabjuləri]
vocabulary   all the words you can speak and write;
        a selected list of words, usually in alphabetical
        order

[vois]
voice   the sound that comes from people's mouths
        when they speak or sing

[vol'keinou]
volcano   a cone-shaped mountain that throws out
        hot ashes or liquid rock from an opening in the
        top

['voljum]
volume a book. The same word also means the
    amount, quantity or bulk of something.

[volən'tiə]
volunteer to offer to do something that you don't
    have to do

[vout]
vote to say which person you would choose to be
    in charge of something or to be a member of
    a committee or similar group of people

[vau]
vow a solemn promise

['vauəl]
vowel the sounds of a language which are not
    consonants. Usually vowels are written with
    the letters *a e i o u.*

['voiidʒ]
voyage a long journey by sea

['vʌlgə]
vulgar rude; not very polite

['vʌltʃə]
vulture a large bird of prey that eats dead flesh

[wod]
wad a bundle of paper, often used for packing

['wodl]
waddle to walk with short steps, rocking from side
    to side, as a duck does

[weid]
wade to walk in water

['weifə]
wafer a very thin biscuit

[wag]
wag to move something up and down or from side
    to side, as when a dog wags its tail

[weidʒ]
wage payment for a job of work

['wagən]
wagon an open vehicle with four wheels, used to
    carry heavy loads

['wagteil]
wagtail a small wild bird with a long tail that wags
    up and down

[weil]
wail to make a long sad crying noise

[weist]
waist   the narrow middle part of your body above
the hips

['weiskout]
waistcoat   a short sleeveless jacket, sometimes
worn by men under a coat

[weit]
wait   to stay in a place until someone comes or
something happens

['weitə]
waiter   someone who serves food at a table in a café
or restaurant

[weik]
wake   to become awake after being asleep; to wake
up someone who is asleep

[wo:k]
walk   to move along on your feet, but more slowly
than running

['wo:ki'to:ki]
walkie-talkie   a radio carried about with you when
you walk, used to send and receive messages

[wo:l]
wall   something built of bricks or stone, like the
sides of a house or a fence around a garden

['wolit]
wallet   a small pocket case, usually of leather, for
carrying paper money, tickets, stamps and
personal papers

['wo:lflauə]
wallflower   a sweet-smelling garden flower that
sometimes grows on old walls

['woləp]
wallop   to hit someone hard

['wo:lpeipə]
wallpaper   a special kind of paper put on the inside
walls of houses as decoration

['wo:lnʌt]
walnut   a tree which has nuts that are good to eat.
The wood is very hard, and is used to make
furniture.

['wo:lrəs]
walrus   a sea animal, like
a large seal with two tusks

[won]
wan   pale; looking rather ill or weak

[wond]
wand   a magic stick used by fairies or by conjurers when they do magic tricks

['wondə]
wander   to roam about from place to place

[wein]
wane   to become smaller, as when the full moon begins to wane

[wont]
want   to wish for or to need something

[wo:]
war   a fight between two or more countries. If two groups of people in the same country fight each other, it is called civil war.

[wo:d]
ward   a large room in a hospital, where there are a number of beds for sick people

['wo:də]
warder   a man who stands guard over prisoners in a prison

['wo:droub]
wardrobe   a cupboard where you keep clothes

['weəhaus]
warehouse   a building where goods are stored

[wo:m]
warm   more hot than cold

[wo:n]
warn   to tell someone to take care because of something that may happen, usually dangerous

[wo:p]
warp   to twist out of shape

['woriə]
warrior   a man who fights for his country in time of war; an old-fashioned word for soldier

['wo:ʃip]
warship   a ship that has guns and weapons for fighting in a war

[wo:t]
wart   a small hard lump on the skin, usually on the hands or face

[woʃ]
wash   to make clean, using soap and water

['wo∫iŋ]
washing   clothes that are being washed or need to
   be washed

[wosp]
wasp   a stinging insect something like a bee with a
   very narrow waist

[weist]
waste   to use something up or spend money
   carelessly. The same word also means rubbish;
   something of no value that is thrown away.

[wot∫]
watch   to look at closely. The same word also
   means a small clock which you wear on your
   wrist or carry in your pocket.

['wot∫ful]
watchful   careful; watching what you are doing

['wo:tə]
water   the clear liquid in lakes, rivers and seas.
   Water also falls from the clouds as rain.

['wo:təklozit]
water closet   a small room containing a bowl which
   has a rushing flow of water to carry away
   waste through a pipe. It is called W.C. for
   short.

['wo:təkres]
watercress   a green plant that grows in fresh water.
   It is eaten in salads and sandwiches.

['wo:təfo:l]
waterfall   a stream of water falling down from a
   high place

['wo:təlili]
water lily   a water plant with large flat floating
   leaves and beautiful pink, white or yellow
   flowers

['wo:təpru:f]
waterproof   able to keep water out. A raincoat is
   waterproof.

[weiv]
wave   water moving in a curved line on the surface
of the sea or a lake. The same word also means
to move something, like your hand or a flag,
back and forth or up and down.

['weivi]
wavy   curving in and out

[waks]
wax   a soft yellowish material used in making
candles. The same word also means sealing
wax, which melts when you heat it, and then
gets hard again.

[wei]
way   a road or path; space to move through. The
same word also means how to do something,
like the way to paint a picture.

[wi:k]
weak   not strong

['wi:kən]
weaken   to make something or someone weak

[welθ]
wealth   great riches; a lot of money

[wi:n]
wean   to train a young child or young animal that
has been living on milk to eat solid foods

['wepən]
weapon   anything used to fight or hunt with, such as
a gun, a heavy stick, or a bow and arrows

[weə]
wear   to be dressed in. You wear thin clothes in
summer and thick clothes in winter.

['wiəri]
weary   very tired

['wi:zl]
weasel   a small wild animal with a long slim body.
It kills and eats other small animals.

['weðə]
weather   what kind of day it is outside. The
weather can be wet or dry, hot or cold.

['weðəkok]
weathercock   a flat piece of metal, often in the
shape of a cock, that turns
in the wind to show you
which direction the
wind is coming from

[wi:v]
weave to make cloth by twisting threads over and
  under each other

[web]
web the lacy net that spiders spin to trap insects

['webfut]
web-foot a foot that has skin joining the toes
  together. Ducks, geese and swans are all
  web-footed.

['wediŋ]
wedding the marriage ceremony, when a man and a
  woman become husband and wife

['wedʒ]
wedge a triangular piece of metal or wood, very
  thin at one end and thicker at the other. You
  put a wedge between two things to hold them
  firm or to push them apart.

[wi:]
wee small; tiny

[wi:d]
weed wild plants that grow where they are not
  wanted in gardens or in fields where crops are
  grown

[wi:k]
week seven days

['wi:k'end]
weekend Saturday and Sunday

{wi:p]
weep to cry tears

[wei]
weigh to find out how heavy something is

[weit]
weight the amount that something weighs

[wiəd]
weird strange and frightening

['welkəm]
welcome to greet someone with joy

[wel]
well healthy; properly. The same word also means
  a deep hole in the ground from which oil
  or water is obtained.

['weliŋtənz]
wellingtons rubber boots

[west]
west the direction in which the sun sets; the
  opposite direction to east

[wet]
wet   not dry; covered with liquid

[wak]
whack   to strike something so hard that it makes a noise

[weil]
whale   the largest animal found in the sea

[wo:f]
wharf   a landing place for loading and unloading ships

[wi:t]
wheat   a kind of grain from which flour is made

[wi:l]
wheel   a large flat circle made of wood or metal. Cars, buses and bicycles must have wheels to be able to move along.

['wi:lbarou]
wheelbarrow   a kind of small cart with only one wheel. You carry leaves and grass and building materials in it.

[wen]
when   at what time; at the time that

[wen'evə]
whenever   at any time

[weə]
where   at or in what place

['weðə]
whether   if or if not

[wei]
whey   the watery part of milk. When cheese is made, the milk is separated into the thick part (called curds) and the liquid part (called whey).

[witʃ]
which   one of two or more people or things, as when you decide which friend to invite or which flavour of ice cream you are going to have

[wif]
whiff   a sudden puff of air, smoke, or scent

[wail]
while   during the time that; as long as

['wimpə]
whimper   to cry in a low whining voice

[wain]
whine   to make a sad complaining crying sound

['wini]
whinny   the noise a horse makes by blowing
      through its nose

[wip]
whip   a piece of thin strong cord or leather
      attached to a handle. The same word also
      means to stir up eggs or cream very quickly.

[wə:l]
whirl   to turn round and round very quickly

[wisk]
whisk   to move, sweep or stir something very
      quickly. The same word also means a kitchen
      tool used for whipping eggs and cream.

['wiskə]
whisker   one of the stiff hairs on a man's face, or at
      the sides of the mouths of some animals, such
      as cats, lions and tigers

['wiski]
whisky   a very strong drink made from grain

['wispə]
whisper   to speak so softly that only someone very
      close to you can hear

['wisl]
whistle   to make a high musical sound by blowing
      through your mouth with your lips nearly
      closed. The same word also means a small
      tube-like instrument that makes a whistling
      sound when you blow it.

[wait]
white   the colour of snow

[hu:]
who   which or what person

[houl]
whole   all; not a part; not divided

[wu:p]
whoop   a loud cry or shout. The same word also
      means the noise made by someone who has
      the illness called whooping cough.

[wai]
why   for what reason or cause. as *Why did you go away?*

[wik]
wick   the twisted threads of cotton in a candle or lamp, which you light

['wikid]
wicked   evil; very bad; the opposite of good

['wikit]
wicket   three stumps in the game of cricket: a small gate or door built into a larger one

[waid]
wide   a long way from one side to the other; broad; the opposite of narrow

['widou]
widow   a woman whose husband is dead

['widouə]
widower   a man whose wife is dead

[widθ]
width   how wide or broad something is

[waif]
wife   a married woman

[wig]
wig   false hair that you put on over your own hair

['wigli]
wiggly   not straight, like this line

['wigwam]
wigwam   a tent or hut that American Indians lived in

[waild]
wild   not kept or looked after by people; the opposite of tame

['wildənis]
wilderness   a wild or desert area of land where no one lives

['waild'flauə]
wildflower   a flower that grows without being planted by anyone

['wilful]
wilful   wanting your own way

['wiliŋ]
willing   pleased and ready to do something you are asked to do

['wilou]
willow   a tree with long bending branches and narrow leaves. Cricket bats are usually made of willow wood.

['waili]
wily   crafty, sly

[win]
win   to come first in something, like a race or a game

[wind]
wind (*rhymes with tinned*)   fast-moving air that blows things about

[waind]
wind (*rhymes with kind*)   to turn or twist something around, like winding up a ball of string

['winmil]
windmill   a machine that is worked by the wind. It is used for grinding grain or for pumping water.

['windou]
window   a glass-covered opening in the wall of a building, which lets light and air in

[wain]
wine   a strong drink made from the juice of grapes

[wiŋ]
wing   one of the two feathered parts of a bird's body with which it flies. Aeroplanes have metal wings.

[wiŋk]
wink   to shut and open one eye quickly

['wintə]
winter   the last of the four seasons of the year, when it is coldest

[waip]
wipe   to clean or dry something by rubbing

['waiə]
wire   a very thin, long piece of metal

['waiəlis]
wireless   another name for radio, a way of sending sounds through the air without using wires

[waiz]
wise   knowing and understanding a lot of things
[wiʃ]
wish   to want something very much
[wit]
wit   understanding, cleverness
[witʃ]
witch   a wicked, dangerous woman who is supposed to be able to do magic
[wið]
with   near to or alongside. Sometimes the same word also means against, as when you fight with someone.
['wiðə]
wither   to dry up, to shrivel
[wi'ðin]
within   inside; in the inner part
[wi'ðaut]
without   not having or using something. The same word also means on the outside.
['witnis]
witness   someone who has seen something happen and therefore can say he knows all about it
['witi]
witty   clever and amusing
['wizəd]
wizard   a man who is supposed to be able to do magic
['wobl]
wobble   to rock unsteadily from side to side
[wulf]
wolf   a dangerous wild animal, that looks like a large dog
['wumən]
woman   a female human being; a girl when she is grown up
['wʌndə]
wonder   to be surprised at something marvellous, unexpected or strange. The same word also means to question, to want to know.
['wʌndəful]
wonderful   marvellous; amazing
['wʌndəland]
wonderland   an imaginary country where amazing and wonderful things happen

[wud]
wood a little forest. The same word also means the
material that trees are made of. Wood is used
to make lots of things like fences, furniture and
some buildings.

['wudn]
wooden made of wood or hard like wood

['wudpekə]
woodpecker a wild bird that pecks holes in the bark
of trees to find insects for food

['wudwə:k]
woodwork carpentry; the wooden part of a building
or furniture

[wul]
wool the thick warm covering of hair on a sheep,
which is made into such things as blankets and
clothing

['wulən]
woollen made of wool

[wə:d]
word a spoken sound or group of letters that means
something when you hear it or read it

[wə:k]
work to do something useful; not playing

['wə:kmən]
workman someone who works with his hands,
often using tools or machinery

[wə:ks]
works a factory or workshop. The same word also
means the machinery in something, such as a
clock or watch.

[wə:ld]
world the earth, the people and things on it, and
the air around it

[wə:m]
worm a small snake-like animal which lives
underground and moves by wriggling in the
earth

[wo:n]

worn looking shabby or ragged. Clothes look
worn when you have been wearing them for a
long time.

['wʌri]

worry to be afraid something is going to go wrong
or that something bad may happen to someone

[wə:s]

worse not so good; more bad

['wə:ʃip]

worship to honour and praise God

[wə:st]

worst most bad

[wə:θ]

worth the price you would have to pay for
something you want to buy. The same word
also means deserving or useful; good enough or
valuable enough, as when someone says a book
is worth reading.

['wə:θlis]

worthless not worth anything; no good

[waund]

wound (*rhymes with round*)   turned and twisted

[wu:nd]

wound (*rhymes with spooned*)   a cut in your flesh

[rap]

wrap to cover something by folding paper or cloth
around it. The same word also means a shawl
or cape worn by girls and women.

[roθ]

wrath great anger

[ri:θ]

wreath a ring of flowers or leaves twisted together

[rek]

wreck anything that has been ruined or destroyed,
leaving only useless bits and pieces. Sometimes
the word is short for shipwreck.

[ren]

wren a very small brown wild bird

[rest]

wrest to pull something away from someone by
force

['resl]

wrestle to struggle with someone to see who is
stronger

['rigl]
wriggle   to move by twisting and turning

[riŋ]
wring   to make water come out of something, like
   wet clothes, by twisting and squeezing

['riŋə]
wringer   a machine with two rollers that wring the
   water out of wet washing

['riŋkl]
wrinkle   a small fold or crease in material, cloth,
   paper or the skin of old people

[rist]
wrist   the thin part of your arm that joins on to your
   hand

[rait]
write   to draw letters or words so that people can
   read them

[raið]
writhe   to wriggle or twist about

['raitiŋ]
writing   something you have written

[roŋ]
wrong   not right; evil or wicked

['eks'rei]
x-ray   a special kind of photograph which shows
   doctors what the inside of your body looks like

['zailəfoun]
xylophone   a set of narrow pieces of wood that
   make musical sounds when they are hit with
   wooden hammers

[jot]
yacht (*rhymes with got*)   a kind of boat, usually with
   sails, used for racing or for pleasure

[jak]
yak   a long-haired ox

[jap]
yap   to bark sharply

[ja:d]
yard　a space, usually closed in by buildings or a
fence. The same word also means a
measurement of 36 inches or 3 feet.

[ja:n]
yarn　thread made from wool or cotton. The same
word also means a story told by someone who
has travelled a lot.

[jo:n]
yawn　to open your mouth wide and breathe air in
and out slowly, especially when you are sleepy
or bored

[jə:]
year　a length of time; 365 days. 52 weeks or 12
months make a year. '

[jel]
yell　to call out very loudly

['jelou]
yellow　a colour. Lemons and primroses are yellow
and so are the yolks of eggs.

[jelp]
yelp　a short sharp cry or bark

[jes]
yes　the word you use to show you agree

['jestədi]
yesterday　the day before today

[jet]
yet　by now. The same word sometimes also means
but.

[ju:]
yew　an evergreen tree, often seen growing in
churchyards

[ji:ld]
yield　to give up, as when the enemy surrenders.
The same word also means to produce, as
when a field of wheat yields a good crop.

['jogət]
yogurt　slightly sour thick milk, often mixed with a
fruity flavouring. The word is sometimes
spelled yoghurt or yoghourt.

[jouk]
yolk　the yellow part in the middle of an egg

['jondə]
yonder　over there; beyond

[jʌŋ]
young not old; in the early part of life

[ˈjʌŋɡə]
younger not as old as someone else

[ˈjʌŋstə]
youngster a young person who is not yet grown up

[jɔːˈself]
yourself you and no one else

[juːθ]
youth the time when you are young. The same
word also means a young man.

[ˈjoujou]
yo-yo a toy in the shape of a reel, which spins up
and down on a string

[ˈziːbrə]
zebra a wild animal like a small horse with stripes

[ˈziːrou]
zero nothing

[zest]
zest joy in what you are doing; enthusiasm

[ˈzigzag]
zigzag moving from side to side, like this line

[ziŋk]
zinc a bluish-white metal

[zip]
zip a long metal or plastic fastener used to do up
clothing and to close purses and bags

[ə]
**   r** another word for zip-fastener

['ziðə]

zither a musical instrument made of a flat board
with lots of metal strings stretched across it.
You pluck the strings to make musical sounds.

[zoun]

zone a large area of the world which is different
from other areas because, for example, it has a
much hotter or much colder climate

[zu:]

zoo a place where wild animals are kept and people
can come to look at them. The word is short
for zoological gardens.

['zɪp]
zipp